T0354609

Rosa Lilia

Scar of Abuse, Heart of Hope
(A true story of extreme child abuse)

Liliana Kavianian

iUniverse, Inc.
Bloomington

Rosa Lilia
Scar of Abuse, Heart of Hope

iUniverse books may be ordered through booksellers or by contacting:

iUniverse
1663 Liberty Drive
Bloomington, IN 47403
www.iuniverse.com
1-800-Authors (1-800-288-4677)

ISBN: 978-1-4759-6280-2 (sc)
ISBN: 978-1-4759-6281-9 (hc)
ISBN: 978-1-4759-6282-6 (e)

Translator: Olivia Holloway Salzano

Library of Congress Control Number: 2012921689

Printed in the United States of America

iUniverse rev. date: 1/2/12

Contents

I would have liked to tell a different story,
but this is mine. I had no other.

Ario de Rosales
The Night of the Fritters

My life has always been marked by death. At only four days old, I had already stopped breathing. After seeing my birth, my father, Vincent Sayavedra, had left for the bar and hadn't been home in more than three days. My mother, Elia Negrete, had come down with a fever and was too weak to leave the bed. My father's mother, Trina, was at home with my mother, helping to care for me. That was when I stopped breathing. My family called the doctor immediately.

"She's dead," said the doctor.

"No! No, my little one!" cried my mother. "You can't die!" she cried, clutching my body.

They notified the relatives, went out to look for a small casket, began cleaning the living room, and moved the furniture in my grandfather's house, all to organize the funeral. My mother, Elia Negrete, knelt down in front of a statue of Christ and begged him to bring me back to life. My grandmother Trina, who cried in the corner of the living room, was pestered by my mother's impulse to take me to the church to bathe me in holy water.

"She's dead, Elia," responded my grandmother Trina. "There's nothing we can do."

"That doesn't matter," my mother asserted. "God can give her back to me."

My mother insisted, so my grandmother finally agreed to take me to the church to be baptized. When my mother was left alone at home, hoping that her mother-in-law would bring back a live baby from the church, she continued praying and made promises to God in exchange for my life. She promised that if I lived, she would dress like Santa Theresa for a year and shave her head.

Trina arrived at the church with my body limp. When they put holy water on my head, I jumped like someone who is jolted from a nightmare and opened my eyes.

When my mother found out that I had come back to life, she shaved her head and kept it that way for a year, but she did not fulfill her promise to dress for a year like the nun Santa Theresa.

My parents had married in 1961, and my mother became pregnant right away. Provoked into depression by my father, she began to go days without eating during the pregnancy. Rafael Negrete and Elpidia (Pillita) Huerta, my maternal grandparents, had sent my parents to live in New Italy, a very hot, calm place that was relatively close to Ario de Rosales, Mexico, and set them up with a clothing and shoe store that would soon go broke because my father dedicated his time to going around to cantinas and brothels. My mother cried every day and stayed in bed. She knew of her husband's ways and accepted them for the time being but continued believing that God could change him. She always kept hope. She loved him as the first and last man in her life, and she came to accept the fact that he arrived home only to sleep and that his presence invaded the house.

Along with establishing the business, my grandfather had sent servants to help my mother maintain the house and to cook and clean. But the servants did not stick around very long. My father impregnated several of them, and they asked to be dismissed. My mother silently pardoned my father because he manipulated her and because she was not courageous enough to confront him. Despite her depression, my mother was a very good wife; she was attentive, faithful, and caring.

By the time they had their first wedding anniversary, my mother's routine was to spend the whole day lying down and crying. She rarely ate and didn't even have the strength to nourish me. Obligated by the pressure of nine months, she gave birth to me. The first few days were a battle to lower my fever and find a way to let me breathe more easily. They called the healers of Ario de Rosales and the doctors of the city. Even though the doctor promptly declared my situation terminal—I had stopped breathing for an hour—a greater power brought me back to life when that holy water touched my head.

A few years ago, when I was able to talk with my mother (without the desire to tear her head off) and told her about many of the things that happened later on in my grandparents' house, where I was sent to live at the age of four, she told me something very painful and confusing. She was surprised by the stories I told her about Aunt Barbara, who also lived in my grandparents' house, and stories that involved Barbara's brother, Uncle Eduardo, and his visits to that house, and all the things I then brought myself to confess. It was hard for her to believe that I was made to work in my grandfather's store and that her own siblings abused me. She had never seen abusive behavior from my aunt or uncle, and although my grandfather had always forced his children to work, he had never beaten them. My mother was regretful for not having protected me, for having left me at my grandparents' house when I was only four years old, and for letting me go like a marble down the mountain.

"After hearing that you went through so many horrible things, I realized that I should have paid better attention to the Bible," lamented my mother. "The Bible says that when a child dies, it's because God wants to carry it away with him. It was not right to make promises to God in exchange for your life. It wasn't right for God to give you back either. It would have been better if he had taken you, my daughter. Look how you've suffered."

But her faith on that eighth day of my life revived me, and I have believed in that miracle.

I do not blame her for leaving me with my grandparents. After all, she left me in the situation that she thought would give me the best childhood, with the comfort of my grandparents' house. She believed that their finances would provide for me the best doctors, clothing, and food. We all have our story and our own frustrations.

My mother was born in Guanajuato and was the third of five siblings: Eduardo, Fermín, Elia, Rodrigo, and Barbara, who is the cruelest woman I have ever met. When my mother was twelve years of age, my grandparents decided to pack their bags and move to Ario de Rosales. It was the custom to have the business in the same house where one lived, and my grandfather hoped for a great future for his business.

My mother had always been close to God. She believed in people's goodness and said that she had a religious mission on earth. She wanted to be a nun and, despite her father's protests, entered the convent. Her childhood ambition was to give love and receive it too, and she recorded this desire in a series of letters that she showed me the day we had that enlightening conversation. I could not believe the quantity of notebooks she had filled since her youth. She placed a title on each letter, like this one, which she wrote just a few years ago while remembering her childhood:

Ambition
Once upon a time there was a girl with a good heart. She was noble, yet timid with reason. She was a dreamer and wrote a ton of little letters. She would have been a good writer, but her heart was broken. She had so much tenderness that the harder heart broke it; since she was full of traumas and damage, she escaped in her letters. She was a girl nine years old, full of sadness and sweetness. Her bitterness was reflected through her eyes. She was a mature girl, very prudent; she exuded a sweet air but dragged her self-esteem at her feet. She wrote tender and beautiful verses with light tones of bitterness. She always walked with a withered expression, full of anguish. This girl never smiled and always hid underneath the counter of her parents' store. She walked very primly and seemed like a princess, but between her jewels, a tear was always falling.

She had a very cruel father named Rafael. He was a great businessman, very wealthy, smart in his work, with refined language. He was friendly and polite but had no heart. His daughter knew that he wrote beautiful poetry yet did not understand where his poems came from since he rarely showed that he had feelings … he was so strong and imperative. He was pleasant only with certain people, particularly his customers. Although he was strict and stoic with business matters, he would cry on the few occasions that tragedy struck the family. His tenderness would especially come through when one of his sons died and when one of his houses burned down.

Rafael's mother died when he was very young, and his father remarried two times. Rafael was forced to begin working as a young child even though his family was not poor. He didn't go to school in his town of Pueblo Nuevo in Guanajuato, and by twelve years of age, he owned his own creamery. His compulsion to work and earn money only intensified as he grew up.

Rafael's children were marginalized—they didn't know what love was. There were no birthday parties, only lectures and reprimands, and there was great pain in their hearts. There were neither Christmases nor candles to blow out. They never enjoyed the dolls they so desired, and remained admiring them in catalogs. The girl's games were played with bills and Centenarios. Now she is so cheerful, whereas she used to be timid and fearful—everything scared her. At night, she got shaky and feverish and would take a spoon of cough syrup to make it go away. She and her siblings never knew a caress or a word of love, and they grew up like robots. Her father was blinded by greed and ambition. Just seeing him made them fearful; this is even considering that he looked like an artist.

When she worked at her father's store, she was dominated by fear and always felt like the air suffocated her and that everyone stared at her. She would quickly take refuge behind the counter, feeling like she was enveloped by heat. She always worked with no pay—her father exploited her like a mule. All that was missing was for her to bray. She wanted to become a doctor, but Rafael and her mother, Pillita, took her out of elementary school. During her childhood and adolescence, she lived in fear of Rafael's angry outbursts, and at the time in her childhood when she could have been learning and studying, she was forced to work in the store like a mere instrument of her robotic father.

One day an aunt was going to do the children's portraits. But at the moment they were to pose, they had to make an effort; they were not allowed to smile or make funny faces—the adults brought out all the sadness in children their age. They never went hungry, yet when they went to the dining room, everything they ate had no taste. Their father walked around with his belt in his hands, and all the while they wanted to go to the bathroom to spit out their *food. The domestic servants were on the children's side because they saw that Rafael was very mean. He would tell his daughter that he would electrify her room so that no one would dare to go in. She had two boyfriends in secret; she would go out through a window, and Rafael would follow her and send the boyfriend running away with gunshots. Then he'd hit her with his belt until she fell to the ground. To the outside world, she seemed like a princess, yet on the inside she was a Cinderella.*

At the age of sixteen, she found refuge in the convent, yet Rafael always tried to get her out with promises and lies to make her to work again, unaware that she had already been marked by the years in his presence. She stayed peacefully in the convent for almost a year until her father's earnest pleas and promises to give her more freedom and be more kind persuaded her to return home.

Ambition was Rafael's vice. Though he had means and roots, he left behind pits, scars, and a marked pain. His wife would faint, or would make herself faint, yet she enjoyed those moments in which she could forget everything. Rafael talked sweetly to his wife, Pillita, and caressed her only when she fainted.

Pillita was refined, cultured and educated, beautiful, charitable and devout. She was friends with Lázaro Cárdenas, the president of Mexico from 1934 to 1940, and made many contributions to society and to her loved ones. When her personal cook of many years aged, Pillita gave her and her sister a house and a pension to enjoy their retirement. Rafael's sweet wife donated a large house the size of a whole city block to be converted into a center for charity to impoverished people in the town. The center provided food, monetary and clothing donations, and free professional classes in mechanics, artisan work, cooking, and other areas so that the poor people could gain skills to make a living. On another occasion, Pillita founded a free school for men studying to become priests at the seminary. Besides donating books to the community religious school, she donated money and arranged for free classes to help the men graduate as priests.

At the time, the local prison did not provide food, clothing, or any activities for the inmates. Pillita spent many years preparing and delivering food to the inmates who had no family members to take food to them. She also provided diversions for them by delivering cigarettes and magazines with which to fill their idle time.

Pillita always used delicate, tender language and spoke quietly. She had magic, she had charisma, and she had an angel or something mysterious that followed her despite the fact that she always wore an embittered, long face. The young girl, Pillita's daughter, remembers that she would sigh while working. She had something enchanting in her sad gaze, with touches of sainthood. How would she have been able to chuckle when she was married to such an ogre? She was saintly and good and proper; what stood out with her was a painstaking politeness.

Her daughter is without words to venerate her. She writes this, a page in her life, to this generous mother—a poem that she wanted to free from something inside her that she has not been able to release. It's about a girl who didn't grow up and who as an adult returned to being a girl and did not mature. Childhood leaves its vestiges, which do not heal and whose wounds do not close. They are like wheels; even though they are well oiled, a patch remains on the ground. Nor are memories forgotten; the mind memorizes them and retains them. They are like a cadaver that is cremated; even if it is burned, the ashes remain.

My mother found her first mission at seventeen years of age, several months after leaving the convent. Clementina, a girl who did the ironing for my grandmother, was married and had seven children. To sustain them, her husband had gone to the United States to work. Clementina had not heard from her husband in nearly three years and did not even know if he was alive. She got involved with an old Japanese man who lived in the village, and she became pregnant. Little Nataly was just a few days old when Clementina suddenly received a call from her husband.

"I no longer have work here," he said. "I'm returning to Ario right away."

Clementina got so scared about her husband's reaction to Nataly that she tried to kill the baby in a silent way. She tried to make Nataly catch pneumonia by putting her in a crib next to the window, but not even the cold could come against the strength of the little girl. She did not die, nor did she even catch a cold. Clementina was desperate—she needed to feed her children, the youngest of which was two years old. She asked my mother to help her turn the baby girl in at an orphanage.

"Not to worry, Clementina, give me the baby," my mother told her. "Give her to me as a gift. I can take care of her."

Clementina trusted in my mother—she was talking to a future nun—and decided to give her the little girl. Hidden from my grandparents, she received the little one and spoke with Chabela, one of the kitchen servants, who agreed to take care of the girl for a time. My mother asked her to let go of her work in my grandmother's house so she could take care of Nataly in her own house. In exchange, my mother would send her money to take care of the little girl and Chabela's seven other children. Just as my mother had planned, Chabela went to tell my grandmother that she would not be able to continue working in her kitchen. Her excuse was that she felt very tired, that her legs often fell asleep, and she exaggerated that she had prepared the last several meals while sitting down. "It will be better for me to dedicate myself to my children," she explained.

It was around this time that my mother, seventeen years old and disappointed by her father's unfulfilled promises to be calmer and give her more freedom, decided to enter the convent once again.

Chabela hid the truth about Nataly for a couple of years while my mother visited her and, as promised, paid all the little girl's expenses. My mother's involvement with the baby, her reentrance into the convent, and her frequent visits and help to Chabela made it seem as though she had taken to the convent to hide signs of her pregnancy and was hiding her own baby with Chabela. A fictitious rumor broke out that a nun had become pregnant in the convent, and a scandal arose. "She went to the convent to get rid of the creature, and besides that, she gave it away!" said the old gossiping women in Ario de Rosales. After my mother had been in the convent for almost two years, the rumors got to my grandfather, and although it was a lie and he learned the truth, he asked her to leave the convent.

"Elia Negrete, my mother."

"To heck with your being a nun! I need people to help me here in my business, not to be out there praying," he told her. "Besides, you need to get out of the convent so that people will put this rumor to rest!" So my mother, nineteen years old, left the convent for good.

When Pillita found out about Nataly, she felt compassion and believed that she herself could give more attention and care to the little girl than Chabela, who was taking care of her seven children. So Nataly went to live with Pillita.

My mother met my father in Ario de Rosales. She was almost twenty years old and passed most of the day helping at the store, from which she saw the civil parades that animated the whole town. My grandfather was so strict that any time my mother went out, she was accompanied by my grandmother or one of the servant girls. Grandfather hoped that his daughter would marry a man of prestige, capable of giving her a life of ease, but my mother had her eyes on the devil himself.

One day she saw a young man walking around the recently remodeled plaza, and she continued to see him for several days. The young man would sit on a bench or stand around, and then would walk around the plaza a few times before returning to the bench. He continued that way for hours. Thanks to the fact that he always chose the same bench, my mother did not have to leave the store to see him.

One day, Mother, with her childish boldness, ordered one of the employees to chat with the young man and offer him money to continue sitting on that very bench, in front of the store. The young man accepted the offer. So while my mother ordered merchandise and attended to customers, she could closely monitor the man's every move. In spite of not having spoken with him yet, she knew she wanted him. My grandfather had already decided my mother's future; he wanted her to be engaged to a Spaniard who owned territories on the outskirts of town. Yet my mother made her choice clear. "This young man from the plaza will be my husband," she declared to Pillita.

She had never been interested in money. She wanted a poor man, or rather, a simple man who loved and respected her, and who would share with her the desire to help the disadvantaged. She had found such a man. In spite of not knowing him and the impossibility of getting close to him, she felt that he was a lost young man, in search of something that would give meaning to his life. On occasion, my grandfather would travel to the coffee fields, and my mother took advantage of the chance to cross the plaza and converse with Vincent —my father in the making—after acquiring the authorization and complicity of my grandmother.

They went months with the same amorous routine, looking for things in common that would bring them together. Even though they never succeeded in finding things they had in common, they continued to get closer. It would be more accurate to call it a solitary search, because my mother had fallen in love with that young man, who received money daily for three months without saying much about his life, let alone declaring love or anything that resembled it.

My grandmother became convinced of the affection that her daughter felt and realized that she had fallen in love, so her complicity became unconditional in order to make it possible for the couple to meet each other more frequently instead of only in the plaza. Grandmother was a huge support until she began hearing the rumors. "Vincent is a bad man who hits your daughter," people told her. The first chance she got, my grandmother confronted my mother. Yet my mother denied everything and said that she knew of those rumors, and that they had been started by a jealous young woman Vincent had visited a couple of times. My grandmother's fears were not assuaged.

When Vincent and Elia's courtship had continued for three months, they decided to get married. Upon hearing the news, my grandmother let out a shout of frustration that reached the sky; she was deeply troubled by the rumors about Vincent's violent streak. When my grandfather found out about the engagement, his shout reached infinity. He was worried by his daughter's plans and even went to the church to ask the priest to help him persuade her to change her mind. But my mother wanted to escape from the house. "Vincent, please, get me out of here. I can't take my father anymore," she said. In reality, what worried my grandfather was that his daughter was accustomed to the comforts of the home, where she had had everything she needed. It was evident that the suitor couldn't even offer a wedding, much less a secure place to live. My grandmother understood that her daughter was in love, but if *she* had been the one choosing, she would have gotten rid of Vincent as soon as she found out about the rumors of Vincent's violence.

"You are accustomed to living a life without poverty. This man is lazy; he does nothing with his life!" sobbed my grandmother.

"Not all fingers on a hand are the same," defended my mother. "I am either going to marry him, or I'm going to marry him."

"My grandparents Pillita and Rafael."

They had no choice but to plan the wedding, meet my father's family, buy the wedding dress and groom's suit, and invite nearly the whole village. When I see the photo of my parents coming out of the church, I cannot help but imagine how nervous my

mother must have been. She looked precious in white but wore
no smile. My father seemed to gaze at something in the distance
while children threw rice at the couple and the women in elegant
hats and stylish handbags applauded. Behind the couple came
my grandmother Pillita, my grandfather Rafael, my grandmother
Trina, and two of my mother's friends, Melanie and Mary. In
front of the wedding party, a few boys played with the rice and
the girls fiddled with their dresses. On the honeymoon, the couple
went to the popular beach Manzanillo in Colima. I had also saved
the photos of that trip, but they were burned in a fire in my sister
Nataly's house. My mother was shown looking at the sea, in a
bathing suit with a light smile, enjoying the honeymoon, or at least
that is what it seemed like.

"My parents' wedding (Elia and Vincent)."

"Look how nice you are in this photo. Where is it?" I asked her
the first time she showed me the photos.

"It was my honeymoon."

Enthused about such an important event in the life of a young
woman, I asked how it had been, but she discreetly refused to tell

me. When I finished looking at the photos, she confessed that it had been a trip full of deceptions. She had all the illusions of a girl in love; she had climbed up on a bench so that my father would help her down. When she asked him for help, he answered, "Oh, what a scandalous woman! Just jump." They had barely arrived at Manzanillo, and my father abandoned her in a park. "I'll be right back," he said, but he did not return until the next day. He had gone to a cantina, had drunk more drinks than he could count, and couldn't return to look for her, he confessed. She showed signs of anger, to which he—who had already shown intolerance for interrogations—yelled, "Shut up! Shut up! You bought me, I didn't want you. Now you will live with this."

These words were the beginning of a life filled with pain. When my mother returned from her honeymoon, she decided to take Nataly from Pillita's house to live with her. A year after the wedding, I came into the world.

I was born in 1962 in Ario de Rosales, Michoacán, Mexico. I did not leave there until 1981, a little after the whole town had gossiped about my supposed love affair with the middle school principal. I left the town bitterly because that story had spread like feathers in the wind, but I also left with the hope of changing my destiny in the city of Morelia. I returned to Ario de Rosales for brief visits—this was more than twenty years ago—but I never stayed to live there again. Nor do I think I will be able to return, even if it is just to visit.

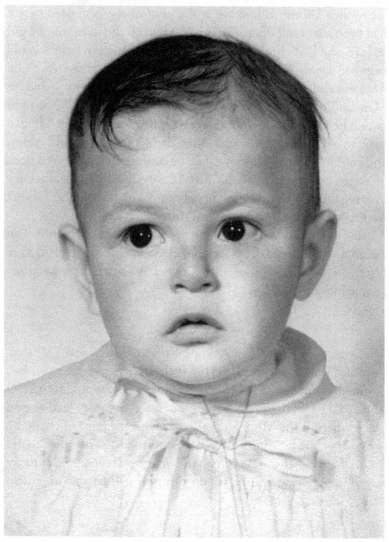

Me, Rosa Lilia, as a baby.

In Ario de Rosales there are no more than thirty thousand inhabitants, although during my childhood it was an even smaller town (in spite of having been founded four centuries before). What had been the land of indigenous *Tarascos* later served as a lodging area for Spaniards, a center of operations for national heroes fighting for independence, and a territory of revolutions. The original name of the town had been just Ario. It became Santiago de Ario during the colonial period, and now Ario de Rosales in honor of the insurgent Don Victor Rosales, a hero from the fight for independence. The majority of the structures in Ario de Rosales are of colonial architecture with beautifully colored roofs. The houses have ample and wide corridors, with many doors connecting to an interior patio like in my friend Teresa Salinas's family's house, which I saw and can still describe from memory: square, connected by brilliantly lighted hallways, and full of hanging plants. From its streets, I remember the stones on which civic parades and pilgrimages to various saints passed all year round: Royal Street, which crossed the city from north to south, would fill up with these kinds of spectacles.

In the main plaza, which had been remodeled many times, grew robust trees that almost made the "fountain of the puppies" disappear. The Santiago Apostle temple had gained a new second wing. Many stores surrounded the plaza, and my grandfather's store was called Downtown Department Store. It was on Portal Juárez Street and sold everything. My grandfather was the first to install a telephone and the first to bring more modern cars to the town. The Villanuevas, the Díaz Barrigas, the Salinas (the family of my best friend Tere, whose father Chucho owned the hardware store), and many other families had businesses and got along well. Their houses were beautiful, and I remember them as being organized and very clean.

I remember Mr. Joaquín Brambila, a short, very serious man with a large nose. He was very famous in and around the town, and many people respected him. Besides being an apothecary, he had been president of Ario de Rosales in the 1940s. In his apothecary La Providencia he sold all kinds of ointments, pills, and creams that served to cure various ailments. With a cream, he cured the whole town of ringworm. His secret formulas brought results—I am sure of this.

If I think about it, I can still see Elia Mares's American clothing store. Elia Mares was a young woman dedicated to having a social life, who enjoyed attending events in the town and socializing with educated people like politicians, professors, and artists of that time. She was a pretty woman, with white skin and a harmonious body. The clothing store did great things for her own wardrobe; she knew how to choose the right articles to draw attention to her figure in any inauguration or social reunion photo. She chose the most refined and modern garments from her store to wear as she posed next to people of authority. That is what she did during the visits from General Lázaro Cárdenas del Rio, who came around the town often.

The general had a special affection for the citizens of Ario; between 1947 and 1970 he was in charge of a project to stimulate development in various localities in Michoacán. The people of Ario (Arienses) called him the General because of his past in the military, and when he passed in the streets, they would go to a lot of trouble to invite him to sightsee, have dinner, or come to meetings to thank him for the changes he was making for the town, especially the improvement of the schools and the drinking water system. Of course, on one of these visits, my grandfather invited him to dine at his house, which is why some photos of the general were hung on the walls.

When I turned sixteen, it was Elia Mares who insisted on introducing me as one of the queens of the patriotic celebrations; each queen represented a sector of development. She proposed that I represent Commerce, and since she had a way with words, she convinced me. It was one of the few moments in which I felt important, despite being extremely embarrassed and shy. On the day of the celebration, they took me around the whole town on a horse. They had put a white dress with fuchsia flowers on me and a flower of the same color in my hair.

"Me, at age sixteen, as queen representing Commerce."

But Elia Mares had a more transcendental role in our family. She raised Oscar, the eleventh child of my uncle Eduardo and aunt Elisa, who was thirteen years old when she married and knew little about raising children and protecting the family. When Oscar was

19

born, things were not going well in Uncle Eduardo's house, which was on the same block as my grandparents' house. The fights were heard from the street, and the plates disappeared in the kitchen, flying in every which direction. If raising ten children had been a drama, one more transformed the situation into chaos. Elia Mares took care of Oscar because she was a friend of Elisa; when the baby was born and Elia saw how desperate Elisa was, she helped her take care of him. Elia felt so much love for the little one that despite her mother, Emilia, whom everyone called El Excelsior, she took Oscar into her home. Elia and Emilia even prepared a room so that the little boy could grow comfortably. Their love for him grew so much that one day Elia asked Elisa to give her the boy.

"I cannot give him away, because he is my son, but you can take care of him and help me with him if you want," responded Elisa.

Oscar's life went on between his true parents' house and Elia and Emilia's house. With time, these women became his mother and grandmother as well. Emilia's nickname, El Excelsior, referred to the second oldest newspaper in DF, or Federal District, the capital of Mexico. Emilia was the first person to find out about what went on and would broadcast it like the newspaper, and just like her daughter, she never failed to attend all social events. She was a likeable woman and was very well mannered, which gave her an enviable level of credibility.

The house where we lived was beautiful, and a few meters away, a river ran through the grounds, which were invaded by avocado trees. Despite the failure in New Italy, my grandfather believed that his daughter would recover from her depression and that Vincent would finally start working. Grandfather also took care—like he had in New Italy—to send them a servant. He gave them the land and put up a store that sold shoes, clothing, perfume, fabrics, and purses. Nataly's presence in the house lasted less than a year, because my mother decided to take her away from the mistreatment and bouts of violence my father inflicted. *This is not the best life I can give you, little one. If I saved you from dying, I cannot put your life at risk again,*

she thought. She talked with my grandmother, asking her to take care of Nataly for just a few days, but something better occurred to my grandmother. Since one of her sisters in Guanajuato had never had children, Pillita asked the sister to take Nataly and raise her. My mother did not think it was a bad idea. She packed a suitcase for little Nataly and sent her to Guanajuato, where she grew, became a woman, and married a man who remains at her side until today. I believe in the saddest part of my heart that my mother was not born to be a mother, and that instead of following her desire to be a nun, she had to raise me and my five siblings in the worst of conditions.

During the first months in that house, my father showed regret and tried to stop drinking alcohol, but his sickness—not just with the alcohol—soon showed its true face. Even the servant girls who passed one after another through our house became victims of my father's hormonal lack of control. He left four of them pregnant, and my mother offered her condolences before having to let them go. Her good woman's heart—or nun's heart—accepted my father without complaints.

Grandfather realized that the business he gave to my father had not been successful. So, although he did not take the house away from my parents, he stopped helping out financially. "This man has to work," he said. He promised my mother that if she left Vincent, he would take care of her; he could set up another business for my mother, and only for my mother.

That house was a home neither for Nataly nor for me. From the age of four onward, I lived with my grandparents and spent the majority of my childhood in my grandfather's store, part of the large house he had bought from some Spaniards before leaving Guanajuato, where he had installed a business. He was not scared to start other businesses elsewhere. He exchanged everything he owned in Guanajuato for the big house in Ario de Rosales. He never questioned the future of his businesses—he always had the confidence and the energy to make them work. He had an energy like no one I have met in my life. As a girl, I thought that he had more energy than Hitler; nowadays it seems so stupid to make that comparison.

The house had enormous rooms and living spaces, where I lived the safest, yet saddest, days of my life. Every day, my grandfather would stay until very late doing business with the ranchers around the area, who bought almost everything that we sold. When I was five years old, I helped him (sometimes until after midnight) to prepare the sacks with kilos and half kilos of sugar and beans. There was merchandise for each of the clients, from beans to hunting rifles. My grandmother Pillita organized the servants and employees to help carry the merchandise, organize the stores, and attend to the customers.

The store was just one of the many businesses my grandfather ran; his whole life was dedicated to the businesses. "I was born for this," he said. In other places in Michoacán he cultivated coffee and sugarcane to take to the Charanda factory, which prepared an alcoholic drink much like tequila, typical of the Michoacán state, and which we Mexicans use as a sweetener. From the sticky sugarcane is extracted a juice and other derivatives like *piloncillo*, a sweet pulp much like brown sugar that would leave me totally stained and sticky when I bought fritters in the town gateway, where men and women sold delicious street food, especially to those who had stayed up all night. At one of these stations worked Evaristo, who sold tacos made of the meat from a cow's neck, called "head" tacos, soups, and other foods to support his eight children. Of course I still remember the little cart that sold fritters with piloncillo. I had always loved the sweet dough, until one night my aunt Barbara had an uncontrollable craving for them. I still remember Barbara's anger about an innocent mistake I made that night; it left an inexplicable emptiness in my heart and a bleeding hole in my head.

One of the properties that my grandfather owned was very far from the town; I have a few memories of this property, only in small segments of dreams. On sunny days, when grandfather let me, I would go to the country with the employees—only to work, of course, never to play. Grandfather used to say that we should all help and that it made us better people. On occasion my grandmother would go along; we would climb up into the truck and go. It was an immense property, full of trees that seemed gigantic, but with the years I slowly discovered that I could reach the tops with small ladders. I would pick the fruit from the coffee trees and eat it with so much pleasure that I would hide away under some tree far away to enjoy it. This sensation of picking the fruit and eating it down to the cores made me happy. On the way we would pick blueberries, which Aurora (a cook who worked forty years for my grandmother) transformed into one of Pillita's favorite desserts. Her son Galdino was the one in charge of organizing the blueberries, just as he was the one who had to put the boxes of blueberries in order when I meddled with them.

Aurora prepared desserts that no one was capable of turning down. She was a very timid woman with a strong body. She had short, chubby arms, but she moved so quickly that in one afternoon she could prepare two custards, two gelatin desserts, and two pies. Life became bitter the day Aurora got sick. She did not like doctors and wouldn't take pills, not even for a strong headache. Every ailment she had was cured with teas and strange mixtures of local herbs.

It was only years later, when the pain from her uterus became intolerable, that she went to the doctor to hear that she had cancer. My grandmother accompanied her to the hospital, promised her a quick recovery, sent her to her home, and paid for her exams and then the operation. She would finally surprise her by giving Aurora a house of her own. Aurora did not stop crying from gratitude for almost three days.

My grandfather had no friends but had many people with whom he did business. I do not know how he met the Spaniards from whom he bought his Downtown Department Store. It was a risky venture, because he exchanged everything he had in Guanajuato for the store in Ario de Rosales. He always said it was a town that would grow rapidly and that he had to be there to grow with it. He knew a thing or two about the Spaniards, and the few things he knew left the whole family with their hair on end.

The Spaniard's wife was sick with arthritis, and the doctor recommended that she move to a warmer climate so that she would not feel so much pain. It rains six months out of the year in Ario de Rosales, and the cold mixes with the fog, leaving people barely able to see. The woman lived afflicted by the pain in her arms and legs. The doctor had advised her to change climate more than ten times, because it was the cold that was provoking all the pain in her bones. The Spaniard, also a venturing type, accepted my grandfather's offer and they decided to do the transaction. My grandparents' house seemed like many in the south of France—which I have seen in photos—except that it had only wood, with many windows, and was full of nooks and corridors.

In the beginning we used the room that the Spanish couple had used, but soon, my grandfather constructed bedrooms on the first floor and added a second floor to the house. The woman's sickness was not the strange thing. Later we found out the truth. Besides looking for a better place for his wife's sickness, the Spaniard and his family wanted to escape the memory of a tragic episode. One of the Spaniard's employees had fallen in love with the daughter and had asked for her hand in marriage. Such a situation would not have been tolerated by the Spaniard, since he already had a fiancé lined up, even though he did not want his daughter to marry yet because he thought she was too young to lose her virginity. Against all odds and everyone's wishes, the day of the wedding with the young employee arrived, and the Spaniard decided to kill the "bastard," as he called him. In the midst of the rush of the preparations, the young man died in the stairway, stabbed. The daughter could not take the pain of the disappearance of her beloved, and shut herself away in her room to mourn his absence. A servant girl who had witnessed the crime noted the daughter's anguish and decided to tell her what had happened to the fiancé, on the condition that the daughter would not tell anyone how she found out. After hearing the tragic news, the fiancée found herself in a state of despair.

"I do not want to live. I want you to bury me where you buried Rodrigo," the girl told her father. "I know that you killed him and you buried him here in the house so that no one would know about the scandal," she told him a few days later.

The girl asked her father to swear that if she died, he would bury her in the house. The next week, still dressed in white, the girl took rat poison and died in her bed, embracing a few mementos.

To follow through with the promise, they buried her under one of the bedrooms. One of the Spaniard's employees stayed on to work for my grandfather and told him the true story. The Spaniard had been the one who killed the girl's fiancé. That story remained like a myth and we never tried to find out the truth, nor did we look for the couple's bodies.

We could say that Nataly took on the role of an older sister, but she was raised by the aunt in Guanajuato. We could say that I was the oldest of my siblings, but I was the only one raised by my grandparents. The sibling who was born next and was raised by my mother was Damián—the only boy—who was soon followed by Mili, Susana, Carmen (who died at nine months), Ernestina, and the youngest: Esmeralda. They lived many years in the punishment of having to share the house with my father. Despite them living near my grandparents, the visits I could make were controlled by my grandmother and prohibited by my mother; she did not want me to experience the violence in her house.

My father rarely showed interest in me. He would call me "trash," and he called Damián "rubbish," yet these were terms of endearment for him. The one who did not escape his violence was my mother; the hate he felt for the woman who had bought him in the plaza was visible, and he had her stuck in a bubble of sadness in a dark, lifeless house. Grandmother insisted on signing my mother up with some kind of shop, or persuading her to take on some business that would give her back the energy she once had.

One afternoon when I was nine years old, I went to the house where everyone in my, family except me, was living. I wanted to play with Damián, and when I arrived, saw that my mother had put on makeup; her lips were red, and she had styled her hair. After seeing her so often with dark bags under her eyes and always having thrown on the first clothing she could find, I was impressed with the beauty I saw.

But that afternoon my father arrived in a bad mood: "Prostitute! Low woman!" He dragged her around through the entire house, hit her a number of times on the ground, and then took her to the patio, where the pigs my grandmother had given her were kept. Damián hugged me and, together, we put ourselves in front of him, like two naive children, to make him stop hitting her. He was drunk and felt even less compassion than normal. He kept dragging her through the yard for several meters until he stopped right in a mud pool. Finding excrements, he took some and spread them on her face. "This is what you deserve," he told her. Damián started to cry and so did I. We tried to take his hands, but we could not dampen his vengeful spirit. "Let her go!" we cried, until the fatigue and the imbalance from his drunkenness knocked him down to one side of the mud pool.

While my mother went to bathe, I had Damián lie down in his bed and go to sleep. My mother appeared timidly in the room and told me to return to my grandmother's house, as she had so many times. I even remember one night that my uncle Rodrigo—sent by my grandmother—tried to leave me with my mother because I would not stop crying and begging to be with her. He knocked on my mother's window.

"I brought you your daughter, who wants only you and has not stopped crying all day. Pillita asks you to please let her stay with you tonight.

"No, Rodrigo, take her back with you. I cannot have her here."

But my uncle insisted, took me in his arms, and put me in the window. He immediately took out a small bag full of candies that he had taken from the store. When my uncle Rodrigo went running away, my mother yanked the bag and threw the candies into the room.

"I cannot take care of you! Don't you understand? In your grandmother's house you have comfort, food, servants ... How is it possible that you want to live here?" she said as she shook me angrily.

It took me a long time to understand her rejection. I believed for many years that my pain had to do with the images of violence I saw in that house, but my greatest suffering came from the rejection by my own mother, the abandonment and loneliness that the separation caused me. My sisters, in a conversation with me many years ago, told me that my mother felt like she had a debt to me for not having raised me. Sometimes she cried and felt regret for not having been closer to me or keeping me close to my sisters, despite the circumstances. I hated her for a long time and refused to see her until I stopped feeling a grudge. But now that more than forty years have passed, I have come to see that leaving me at my grandparents' house when I was four was the best alternative that my mother had at the time. I was a lively girl, always wanting to learn, but I made my mother nervous because every word I spoke could end in an episode of rage from my father. My mother tried to protect me, just like she protected Nataly, and did what she thought was best.

There were so many bedrooms and living spaces that my grandfather built in the house that I would use them as hideouts; I disappeared and chose any one of them when I did something bad or when something happened to me. In one of the rooms, I set up the restaurant that I had always wanted to have in my eight long years. I gave the name The Bonfire to the place that gave me such peace and space to feel free in a house that was so large yet so limiting. I had very clear ideas; there were so many things in each room that when I started looking around, I always found what I wanted. Some pieces of iron served to simulate a fire, and an old table would be to serve the clients. Although my setting was largely imaginary, my cooking was real. My grandfather had all kinds of things in the store, but I wanted to have everything—or almost everything—to be my own, so I adapted sardine cans to be my trays. I made tortillas by hand, fried enchiladas, and made my own chili. On the second floor there was a room full of dried fish, or *guachinango,* that my grandfather hung up on lines to dry. He had so much that he couldn't keep track of it, so I took a few to prepare with garlic and flour, fried them, and served them with whatever I had on hand. It was marvelous to play this game and feel like a business owner and cook. No one bothered to ask about me, and the house was so big that I did not bother anyone anyway.

The only client in my restaurant was my uncle Rodrigo, my mother's brother, who visited our house daily. He was an alcoholic who would have little luck in his future. He had been spoiled by my father, who said to him since he was very young, "Don't work, little guy, that's what your dad is for." Mireya, Rodrigo's wife, was very white and had the air of an actress. Together, they had three children. My uncle Rodrigo never knew his youngest child. Mireya frequently came and went from her mother's house and took her children along when Rodrigo drank, because my uncle—even though he did not hit her—had the habit of breaking everything in his path if the alcohol took hold of his body. When he was sober, he worked and helped my grandfather; when he wasn't, however, he would either go around the town with his friends or shut himself in the house with a bottle, his friend in hard times.

Uncle Rodrigo spent a lot of time with us, but when it was time to eat, he grabbed his bag and left. He would say that the soup needed more salt, or that the meat was overcooked. When he did not leave because of the food, he would go because my aunt Barbara and my grandfather began with their sermons of rehabilitation. One time, in the middle of an argument, he choked on a piece of chicken and we all had to hit him on his back. He liked to go to my restaurant because I followed his drunken jokes and conversations.

"What do you have to eat? Show me your menu," he would say, as if acting.

I knew his routine very well, but soon his spoken routine disappeared.

"I'll be right back," he would say hurriedly. He would open a storage room, uncap a bottle of Charanda, and drink it. Then he'd return as if nothing had happened, but with a scent on his breath that I would disguise with my cooking. In times of desperation—as

I discovered a couple of times—he would open bottles of perfume, daydream while taking in the scent, and drink down the liquid.

"I have enchiladas and fish in garlic sauce, and I have beans simmering in the pot and a salsa in the stone mortar."

"I'll take it all, Miss," he responded. "I like everything you prepare in this restaurant."

I saw him suffer and I also suffered (silently) with his alcoholism. I never asked him to stop drinking or to check into a rehabilitation clinic; there were plenty of people to make those suggestions. My grandfather locked him in a room on the second floor many times so that he would not continue slowly killing himself. My uncle Rodrigo went crazy; he would tear the room apart, breaking the windows and walking on the neighbors' roofs until finding a lamppost and lowering himself like a monkey. The fact that he drank perfume seemed horrible to me; he would inspect each room until finding the smallest bottle with the smell of alcohol. After the third time he broke the windows, they shut him in a room without windows.

One afternoon while he was shut in that room, he heard my voice in the hallway, knelt down, and, through the large slit under the door said, "Rosa Lilia! Go to the pharmacy and bring me alcohol—please, I am begging you." He sounded desperate, so I ran to the kitchen and asked Aurora to fill a bottle with water, which I soon had to trade again because the first bottle did not fit under the doorway. I slid the second bottle under the door and stayed around for a moment expecting to hear him complain, but he said nothing; he thought the water was alcohol. *He's going crazy for real*, I thought. I had suspected this days before, when they let him go to the kitchen.

That morning, he opened all the cabinets looking for something that smelled like alcohol. Since he didn't find even a perfume bottle, he started running in circles around the table: "Follow me!" he said to me. At first I felt embarrassed, but then I fell into his game, and we went so many times around that we ended up laughing on the floor. Aurora slowly shook her head. Taking care of Uncle Rodrigo was entertaining; I learned to love him and also discovered that I have a special way with taking care of sick people.

Since then, I believed that my destiny was to be a doctor. I wanted to grow up quickly, go to preparatory school and then to college, and to work in a hospital that could cure my uncle, my grandmother, and anyone who got sick. In that way, I could also please my grandfather, who almost hit me when he found out that I had a restaurant and dreamed about being a chef. My grandmother traveled almost every month to Guanajuato; she took advantage of those times to see her sisters and consult her doctors. I never knew exactly what she suffered from, but she always complained of dizziness, pain in her bones, and strange episodes of the sensation of suffocating—like one day in the middle of the street and in front of a house of handsome young men. Later she described the suffocating sensation as "spiders in my throat."

On one of her trips, my grandmother found a psychiatric clinic in Guanajuato, which everyone knew as a madhouse. Given that Uncle Rodrigo's bouts of craziness were getting more critical, Grandfather thought the clinic was a perfect idea. One night, when Uncle Rodrigo would not stop yelling, they gave him a little bottle of alcohol, I don't remember which kind. I saw that my grandparents and my aunt mixed in something yellow that they had asked me to buy at the pharmacy. An hour later, my uncle Rodrigo had fallen asleep. Aunt Barbara accompanied my grandparents up to the door, helped them lift Uncle Rodrigo into the car, and yelled after them, "Have a good trip!"

She came back into the house and saw me crying, sitting in a corner of the room … I don't know if I cried because of the uncertainty of my uncle Rodrigo's destiny or because he was the only client for my restaurant. Aunt Barbara lifted me up by my arm and pushed me through the hall.

Two months later, Uncle Rodrigo was able to escape from the mental hospital. The hospital called my grandparents' house to inform them, and the hospital security staff began the quest to find my uncle. A few days after the quest began, my uncle appeared in my mother's house in Irapuato, asking her for money to buy a bottle.

"Rodrigo! How did you escape? Everyone is looking for you, little brother."

"Elia, please, I am dying, I need money. I promise I won't tell anyone that you helped me."

My mother hugged him and gave however many pesos were necessary to buy a glass of tequila in the nearest pub.

That night, Uncle Rodrigo got revenge for having been tricked. It was a rainy, foggy night. I was in my room with the lights off, trying to sleep and ignoring a headache. I felt tired and weak because I wasn't eating; I couldn't stop thinking about how many things went on in this house and in my family. All of a sudden, I heard yelling. I sat up in bed, waiting for it to happen again. I walked toward my door.

"Let him go!" I heard. I had no doubt that my grandmother had said it. I ran to the room, and when I opened the door, I saw that my uncle Rodrigo was grabbing my grandfather's neck. Pillita tried to separate the two but couldn't.

"Why did you lock me away, you evil old man? I am not crazy! Let me die if that's what I want."

I helped Pillita in her effort to separate them until my uncle Rodrigo fell to the floor. Grandfather had turned purple and lay still on the bed. My uncle stood up and walked out of the bedroom, furious. He repeated, "Evil old man." We didn't see him for days.

Even though I didn't have clients in my restaurant, I continued to cook. I had added to my assets a hen that laid two eggs each day. I don't remember her name; in fact, I am sure that I never came to name her. I kept the hen in the little house next door—where Buki, the famous Mexican singer Marco Antonio Solis, lived—so that my grandfather wouldn't punish me for having it. It was better that the hen didn't have a name, because one day my grandfather discovered the hen on our patio. He saw it eating bread crumbs that I had thrown down from a window on the second floor, and yelled for an employee to kill it.

"Take her to Aurora to use for tomorrow's lunch," he said. The next day, I went to the kitchen, but there were no traces of the head or of the feathers. But there *was* a pot full of soup. When Aurora saw me spying on her, I asked her what was in the pot; she confirmed the tragic news for me. I closed myself in my room for hours and passed the following days without eating. I already had problems digesting meat, but after the hen's murder, I hated having any type of animal on my plate.

During those days I dedicated myself to eating fruit, especially when I went out to Grandfather's land in the country. I began to get thin and pale and to have stomachaches and fever. Cucumbers with hot pepper, salt, and lime became my favorite food; I enjoyed it as though it were the last food on earth. Later, at home, I would end up vomiting in my bed. Grandmother believed that it was some bacteria that the hen had passed along to me, or something I had cooked improperly in my restaurant.

Buki's house, which had served as the hen's hiding place, also was useful because of the medlar tree on which I used to throw out the meat, milk, and eggs that Aurora brought me to eat. Elenita, Buki's mother, was a very reserved woman, friendly but not sociable, and very different from her husband. Surprised by the adornments in her tree, she decided one day to show up at my house to talk with my grandmother.

"I am very worried about your granddaughter. I now know why she is sick and malnourished," she said to my grandmother. "Come with me."

Elenita led her to the yard.

"Here, Pillita, look. Your granddaughter throws food out the window into my medlar tree. Do you see the scraps of meat and eggs?"

My grandmother felt embarrassed, but Elenita was a patient woman and told her not to worry but to talk to me because this situation was serious for a girl. When Grandmother entered my room, I guessed from her body language what she wanted to say to me.

"I'm sorry," I told her. And I had to confess that I had barely eaten anything for weeks, that some of the medlars were missing because I had eaten them, and that then I had begun to throw what Aurora cooked onto the tree.

Buki's family lived from the fabric business. From the few times that I entered his house, I was left with the memory of a long, narrow hall, with many rolls of cloth all around. Buki lived there, along with his parents, Antonio and Elenita, his six brothers (Buki was the fifth of the boys) and the only sister. Buki's aunts lived in one part of the house, two famous elderly ladies who had transcended from a joke to a myth for having hidden golden coins under the chimney.

They told everyone that in the time of the Mexican Revolution—since there were no banks and it was dangerous to keep money in the house because *Zapatistas* and *Villistas*, followers of revolutionaries Emiliano Zapata and Pancho Villa, could appear at any moment—possessions in the form of money and other assets were hidden. Because of this, Buki's aunts put their gold in clay pots, wrapped the pots in paper, and dug a hole underneath the chimney. It was also said that the old women had riches but did not want to share with anyone, that their only occupation was to stay in the house to guard their possessions. I do not remember if Buki's aunts were from his mother's or his father's side of the family, but I do remember that they seemed mysterious and rarely let themselves be seen by outsiders.

Business in the town was not easy, and required respect and trust from clients. Above all, it needed a closed fist and a watchful eye to make sure the merchandise was sold at a fair price and not given away. Sometimes sales in the Solis's house did not go well, so Mr. Antonio visited my family's store when my grandfather was not around. My grandmother greeted Antonio cheerfully. He was a fun man who like to converse with everybody and was very good at telling jokes; he was so crafty, or *pícaro*, that people in the town ended up calling him Pikirín. It was impossible to avoid helping him, and Pillita had no problems with this.

Another business that Antonio managed was with roosters, but he raised them in his brother's house fifteen minutes outside the town ... I'll call him Miguel Angel because I don't remember his name. The roosters, fine and colorful, were used in clandestine cock fights or were sold. I remember that some of them were very pretty, but it was not a profitable enough business to support a large family. Miguel Angel had a daughter with very creamy skin, who was beautiful and almost perfect, whose name was Rosa Lilia. When my aunt Barbara met this girl, she was enchanted. She said the girl's white skin and light eyes were a manifestation of the Aryan race, "the most lively and intelligent," she would say. My aunt was a faithful follower of the racial paranoia of Hitler, which is why, when I was born, despite my mother's desire to name me Dalila, I instead received the beautiful girl's name.

The house with the medlar tree would become unoccupied some years later, when Buki became famous. Marco—the name by which I met him and remember him—became interested in music very young, and had the habit of singing and transforming all objects into musical instruments. He was always going around with his cousins, looking for something to do. Among the objects he would use, according to his friends, were glass bottles to see the eclipse. Along with a friend, besides cutting our fingers on the bottle parts, we had to pay Marco and his friends to use the invention. On another day, the boys persuaded us to spend an afternoon watching movies, supposedly horror films, at Marco's house. When we entered the house, they turned off the lights and began to yell like ghosts. They chased us, saying they were the reincarnation of the devil; that was the horror movie. It was a fun group, and the youth were daring but respectful.

In his adolescence, accompanied by his guitar and his inseparable cousins, Marco would spend hours in the plaza, where there was always a rancher who would leave a coin. I don't know how far into high school Marco went before he decided to test fate in the Federal District of Mexico, the capital DF, but he went with the certainty that he would triumph. In 1970, Marco was eleven years old and had already formed his first duo, Solis, with his cousin Joel. Marco was three years older than me, but his ambitions seemed like that of a grown man. With the name *Solis,* the duo performed in Raul Velasco's program *Always on Sundays.* This live show featured various international celebrities. The duo's success was indisputable, so that in little time they expanded into a band and changed their name to The Bukis (which meant "youth" in the *Purépecha* language). Since then, Marco's career has been successful and everyone in our town holds him on a pedestal. I remember that one of their first songs was "Cardboard House," in honor of the poor and the abuse they suffer from the rich. This very song was heard by the whole town, and its inhabitants said proudly that Marco was a child of this land.

People say that when Marco visited the television program, Luis Echeverría's wife (the Mexican first lady) was in the audience. She thought the two were good musicians and that they would have a future in the music business and promised to help them. When they were on their way to fame, Buki's family moved out, and my grandfather was able to buy the house to expand his property.

When I was eleven years old, my restaurant saw a sad ending. It was a day in which my grandfather began to organize the storage rooms—this had never happened, because that particular task belonged to the servants. He complained for days that the piloncillo storeroom smelled like urine, so he began to take inventory of all the storerooms to confirm that only the one with the piloncillo had that problem. I saw him irritated, going around to each of the thirty narrow, tall storerooms, and I followed him. I begged God not to let my grandfather discover my restaurant. He looked around the whole house until he found the room with a little sign that said THE BONFIRE. I was beside myself when I listened to what he did. He took the pots, inspected the boxes, kicked the table, and yelled, "Rosa Lilia!" When I heard my name, I ran to the first floor and stayed hidden behind a door. Grandfather came down, furious, and told the first servant he saw, "Go take down the trash that's up in that room."

Pillita seemed startled.

"What's going on, Rafael?"

"This girl is doing her things again. Upstairs I found scraps of rotten fish, chili, pots … She was playing restaurant … Let me find her … She'll see…"

"But she is just a girl …," my grandmother tried to defend me.

"She is a girl who lives with us and has to help us. She can't be doing foolishness and wasting products from the store."

Grandfather left the house and I ran to Pillita's arms. We both followed the servant and saw that she threw everything into a cloth bag and threw the bag into the trash. There are times in my life that I don't remember; I confuse them or I complete them with dreams, but other moments were left marked like scars. When I saw my restaurant destroyed, I felt that everything had lost sense and purpose. I did not eat well, Aunt Barbara treated me like a fool, Uncle Rodrigo was sick, my mother had asked me not to visit her, my grandfather did not let me play, and my grandmother did not protect me like I needed her to. The room where my restaurant was had been my life, my own idea. I hated Grandfather. Everyone respected him, but on more than one occasion, we all hoped he would die. Dedicating his life to business had transformed him into a cold man who always looked at the most convenient way to make more and more money, to buy properties and manage them at his whim. He was not selfish, but he liked to control everything.

Pillita sighed daily; she seemed so tired of Grandfather that many times I feared that one day she would pack her bags and leave me there alone. Like a good woman submissive to sexism, she never showed her opinion but always found a way around his rules. She didn't trick him in order to be with other men but rather to do social deeds. She modified some things to benefit other people with her acts of kindness. She would leave the house dressed up, claiming to visit her friends, the Karrases, a Greek family in town, when instead she was leaving to do charity. Grandfather Rafael paid too little attention to her at those moments, so he never suspected that he was being tricked.

In a certain way, Pillita understood that Grandfather was the way he was because of his history; he was orphaned at the age of nine. At twelve years of age, he sold ice cream, and a few years later he had installed his first creamery in a town smaller than Ario de Rosales, named New Town in Guanajuato, where he met Pillita. A few years later, they married in León.

Grandfather liked women, but my grandmother kept an eye on him as much as she could. She had experience ever since before getting engaged because Grandfather was confused. Pillita had three sisters: Consuelo, Emilia (or Milla), and Esperanza (or Lancha). He dispensed of Consuelo because she was not attractive and had a bitter character, but he conquered both Milla and Lancha, who were more cheerful. Yet because of so much confusion about which one to choose, he ended up marrying Pillita. In the conversations in the living room, with friends, authorities, or distinguished clients—those conversations in which children have to keep their mouths shut—Grandfather would say very naturally, "Truthfully, I didn't know which one I should choose. First I chose Lancha, and then I wanted Milla, but in the end I married Pillita." He would chuckle thinking of his achievement.

Grandmother laughed at his joke, but her laughter sounded forced.

The ranchers were the people who really adored my grandfather; they themselves had taken on the task of publicizing the hours of operation of his store: "Don Rafael is open late at night," they commented. Sometimes he did not sleep because the ranchers began their commercial pilgrimage in the wee hours of the morning. They would travel miles in search of merchandise to take to their towns. They brought pickup trucks or horses loaded with seeds, clothing, tools, gunpowder, and even firearms for hunting. My grandmother was in charge of the staff; she supervised the work in the store and in the house, hiring and firing (according to my grandfather's instructions), confirming that all the merchandise was in order, and removing the money that had accumulated during the day. The one responsible for training the sales employees was my grandfather; in this area, there was no better teacher. I witnessed it one morning when I was walking around the store.

I stayed in a corner so I wouldn't bother anyone. A merchant came in and asked one of the attendants if she had a nail, bringing one out of his pocket to show her. She looked in all the drawers and laid out ten types of nails on the counter—none of them was like the nail the customer needed. The attendant said, "I'm sorry, sir, we don't have that kind of nail." Just as the man was walking out of the store, my grandfather appeared.

"What did the gentleman want?" he said hurriedly.

"A nail, but we don't have the right kind," the employee told my grandfather, who had been spying on her.

Grandfather became furious. No one could leave the store without having bought what he needed or even an item he was not looking for. When something like that happened, Grandfather became so angry that he always repeated the same strange phrase.

"Charap camea camon chuchirimico!" he yelled.

I don't know where that saying would have come from; I can't even write it as it should be written, but it sounded like *"Charap camea camon chuchirimico."* It was the first thing he would say when he became angry. The young woman was frightened.

"Charap camea camon chuchirimico!" he yelled, this time more forcefully. "Go bring him back here!"

The girl almost started crying. She went out and came back into the doorway, responding, "He is already going around the church" as she tried to catch her breath.

"Bring him here!" he yelled back, snapping his fingers.

The girl ran to bring the customer. I had continued in the corner of the store, almost behind a box. I watched as the merchant returned. Grandfather apologized for not having the nail for which the man was searching and said, "I am sure that I can help you with something else." They chatted for several minutes about the town, the planting season, the weather, and any other subject that occurred to my grandfather.

The merchant ended up buying shearing scissors, a sack of fertilizer, and even a pair of shoes. I was impressed by my grandfather's transformation and his capacity to smile, ask the right questions, and make sure the man did not leave empty-handed.

"See you soon, Mr. Rafael," the man said.

My grandfather shook his hand, gave him a handful of candies—the kind that he no longer sold—and responded, "Give my regards to your family."

"I don't want anyone leaving here without buying something," he told the young woman, and then left.

This very strange phrase that Grandfather would say was surely in the *Tarasco* language or *Purépecha,* a language that can still be heard on an island named Janitzio in Lake Pátzcuaro. There are many meanings of the word *Janitzio,* among which are "place where it rains," "place for fishing," and "cornflower," but without a doubt, it means a magical place, full of cultural wealth. Many of its inhabitants have conserved their clothing and the Purépecha language. Every year on November 2, the island receives thousands of people who celebrate their dead, a deeply rooted tradition in all of Mexico and well known around the world.

Hundreds of tourists arrive to see how the town remembers their dead. The cemetery fills with decorations and *cempasúchil* flowers or Chinese carnations with yellow tones, popular for use in these types of celebrations. In addition, the visitors take along pozole, a Mexican stew; skulls filled with sweets; and, of course, the dead person's favorite food, all in an atmosphere illuminated by candles. On November 1, the inhabitants celebrate the angels, the youngest children who have left the world of the living. If an offering is being made for the first time after the child's death, the godfather takes the dead child a kind of bow made of yellow and orange flowers, and the skulls filled with sweets are exchanged for figurines of little angels or animals. The whole ritual begins in the houses where the dead previously lived and ends in the cemetery with the delivery of the offering and prayers for eternal rest. It is truly magical.

My uncle Rodrigo, a little time before being committed to the mental hospital, asked me to learn a phrase in Purépecha.

"When we go to Janitzio and you see a Tarasco, you will say to him, *'Nani ranchi conconchures tachines con chiriwisky whisky,'* my uncle said in a natural way. Even though I don't know how exactly to write the phrase, I do remember how it sounded. I learned this phrase with all my heart, and on a day when my uncle was not drunk, we went to Janitzio with my cousin Rodrigo. When we arrived at the beautiful place, I said to a man there, *"Nani ranchi conconchures tachines con chiriwisky whisky,"* meaning, "Give me beans with a tortilla, *charalito* fish, and chili, please."

I was thankful that I was able to repeat these words and enjoy a delicious meal. I still remember the scent and the taste of that dish, and have even greater reason for remembering the place because it was my favorite for a long time. I had fun with each thing I saw. Janitzio's streets were full of surprises, like the dance of "the old men"—men dressed in white pants with embroidery, white shirts, and colorful ponchos. They were dressed in the attire of countrymen from the region, accompanied by a staff and a mask imitating the face of a friendly, cheerful old man. Their hunchbacked, ailing bodies contrasted with the rhythm, the twirls, and the quick stomping that produced a peculiar sound. It is still possible to see them dancing; there are dancers of all ages who pass hours on end near the lake, entertaining the visitors.

My aunt Barbara also took me there a couple of times, but those trips were not as fun as they had been with Uncle Rodrigo. First, I had to persuade her to take me, and since she liked to see me humiliated, she would say that I couldn't go until all of my cousins were in the car, ready to go. "You are too ugly to be taken out of the house," she would say. "It would be better for you to stay so you could clean and take care of my cats."

In any case, I did everything she wanted; I cleaned her room, fed the cats, and even shined all of her lamps. Despite her cruel game (and it wasn't worth it to talk about her mistreatment on the way), the trip seemed beautiful, and the destination, a paradise. Janitzio Island is one of seven islands in large, beautiful Lake Pátzcuaro. In order to cross, we had to take a motorboat for thirty minutes, always with the same boatman. Since my aunt had an obsession with light-skinned people, she would always pick the same man. I remember that in Lake Pátzcuaro there was a fish that was exclusive to this lake and to Japan. It was a very different species, white, and the most delicious that I have tasted in my life. It was the only fish that my grandmother could eat; any other seafood would produce an allergy. Upon arriving back at the house she would ask, "Did you bring me fish?"

On Janitzio was constructed a 130-foot monument dedicated to Morelos, a hero from the Mexican independence movement and a native of Michoacán. It is a gigantic sculpture with spiral stairways that go up inside the statue. Its left arm holds a sword that serves as a support, and its right arm is raised to the sky in a gesture of triumph. From that very arm and its fisted hand, one can see the whole Lake Pátzcuaro.

I told of that trip and other happy things when my mother visited me at my grandparents' house. I was nine years old at the time. I would never tell her about the things that happened with my aunt Barbara, not while I still lived in that house. Yet my mother knew how her sister was. When she would finish the visit, I would cling to her so that she would take me with her. I wanted to be with my brothers, and I didn't care about the conditions in her house. On each occasion, her visit ended in a crying fit or a tantrum when I had to say good-bye. I tried to cry but did not succeed; instead, it seemed like I would suffocate, and would have to run to the bathroom to throw cold water on myself.

I tried not to let my aunt see me, because if my crying got out of control, Barbara would hit me. Though I didn't understand it then, I later realized later that Barbara resented me because she was both hateful toward and jealous of my mother. Some of Barbara's anger stemmed from my mother's marriage to a poor, abusive man of whom the community spoke badly. This marriage was not only unfortunate for my mother but also brought negative attention to her family. Barbara took out her resentment toward my mother on me.

One day Pillita spoke with my mother, asking her—again—to accept me back into her house, but my mother said that she couldn't and told of a new drama.

"Vincent killed two men in a cantina," she said. That day Vincent had arrived at home full of rage. "I am going to hang you!" he cried, furious, and began to chase her. My mother took my two brothers and lifted them up to the roof, and then she went up too and was helped by her neighbors, who had heard the screaming and come out to their yard. At that moment they realized the truth about my mother's life, and in the future they would call the police each time they heard screams. Their calls to the police and my mother's prayers saved her life more than once. I do not like to criticize religious people, but faith itself and my mother's conviction led my mother to tolerate the beatings.

"God has sent me this suffering and I have to accept it," she would say. She felt guilty for not having become a nun or turning her soul over to God. After that conversation with my aunt Barbara, my mother decided that I could stay a day or two with her, whenever my father was not angry. On those days, I watched her pray the entire day, clinging to a rosary with which she would pray for Vincent and her children. She would spend the whole day in penitence while the house seemed like a pigsty. Damián and Mili would stay alone in some room or play in the patio. At night no one would bathe them. During those visits, I became convinced of how cruel my father was.

My father could surely be found in a cantina named Little by Little, You'll Get There, Bastard," a place full of death and prostitutes. One day when I was six years old, my mother sent me and Damián to follow my father. We waited outside after he went in, sitting nearby until a man came out and left the door open. Through the open doorway, we saw my father with a bottle in one hand, caressing a woman with the other hand. The women at the other tables had their dresses undone, and one was sitting on a drunken man's lap; he barely touched her.

We returned home excited, because the scene was quite new for us, and told my mother what we had seen. She wasn't at all surprised, and seemed numb when we told her the details. She continued praying. When my father returned from the brothel, he would tell my mother that he had slept with three women, and that they were all better than her. Other times, he would grab her arm and pull her into the bedroom; my other sisters were born from those encounters. When I saw my father with those women, I hated prostitutes.

One night, in that very cantina, my father got involved in a fight for a young woman. He was so out of control that he had no time to realize that the badly wounded man whom he was on the verge of choking was a well-known politician in the town. My father had him on the ground, almost dead, when the owner of the cantina—who never intervened in drunken arguments—shot a gun into the air. Everyone returned to his respective table. The politician got his breath back, stood up without a word, smoothed his clothing, and hobbled out of the cantina. After that fight, the politician's brother sent a message to my father: "If you don't leave this town, I will kill you."

My father knew quite well with whom he was dealing and that the threat was sincere; he had hit many people without any serious consequences, but he was sure that the politician would send killers looking for him. Besides, he had to consider the threat that my uncle Eduardo had made a few days earlier: "If you hit Elia again, I will personally make you disappear."

That night of the fight with the politician, my father came home and saw that my mother and siblings were gone. My mother had left a few hours before for Irapuato in the state of Guanajuato. She was going to the house of my grandfather's niece Delfina because she was convinced that Vincent was crazy and nothing could be done for him. She was scared because she was sure that my father would do anything necessary to find her. This story would be repeated years later, when I escaped from my first husband, Leandro. "I bought this gun to use on you," Leandro would later say to me. "If you don't leave, I will kill you."

Delfina was a caring woman who liked living in Irapuato because it was the second-largest city in Guanajuato, not too big, not too small. Agriculture provided work for almost everyone, especially from the production of strawberries, grains, and vegetables. The city's architecture was beautiful, with adobe houses that remained intact until the Presa del Conejo dam ruptured in 1973 and resulted in a flood that wiped them out.

Delfina read tarot cards. She had not seen Irapuato's natural disaster in those cards, but when she read for my mother, she saw another tragedy.

"Vincent is going to die," she said.

"When?" my mother asked.

"He will not die soon, but when he does, his death will be bloody and will take place outside of Mexico."

Pillita was calmer when she found out that her daughter had finally decided to abandon Vincent. Grandfather insisted on setting up a business for my mother in Irapuato, which is why it did not take long to start one that fit her well: a hair salon.

Everything continued as normal in Ario de Rosales, except for Pillita's health. We had left to buy some suits at Elia Mares's store, but when we came back, she had an attack. We often passed outside of a pharmacy owned by a family of French origin. The woman had twins who were tall with blue eyes. Every time I walked by there, I would say, "One day God will give me twins." The twins' house was enormous, with a lateral passageway that connected to the patio. Sometimes the twins were outside. They were nineteen years old, and I saw them from the viewpoint of a timid eleven-year-old.

But I felt even more embarrassed when the spider attack began. We were outside the house where the twins lived when Pillita began to feel choked by imaginary spiders in her throat—I don't know what caused these attacks, and neither did anyone else. Her face would turn red, and she began to make peculiar sounds. I entered the twins' patio, grabbed a bucket, put water in it, and went running back to soak Grandmother.

"The spiders have calmed down," she said. After she was completely wet, the spiders (or whatever they were) had calmed down, but my heart was still beating from fright and embarrassment;

the twins were standing behind me. I grabbed Grandmother by the arm and we went hurriedly on our way.

When we arrived home, Pillita told Aurora and my aunt Barbara that the spiders had begun attacking her again. I began crying from fear that I would be totally abandoned in life if anything happened to Pillita. She was one of the people whom I loved most. She didn't give me affection like I would have wanted, didn't take time to caress my hair or ask me how I was feeling, nor did she play children's games with me, but when I imagined her death and saw her in a coffin, I would lock myself in some room in the house and cry for hours.

Uncle Rodrigo had come back. He forgot about the animosity between him and my grandfather, but not about the alcohol; he continued just as much a drunk, but much sicker. Since I no longer had a restaurant and couldn't invent another, I entertained myself in the store or on errands for remedies for Uncle Rodrigo. I would go through the fields and up the hill, where a woman who harvested mushrooms lived in a small house of wood. They were mushrooms with healing properties, which Aurora cooked for many hours. When they had cooled down, she would put them under the sun and drain the liquid in a bottle to be locked away.

One day I wanted to try one of those mysterious things; they were delicious, but my brain started to tremble, and I believed I was dreaming. I went running (or flying) back to my room and slept. I am not certain that it was the same effect that Uncle Rodrigo would feel when he ate an entire pot of the mushrooms. But the anti-alcoholic remedy didn't always work and was sometimes even counterproductive, because Aurora had to put a considerable quantity of alcohol into the pot of mushrooms to make my uncle eat them. He later became so thin that he couldn't continue eating just the mushrooms.

My family thought it better to opt for the creative medicines of the folk healers to address Rodrigo's health problem: we hired two men with long hair who came over one evening and took over

Aurora's kitchen to prepare their concoctions. While they began the potions, they sent me to the store with a list of items to bring back. Grandfather had already closed the store for the night and wanted me to help, so he gave me the keys and sent me to the store. While searching for the dried skin of a colorful snake—besides finding the rattles from snakes that Grandfather collected—I went through a box full of mementos: photos, stones that had no significance for me, and jewels. It was the perfect place for an indiscreet girl.

Neither the serpents nor all the mushrooms in the world would work to cure my uncle Rodrigo, not even the iguana that they told me to clean one time to make a soup. After cleaning the iguana almost ten times, I gave it to Aurora. After she had finished the soup, everyone said to me, "You are going to serve this soup to your uncle without telling him what it contains; do you understand?"

I sat in the kitchen waiting for the soup with the mystical healing properties of the iguana meat. The plan was that Aurora was going to offer me a bowl of delicious chicken soup whenever my uncle entered the kitchen. Just as we had planned, Uncle Rodrigo, who came in staggering from one side to another, took hold of a chair, then held the table and sat down. I sat down next to him and Aurora served me a bowl.

"The soup is delicious!" I said to Aurora after I pretended to try her soup.

"Would you like some?" Aurora asked Rodrigo.

"If it doesn't have alcohol, I don't want it," responded Uncle Rodrigo.

"Why would it have alcohol if Aurora made the soup for me?" I countered.

"Then I don't want any. You eat it … You're looking like a noodle. Look, I can see your bones," he said, squeezing my arm.

I had the urge to throw my bowl at his head. Aurora murmured to me to be patient.

"Look, if you want, we can throw a bit of wine in, but you have to promise you will eat every last bit," she said.

"Okay, but put in plenty of wine," he responded, irritated.

He tried to eat by himself, but he stuck his spoon in the bowl three times and splashed out almost half the soup.

"Open wide," I said. He seemed like a child. I lost my patience when he told me, "I can't open my mouth wide because I have lips like a minnow, just like yours."

I became furious like I did every time he told me I had fish lips. His drunkenness did not let him see that he was facing a timid, fragile girl.

When I finished feeding him the soup, I gave him the piece of meat that was left in the bowl.

"Did you enjoy it?" I asked, cheerfully vengeful.

"Yes, it was delicious. Was it freshly killed hen?" he asked.

"No, it's better than that. Don't you know what you just ate?" I asked him, laughing.

In addition to telling him the truth, I took the iguana out of the refrigerator so that he would believe me. Then I ran out of the kitchen. Aurora stood there, startled. Uncle Rodrigo went to the patio to throw up.

After that scandal, Pillita, Aunt Barbara, and Grandfather went searching for me throughout the house. I hid myself under one of the boxes in the piloncillo storeroom; when I heard Grandfather's steps, I urinated in the same place where, years later, I would be Uncle Eduardo's victim.

Uncle Eduardo, my mother's older brother, owned the Canada Shoe Store, another store Grandfather had helped to construct and above which was a house where Eduardo and his family lived. He was a drunk, but unlike Uncle Rodrigo, he drank only on occasion. He had the habit of sticking his nose in other people's business, just like his wife, Elisa, whom he married at the age of twenty when she was only thirteen.

"You are too young to be getting married. Are you sure about this?" the priest asked her.

"Yes, whatever Eduardo says," said the girl who had come from a little farm outside the city.

They had thirteen children.

Uncle Rodrigo never again trusted me, and the family didn't send me on any more errands to pick up remedies for him. Aunt Barbara still sent me on errands, which I did not refuse because those were my chances to get out on the street. Above all, I liked to run errands in the morning. At that time, many people were circulating, doing business, buying things, or simply strolling around the plaza.

The most disgusting errand I had to run was to buy filet mignon for the cat. Sometimes I would go at the very time that the truck was unloading the meat, and I saw the fresh blood dripping down on the pavement—in those years the dirt roads had been replaced by pavement. Besides, when the butcher handed me the fillets, I could feel the animal's heat in my hands. I felt like vomiting, and I remembered my hen; what had she done wrong?! If my grandfather had known that the hen laid eggs every day, her fate would have been different. But he did not give me time or the opportunity to tell him.

Whenever I got up my courage, I would run a few blocks out of the way to my paternal grandmother Trina's house; her hug and her sweet gaze were so affectionate that I felt like staying with her forever. Trina was a humble woman with a generous heart. In her house, she sold cheeses and honey-soaked dumplings. Every time she said good-bye to me, she loaded me up with gifts, especially cheeses from other regions of Mexico where the climate was not as hot. I would take them home and quickly hide them away under my bed. One day Barbara discovered them. She did not hit me. She said, "You can visit your grandmother Trina, but only when I allow it. And I don't want you to talk with anyone else from that family, not even your uncles or cousins." Barbara preferred to socialize only with wealthy people from high society, and since my father's side of the family was relatively poor, she did not want anyone near her, including me, to be associated with the Sayavedra family.

Trina made me feel happy and beautiful. She would compliment me on my nose. I felt like I was dreaming, because I was accustomed to hearing that I was an ugly girl. And I believed it. Sometime Trina would allow me to climb trees to pick peaches, which I would eat while walking. She was so different from my father, although she was partially to blame for raising him the way he was.

"Your father is lazy," she would say. She told me that when he was a little boy and did not want to go to school, she would not say anything to him. She protected him so much that she did not allow him to become an independent man; she took care of every detail so that he would be comfortable at home. She gave him everything, let him get used to sitting down and waiting for the world to revolve around him. That is why he spent his life sitting down, just as he did when my mother would pay him to sit on the benches in the plaza.

Despite Grandfather being an ogre, verbally and emotionally aggressive, he hit me very few times. On the day of the iguana incident—even though he was dying to hit me—he could not because I wouldn't leave the piloncillo storeroom until he left the house.

One day my cousins (Uncle Eduardo's daughters) came to visit my grandfather's house and the store. We were running around the store, weaving in and out of all the doors. On one of the laps around the store, Grandfather grabbed me by the hair, put me on his lap, and hit me on my behind with his belt. I urinated on myself. My cousins laughed. Then he sat me down next to him, saying, "Poor girl," and gave me a candy. On the other occasions that he hit me, he would do the same thing.

The only times I could play without problems were during the town festivals, one of which was the celebration in honor of Apostle Santiago. Every July 25, the town would fill with dancers, mariachis, other types of bands, and people going through the streets to adore the apostle until they ended up in the parish named after him. The ranchers would come into town in their best dress, and others sold their products, lighted fireworks, or simply enjoyed the music, games, and food. I really liked these types of celebrations because I felt free; they were parties for the entire town, even though the people were from different origins and had different customs. There was a lot of cultural mixing among Greek, Argentinian, French, and Italian families that had immigrated to Mexico late in the nineteenth century.

On the corner of my block lived the Karras family, who were of Greek origin. Upon arriving in town, they had set up the Athens City clothing store. They lived comfortably with their three daughters: Sara, Marta, and Laura; they were pretty girls whom I admired and wanted to imitate, but the only thing we had in common were a couple of lunches and the Catholic school. Sara was the only one with whom I had problems. I wanted to show off like them with my nose in the air and with graceful gestures. Their house was beautiful and stood out from the others because of its modern decorations. They ate well, not because of the food itself but rather because of how they interacted at the table with their parents. Their world was filled with an enviable harmony. The few times I ate meals as a guest at their house, I looked upon the situation as though it were a dream, and experienced emotions I had never felt in my life.

On one of Marta's birthdays, the family put on a costume party. Aunt Barbara adored those girls; she especially liked their blond hair. She would say, "You should be like them." She lived with the old trauma of Achulo, her mother's father, a dark-skinned man with an Indian's face, who had married Nina, Pillita's mother. Every time she remembered, Barbara would repeat the same story:

"Achulo broke up the family. I don't know what Nina saw in that ugly man." What was the poor man guilty of? On top of everything else, he died at the age of fifty, in the mountain, fleeing from criminals who wanted to rob him of his horse and his few belongings. Nina would die at 114 years of age, so white that her veins seemed to rest on top of her skin, and with long silver hair and a doll's face.

Besides the Karras family, I also remember the Manzur and Yafar families. Among the mix of foreigners in the town were Asians. The most famous Chinese man who lived in the town disappeared one night. He left his huge house abandoned for a long time, until someone bought it many years later. No one knew where the Chinese man had gone. People came to Ario de Rosales from many places, and others went away to just as many faraway places. Many people in town had emigrated from other places in Mexico, just like the elderly man who had been born in the Federal District of Mexico and whose parents were of German descent. Maybe that is why my aunt believed herself a descendant of the pure race.

Grandfather told us that many people in the town were descendants of refugees—emigrants who had escaped from the war and came in search of better lands for their businesses. The Gypsies also arrived many times. They would set up their typical tents and colorful carriages on the outskirts of the town. When this happened, more than one person would take it upon himself to yell, "Prepare yourselves! The Hungarians are coming!" in reference to the Gypsies.

The Gypsies would go around the town, up and down the plaza, looking for someone whose hand they could read. They would eat there and stay until the sun hid beyond the horizon. They left everything dirty, which is why the people said the Gypsies were pigs; the store owners tried to keep them far from their stores. I remember that the Gypsy women would get together in groups of three or four. They did not sit on the benches; rather, they gathered their long skirts to sit on the ground. They could sit there all day while their children played with the water of the fountain or asked for money.

One day, the Gypsies entered our store. The girl working that shift was startled because Grandfather had gone to the country and there was no one with enough authority to throw them out. I was at the counter playing with some old coins. Just like the girl, I froze, not because I was scared but because they looked like they had been torn out of a story. I closed and opened my eyes to prove that I was not dreaming, and then I greeted them. There were two women and a little girl. Their long skirts seemed like butterfly wings. I scanned one of the women from her feet to her head, until I was startled with her eyes painted like a party. They seemed happy, and I wanted to be like them.

"I am going to read your hand," one of them said to me. "I won't charge you a thing."

While the other woman harassed the girl at the counter, I was happy to be meeting the Gypsies. I extended my hand over the table. The Gypsy with the playful eyes took my hand and placed it over hers. She passed her finger, or more accurately, her fingernail, over a line and closed my hand. She reopened it and said, "You are going to get married far away from here and you will have twins."

On Marta Karras's birthday that year, her family put on a costume party. I was inspired by the style of the Gypsies who had visited my grandfather's store. I thought their clothing would be the perfect costume. When the costume party and contest came up, I reminded Pillita of the Gypsy and asked her to buy me a skirt of a thousand colors. I took ownership of that character so much that the girls would come to me so that I would read their hands; I won the prize for best costume.

In Ario de Rosales all kinds of things happened; it was a town marked by historic happenings, which were very important for the liberation of Mexico. During the war for independence, it had been the center of operations of the insurgent army, and many *Arienses* (people from Ario de Rosales) had supported the liberation. So much was the participation of the town that in 1815 the National Supreme Court of Justice was set up there to designate who, from that point on, would represent the three branches of power of the state. Since then, Ario de Santiago, the name the colonizers had designated for the place, was left in the past, and in honor of General Victor Rosales, all would call the town Ario de Rosales.

In 1956 the town passed from the category of village to city, which meant development and modernization for its inhabitants; for me it was and always will be a town. More roads were built, structures were remodeled and so was the church. Many projects for growth were successful between the 1960s and 1980s, rather, between my childhood and adolescence. In her zeal for helping the community, Pillita made huge donations. A copper plaque with her name was put up on Arista Street. In addition to donating a school for the men studying at the seminary to become priests, and taking cigarettes and food to prisoners who were in jail for "errors of ignorance," as Pillita would say, she donated a property to the DIF, a governmental institution that used the house as a large workshop.

I remember that it was an enormous house, although everything is big in a little girl's memory, with many rooms that the government adapted for a kitchen workshop, an infirmary, a sewing workshop, and for other purposes. Pillita signed me up for cooking and first-aid classes. I was eleven years old and I learned many things. Part of my interest and success in the kitchen were thanks to these courses. The first dish that I made was "four-cup chicken"; since then, every time I mention that dish, I inevitably relate it to the DIF house and that whole period.

I went to kindergarten and all of elementary school in the Vasco de Quiroga Nunnery, a property of some Spaniards. Pillita said that that place would be very useful for the rest of my life, and that I would learn things that only nuns could teach me. In the same way, for some time Pillita paid for Yuri, Eduardo's oldest daughter, but she did not take advantage of the opportunity. She did not even last a year. Sara, the Karras's youngest daughter, hated me and got together with Yuri to bother me. The school was surrounded by trees; I remember that many of them were custard apple, or chirimoya, trees. The nuns also raised rabbits and hens. Every week I took corn from the store and gave it to the hens; if my grandfather had found out, he would have asked for a hen to cook. In the back of the grounds there was a pond, in which Yuri tried to kill me.

It was a day when we were learning how to swim. I was on the bank, waiting my turn to enter the water, when Yuri pushed me. The water was not deep, but I fell hard and hit my head. I lost my sense of time and space, and did not know where to get out of the pond. I thought I was going to die, until I felt cold and saw that a nun had me in her arms. I fainted right after seeing her, then awakened later, scared but in a bed. I dreamed many nights about that pond, and saw myself floating in the pond full of blood.

Every Monday we would pay homage to the flag. I went in the escort and Sara carried the flag, which made her feel more important. We had to pray daily in the chapel; there, we were taught the messages of the Bible and how to talk with God. I did not like to repeat the prayers; I preferred to say what I felt with my own words. Whenever I could, I would go to the chapel to pray for my mother, my siblings, and Pillita. In that place, where I felt calm and protected, I asked God many times to make me happy, to would send me a good man (not like my father) in the future, and to make me into a good person, capable of helping humanity. In addition to going with the escort, I learned to play the drum, knit and sew.

Being with the nuns was not unpleasant; in that period they prepared you to become a good wife and mother. Near Christmas time, we made mosaics, which we broke into a thousand pieces, and colored drawings. One Friday, I did not like how my design had turned out, so I began to take off the little pieces of crystal until one of the glass pieces splintered my finger underneath the fingernail. Even though it bled a lot, I did not tell anybody. When I arrived at home I patched up the small wound.

"What happened to your finger?" one of the nuns asked the following Monday.

"Nothing, I got a splinter and bandaged it up so that it would not get infected."

"Let me see," said the nun, putting on her glasses. "My goodness! Your finger is rotting. I am going to call your grandmother to take you to a doctor."

The color was undecipherable, and varied between blue, green and yellow.

"We will have to amputate the finger," said the doctor. The three of us looked at one another with expressions of anguish. "It's just a joke so that this little one will learn," he continued, chuckling.

My finger was infected, but the doctor assured us that, with good hygiene and a cream, it would soon be as good as new.

It was good that they took me to the doctor because the nuns were preparing a theatrical presentation about "fruits and vegetables," and I enjoyed such activities.

What I *didn't* like was when my grandmother would go to Irapuato to see her doctors. Since my Aunt Barbara frequently traveled to DF, Pillita would leave me with the nuns while she was gone in Irapuato. Every day I spent in the nunnery I cried. It's not that the nuns mistreated me; rather, it made me sad to be outside of my house and away from my grandmother. I felt abandoned all over again, even though I was not really abandoned since Grandmother always made sure that I was well. Of course, she looked out for me in her way and was blind to a few things, but she loved me infinitely and demonstrated her care once again with the strawberry costume.

Upon returning from her trip, she showed me the giant strawberry I had asked her to make. It was beautiful, almost real.

On the same afternoon that Pillita returned from Irapuato, my father showed up. After the episode in the cantina with the politician, he had taken refuge in various different houses. He came running into the store and hugged me. I was astonished. He had a scared look, and his shirt was totally wet. Everyone had prohibited me from telling him that my mother was in Irapuato, but his words and hugs convinced me.

He arrived in Irapuato a repentant man, promising my mother that he would change, would let go of alcohol, and would look for work. No one believed him except for my mother, who looked beautiful and happier with her studies at an Italian beauty academy. On one of the occasions when I went to visit her, she gave me a hairstyle that was beautiful but did not fit me. It was too old; it would have fit a twenty-year-old, and I was eleven. When I saw myself in the mirror, I got so angry that I undid the hairstyle. My mother was saddened.

My mother took my father into her home and found work for him in a clothing store; he was put in charge of payment collections. Everyone wanted to witness the abnormal phenomenon of seeing my father work, but his effort lasted only three days. They were the only days my father worked in his life. He said that he left the job because he fractured his foot from walking so much; he put on a bandage and got a pair of crutches. No one knew whether they should believe him, but my mother did not stay silent: "You promised to change, Vincent; you should not lose this job. Tell me if this thing about your foot is true."

"Shut up!" he said to her. "I should go back to the prostitutes; they are the ones who understand me."

"The Bible says that a curse made by a wife or a mother comes true," my mother responded. "Listen to me, Vincent. One day you will die in the street like a dog."

And that's how he would die November 7, 1992, when the drug dealer gave the order to turn out the lights. I was thirty years old at the time.

My father had a problematic character, but nothing and no one could change his tragic destiny. He was sick, possessed by rage against himself and against the world. He was capable of yelling at anyone, without worrying about who it was or what consequences would follow. When the situation was even tenser, he would start to yell like a crazy man. That is what happened during the disaster in Irapuato, when he went against the president of Mexico himself.

It was 1973, and the late summer rain had become so menacing that on August 18 various dams collapsed, including the one closest to Irapuato, named Rabbit Dam. The water came in between the streets and houses like a tsunami, leaving destruction, cries, and death in its wake. Irapuato residents who took refuge on their roofs were ingenious to get food and to escape from the wave of robberies that followed.

Three days after the disaster, President Luis Echeverria went to see the damages, encouraged the people, and promised them the reconstruction of Irapuato. My father got closer to the president from behind and yelled at him, "Hey, Luis! My daughter has no milk! Why don't you leave her a coffin, you bastard!"

The president turned around.

"Should we take him out?" asked one of the guards.

The president replied, "Forget him. His insult is a product of the madness of this disaster." My father was referring to my parents' youngest daughter, Ernestina, who was less than one year old.

The disaster mobilized the whole country. For days, my parents walked on their roof, escaping the water and the rain that would not let up. It was a very sad occurrence for all Mexicans. The inhabitants of Irapuato were scared and abandoned; they felt that the government was not reacting appropriately in response to the disaster. Even months later, the government announced that there were no deaths to mourn, whereas the families complained of their relatives' bodies in the sewers, which had been left open with the passage of the water, or in the secret public grave in the municipal cemetery.

With the disaster of the dam, things got harder in Delfina's house. She had to pitch water out of the house, dry the furniture, and feed her children. My mother and Delfina began to argue about the present and the past. Delfina was tired. My mother's suffering ended the same year of the disaster, or at least the suffering caused by her husband. My father decided to leave Mexico without a known plan; my mother was three months pregnant with Esmeralda, the last souvenir he would leave. My father did not meet Esmeralda until she was thirteen years old, when he returned to the town to attend the funeral of his father, my grandfather of the same name, Vincent Sayavedra. Only then would we find out that my father was living in the United States with his new family in Los Angeles. Six years after that encounter, he would lie dying at the exit of a bar soon after a drug dealer had shot him and left him in the street like a dog. Before dying, Vincent would be helped by a bar employee, to whom he would whisper his last words: "Tell my daughters that I've been killed."

A few months after my father left Irapuato, Delfina said, "I am very sorry for your children, Elia, but I want you to leave my house."

My mother left Delfina's house around the time that I was preparing for the grand fruit theater at school. I was so concentrated on the day of the theater performance that I gave my best performance. Every time I see strawberries, I remember that day. All of us fruits and vegetables were behind the curtain, waiting our turn, until I came out on stage with my skinny green legs and a fat strawberry on my body. Then a carrot, a fresh lettuce, and a juicy orange appeared; the whole market was on the stage. We gave our speeches and then heard applause from the audience. One of the nuns put us in order and the people began to applaud for the best costume. The strawberry received an ovation. My grandmother looked on proudly from the first row. When the nun announced that the strawberry had won first place, I felt glory; that was a moment of great fame and also served to help me realize that I had some talent.

Days later I spoke with the head nun so that she would allow me to train a group of girls for the dance at the end of the year. We got together one time per week, and I taught them choreography until one day before the show. Everything came out perfectly; the audience liked it so much that Tere Salinas's father improvised a theater stage inside his house.

I had the makings of an artist, but what was hard for me was reading. No one had noticed until Master Juana arrived at the school. She was not a nun, so she naturally lacked patience and joy. One day, she dedicated herself to listening to each student reading. On my turn, she gave me a small book with writing and pictures; I did not understand the letters, but I managed to begin inventing a story.

"What are you saying, girl? You are making this up. How is it possible that you don't know to read in fourth grade?"

I lowered my head. It was true; I did not understand the letters. My mind was always somewhere else, and it was impossible to concentrate. I was constantly thinking about fantasies. I daydreamed scenes, and would lose myself in all kinds of imagination. In Grandfather's house, no one helped me study, and I did not do so on my own. In order to pass each grade, I stole things from Grandfather's store and paid Elizabeth, a classmate, to do my homework. I had straight A's on exams because she let me copy her page or would trade pages in exchange for gum, pencils, and toys. The nuns were worried about us being good people and made sure to have us pray. They never suspected otherwise of their sweet pupils' virtues.

Master Juana had the head nun make me take a special test; I had to take several extra classes and study at home. Yuri and Sara made sure to make me feel even more stupid. They followed me with their jokes all year long. One day, I had just entered school and they came up and stood in front of me.

"Pick one," Yuri said, sticking out her index and middle fingers.

"Which one do you want? This one or that one?" Sara chimed in.

"This one," I responded fearfully, anxious to get out of the situation.

"*Screw your mother!*" they yelled at the same time, showing me their middle fingers.

I became very sad because the other kids had heard. I went to the classroom with a knot in my throat, looking at the floor and wondering why they felt so much hatred for me. In spite of their clear cruelty, I never spoke up to confront them, nor did I do anything to get revenge.

Destiny taught Sara a lesson. Two weeks after that joke, she was playing in the hallways of the school. After passing near the head nun's office, Sara decided to run ahead but did not realize that the glass door was closed. She ran her head and hands into the glass. It was horrific; many of us were playing in the schoolyard when we saw her bloody face and hands full of cuts that would remind her of the accident for many years. Yuri left soon after. She did not want to study, and Grandmother got tired of paying her tuition after finding out that Yuri had escaped from school through a window to go to the movies.

"Hey girl, you are from the Negrete family, right?" a janitor said when he saw her sleeping in the theater seat. "Go home."

Yuri went to the Melchor Ocampo School, a few blocks from the Catholic school. That was where all of Uncle Eduardo's children studied. In front of the school there was a plaza where we would all get together to play basketball. In that very plaza I would fall in love for the first time as a fifteen-year-old. One year before that romance, I liked a boy named Alberto who lived in DF but took school vacations in my town, visiting his grandparents. He existed in my head and in my fantasies. All of our relationship was imaginary, because my grandfather did not allow those kinds of things. One time Grandfather even threw Alberto out when I was talking to him from my window. It was a kind of courtship, but we never even held hands, much less kissed.

If my mother had raised me instead of my grandmother, I would not have grown up feeling the rejection I felt from my mother. Maybe I would be better off financially, like my siblings who grew up with my mother. But ever since I was born, Pillita wanted to take care of me, especially since she found out what my father was like. I was lucky to have the opportunity to study with the nuns; had I not been able to, my childhood would have been much crueler. My experience at school helped my spirit and my soul and helped me combat the difficulties I experienced in my grandparents' house. This is something I can say now, but I couldn't when the only thing I wanted was to go back to my mother.

I was four years old when my mother decided to leave me. That day she went to Pillita's house because she had fought with my father. Her hair was messed up, and one purple eye was half closed.

"Stay here, Elia. That man is going to kill you," Pillita said to her.

"I cannot abandon him. He needs me."

"That man does not need anybody. Give me the girl and go away to the house in DF," Grandmother said to her. "There you can help at the pharmacy, I have told you this hundreds of times. The girl will be better taken care of here."

Pillita convinced her. The next day, hiding like a criminal, my mother left me on the corner by the store and went to DF. Three months later she came to get me because my father had found her and as always, she had forgiven him. She went to Grandmother's house to get me, but I rejected her. She told me that, instead of hugging her, I began to cry and stamp my feet when she took me in her arms. Since that day, it was Pillita who made decisions in my life.

She had no control, however, over the moment in which I lost my virginity at the hands of Uncle Eduardo. On that afternoon, I was in the kitchen looking for something that I don't remember. The door opened slowly and my uncle appeared. He took a few drunken steps, and with red eyes and a strange smile, he came to where I was. There was no one nearby. He took a few more soft steps as he spoke to me affectionately. When he got close, I could smell the bitterness of the alcohol. I ran to a table and hid underneath, without too much effort for a seven-year-old girl. I could see his shoes getting closer while he kept fighting his saliva to say affectionate words.

"Where are you?" he said with his strange sweet voice. "I found you!"

Nervous, almost shaking, I asked him if he wanted something: water, tea, or ...

"I can prepare whatever you want, Uncle Eduardo," I said. I did not know what to do. My heart began beating quickly, and I felt a knot in my stomach, telling me something bad was going to happen.

"Come here, Rosa Lilia. I need your help; I'm not feeling too well. Come here."

"How can I help you, Uncle?" I asked him as I came out from underneath the table. "What do you want?"

"I'm just going to cuddle with you. That's all," he whispered.

He grabbed my arm roughly, brought me close to his body, and began to caress me. I looked at him as though looking at a drunken giant. I tried to cry, but I couldn't even breathe. He continued with the torture until I began to bleed. When I saw the blood, I finally started crying. He held my face and tried to comfort me, saying that it was a game. He said everything was all right and grabbed a cloth to clean me.

"This is a new game. You don't have to tell anybody about it, because no one will love you. They are going to hit you and punish you if you tell what you played with Uncle."

He made me drink from the bottle in his hand and took me to a dark storeroom where I would be alone and no one would hear me or come looking for me. When he left, I turned on the light and discovered I was in the piloncillo storeroom. That place was filled with little girl's mischiefs and macabre games like the one I had played.

I went to my room and cried all day. After that, when I saw my uncle in the house, I ran and hid from him as fast as I could. I never said anything. Besides being embarrassed, I didn't want to be punished or for everyone to stop loving me.

The only person who suspected something was my aunt Mary. She was married to Fermín, the son for whom my grandmother had paid to go to DF to become a lawyer. They were a very happy couple and were brilliant together. I could really talk with them. Mary was from Matamoros, a city on the coast of the Gulf of Mexico. She was very realistic because she saw the world how it was. She did not make things up, nor did she just believe what people told her. She was sensitive, capable of saying what she thought, and understanding; she believed in second chances. She met me when I was eight, when she came from DF to visit my grandparents. She got very close to me, but I felt more like she wanted to interrogate me. Maybe she guessed what was happening.

On one occasion she said, "When you see Uncle Eduardo drunk, get away from him. And if he touches you, grab a knife and threaten him." I was surprised and thought about what she said for several days. I couldn't sleep, imagining *what* I would cut off of Uncle Eduardo with a knife in my hands.

I told Grandmother what Mary had said to me, but everyone was blind. Grandmother told my aunt Barbara, who hated Mary because she never stayed quiet. "That stupid woman has a fly's brain," Barbara said as she always did to insult people. "How is it possible that she could tell that little girl to kill my brother?"

I stayed silent and did not talk about the subject again. Knowing my grandfather, I think he might have confronted my uncle, but only in private, without anyone finding out. He would have hidden anything from the public in order to maintain the store's prestige.

Telling was not worth it. Grandfather would have just done the same thing he did with me: hitting me and soon making me laugh Obviously the rumors that my uncle Eduardo abused his children were also not heard by Aunt Barbara. It was even less effective if Mary was to make insinuations. Barbara couldn't stand Mary, especially when she married Fermín, and really as I grew and got close to Mary. When she got pregnant, she talked about the long wait, told me the truth about the stork and the importance of loving the children. I was surprised, because the nuns had lied to me. When Mary's children were born and she would come to visit us, I stayed for hours with her children while she took advantage of the chance to go out or to finish chores.

"You are not her nanny. You have to wash the windows and do what I say. You are not here to take care of children!" Aunt Barbara yelled one time.

Barbara couldn't stand it that I loved Mary and dedicated my time to her children, Rolandín, Rafaelín, and Rogelín, as they were called. Barbara was so jealous that she always found a chance to bother us and to launch her poisonous comments, which had no ill effects except to make us die of laughter from time to time.

"Rolandín, Rafaelín Rogelín ... Well, you should name the next one Valentín," Barbara would ridicule.

Everything seemed distasteful to Barbara. She was so strict and cruel that she could make anyone's existence unpleasant. Ever since she was young, my mother would say to her, "Stupid, crude, pig, fat and ugly."

Now that I am a grown woman, I would love to return to the times of old Ario de Rosales. I could return with my knowledge, reverse to being a girl but with more strength to defend myself and the strength to protect my rights. It's impossible, I know. I also know that I should go back to that land to heal my wounds. One day, perhaps.

When Grandfather got sick, he decided to sell the store and to continue with his other businesses, as much in the town as in other states in Mexico. He was tired, so he sold the store to an Arab family that had arrived a few years before and was risk-tolerant with business; they decided to take on the store. The family's two daughters were my classmates at the Catholic school. It was an excellent business for them, because they inherited my grandfather's clientele. We quickly moved to the part of the house that looked upon Arista Street. The Arab family took the other side, which looked upon Portal Juarez Street. It was that very side that caught on fire.

A few months after the move, on a night that seemed still, the church bells rang. It was not a wedding, but rather signaled to the whole town that there was a fire. At two in the morning, the fire lighted up various blocks in the area. Everybody came out to help. They would go to the fountain in the plaza and come back with buckets while the firefighters from Morelia arrived. But a bunch of explosives, gunpowder, and gasoline began to explode. A hardware store, the pharmacy, and the house where Buki had lived all burned down. Two people died. I stayed frozen in the street and urinated on myself.

Grandfather had given them the property in exchange for monthly payments, but the Arabs had insured the merchandise and the furniture, not the store. The house ended up full of smoke and a couple of walls burned down, but we all ended up okay—traumatized but okay. Grandfather cried. It was said that the fire had been caused by a short circuit and the house being so old, but my grandfather was sure that the Arabs themselves had provoked the fire to receive benefits for the insurance on the merchandise. My grandfather was so disconcerted that he left the property just as it was for many years after the fire.

When the fire happened, Barbara had been in DF for more than one year, in charge of the pharmacy. Grandfather did not ask Barbara to come back, but she *did* have to anyway when, months later, she received the sorrowful news from my grandmother: "Your brother Rodrigo died." None of the creative treatments could save him from dying at thirty-three years in the Social Security hospital after several days of agony. His liver couldn't take any more. He died on a blessed Friday at three in the afternoon. They put him in a metal coffin and transported him to the house.

Since he was well known in the town, many neighbors came to pay their respects. At night my aunt Barbara and my mother came, and of course Rodrigo's wife had been sitting there for a while—she was four months pregnant. Next to her was Pillita, who looked sad, inconsolable, and didn't want to leave the coffin.

Seeing my aunt Barbara gave me chills; her presence reminded me of the humiliation of my childhood. Aunt Barbara stayed for three months because Uncle Rodrigo had left her as the executor. She was put in charge of distributing money from the ten properties— who would have believed it—and giving the monthly income to his children. This was money that Rodrigo and Janet, Rodrigo's children, would come back and claim years later as adults.

Pillita couldn't be comforted, and everybody's lives changed. If she looked sad before, after the funeral she seemed like a soul in penitence. Unable to overcome the death of her son, she wore black for ten years.

When Uncle Rodrigo died, I was fourteen years old; I was taller, more independent, and more traumatized. Yuri, one of Uncle Eduardo's daughters, had changed; she did not hit me anymore or say cruel jokes. Rather, we were friends and companions in mischief.

We went to the Lázaro Cárdenas Middle School, the only one in town. Its principal, an old man who liked young girls, would later involve me in a tremendous scandal by trying unsuccessfully to have a relationship with me. Yuri laughed about the ordeal, and the women of the town believed that I had snatched the old man's affections and that I surely wanted to take his wife's place. Every day they came up with new versions of this story and alleged that I was not the saint I made myself out to be.

The fame of "crazy girls" had begun a couple of years before outside my uncle Eduardo's shoe store. Yuri, her sisters, and I put on swimsuits, took a carpet to the street to use as a stage, and began to dance. "Small town, huge hell," the girls from the newsstand said, accusing us of being pornographic.

I shared many hours with Yuri, but I did not like to enter her house. Aunt Elisa did not worry about her children; her house seemed like a pigpen, all messy and smelling of urine. What did she know about taking care of them, when she spent hours playing cards and the children were no little angels! To punish them, she put them in a dark room for one, two, or even three days at a time; Yuri was the one who lasted more time locked away. Despite her life being torture, she lived in a fantasy world in which I also participated.

"Go out of the window of the second floor," she told me one day. "We are going to travel on the roofs, and at the Villanuevas' house we'll stop and spy.

Mr. Villanueva saw us and went to talk with Pillita. "Tell them to be careful, because I thought they were delinquents and almost shot at them."

Yuri was Uncle Eduardo's oldest daughter, tall and uncontrollable—Grandmother did not waste time scolding her— and I think that she had a great influence on my compulsive attitude. I followed her lead in many mischiefs.

Before Grandfather closed the store, I began selling candies and gum on my own. I would call my cousins to sell to the *guares*, which is what we in Michoacán call people who belong to the Tarasco culture and do not mix with other races. The guare was a woman with an indigenous appearance who used white clothing, typical of her culture. She had a store at the other end of the plaza where my cousin Miguelito would go to deliver the merchandise. He would return with the profit and I would separate everyone's commission, until one day the guare saw my uncle Eduardo and asked him, "It's been a while since your son Miguel has come around here to bring me the candies."

"What candies?" my uncle asked.

"Those candies he sells; he used to bring them around here almost every day."

Miguelito had to tell the truth; otherwise he would have had to spend three days locked in the dark room. Uncle Eduardo told

Grandfather, but I never received a punishment because the cancer had begun to bother him. Some days he looked pale and weak; other days, he seemed to have the same energy he had had while doing business.

Yuri continued with her mischief, and I celebrated them until one night, when she got into my bed. We had asked Pillita to let Yuri stay the night in my room because we wanted to continue putting together puzzles, and besides, it was raining. When we completed the puzzle, she turned off the light and lay down in the other bed. A few minutes later, I heard her get up, and when I turned around, she was getting into my bed.

"What are you doing?" I asked, angry. And I got up.

"Wait, wait," she said, grabbing my arm roughly. "Don't make noise. You are going to like it."

She grabbed my shoulders, laid me down in the bed, and began to touch me. I don't want to remember what happened after that, because I continue to ask myself how it is possible that these things happen. Where was I to muster the strength to face them when I was a girl? Yuri had been a victim of her father; I don't blame her. Uncle Eduardo abused her and some of her sisters. Araceli did not go through the same thing, because my aunt Lancha, Pillita's sister, took her away to live in Irapuato when Aunt Elisa took on the management of a business in DF. The rest of the siblings stayed on with the servant girl and with Uncle Eduardo, who confused his wife's body with those of his daughters when he arrived at home drunk.

After the incident with Yuri, I was ashamed for letting it happen and couldn't look her in the eyes anymore. She noticed that I couldn't bear being in her presence anymore and also became distant. We never talked about the incident, nor did we become friends again.

Years later, Yuri married a Cuban, and they ended the marriage without any children. The townspeople would say that the Cuban was a drug dealer and that Yuri was a lesbian. Later she married Luis, but they also divorced without having children. Yuri ended up serving in the army, searching for drug dealers from a helicopter.

The majority of women in my life were never my allies. I was the target of their abuse, their rage, and their revenge. One of the memories that most greatly damaged my life was the rejection by my mother. Her abandonment hurt me more than the beatings from Aunt Barbara, which were not few. If I had been able to choose, I would have chosen to tolerate my father, live in anguish with my siblings, and run away with them if necessary.

Pillita and Rafael, my maternal grandparents, taught me to work, to be clean, and to respect other people, but they did not teach me how to love myself or how to defend myself. If anyone asked me what the key to happiness is, I would say that it is love, even though that answer seems redundant or cliché. That was what I needed in order to feel strong. My grandparents loved me, but not in a way I needed. They fed me and gave me all the clothing and education that I could ask for, but I was raised without feeling loved or developing the confidence to defend myself. One loving hand or a sweet word would have helped me.

I never told anyone, not even my mother, about the abuse by my uncle Eduardo. But I did eventually tell her years later—in the middle of a drunken conversation in Morelia when I was eighteen years old—about what happened with my aunt Barbara:

"What commitment did you have to me? What responsibility did you take on when you abandoned me, when I begged you to let me stay with you?" I screamed.

"You cannot blame me like that, Rosa Lilia. Your grandparents gave you everything."

"They gave me everything except what I needed. You don't know what happened there, in that house. You never knew about the beatings and abuse."

"What abuse?" she asked, wary.

"You let them take me because I was apparently well, because they had money, and because they dressed me well. But no, I needed love. I did not want all that for me; I wanted my parents!"

I told her about the night of the fritters.

I was eight years old, and it was nighttime. The store was closed because Grandfather had gone to the movies with Pillita. I think

Pillita was really the one who wanted to go, because she would always return saying, "Rafael slept during the whole movie …"

Close to midnight I was still awake. I was used to the sleeplessness, especially when my aunt Barbara and I were alone. Either she talked to me like I was a servant or she made fun of my faults. That night, she had been quiet until she appeared in my room. In one hand she was jingling some coins, and in the other, she held her cat.

She said, "I want fritters, so put on your dress and go buy some at the food carts."

The fritters were fried pieces of dough, made of sugar, eggs, and butter; they were delicious, but from that night on, they became bitter for me. Men and women would set up near the plaza to sell food and stay there until four o'clock in the morning.

"I want fritters without piloncillo," my aunt told me. I put on the white dress that I had worn that afternoon at the dinner with the Karrases and the shoes that Pillita had bought for me in Irapuato, all while Barbara looked on impatiently. I went out of my room and Barbara came out behind me to open the front door for me.

"I'll wait for you here; don't take long."

As always, I went on thinking about how scared that woman made me. I walked through the Juarez gates, and then I began thinking about the stars, my grandfather's country property, and my mother, until I got to the spot where fritters where sold. I don't remember how I ordered them, whether I ordered incorrectly or if the woman hadn't understood me. It is very likely that I forgot to say "without piloncillo" since I was always worried when I was out around the town; I lost myself in time and space as I daydreamed. In general, my family would write down the errands on a piece of paper because I would return home with pork when they had asked for chicken. I never understood why they gave me responsibility if I did not do anything well.

On the way back home, I could feel the piloncillo syrup dripping between my hands; the fritters seemed like dough soaked in water. I began to tremble and sweat; I imagined that my aunt would lock me in a room, or worse, fill the bathtub with cold water and put me inside, as she had done one afternoon when I had not wanted to clean the cat.

Facing the front door, with the fritters in my hand, I began to think about a solution. If I entered, I had to tolerate whatever my aunt thought was an adequate punishment. The next day, everything would be back to normal. If I escaped, however, I would have to hide away in the woods or even farther away from the town. My grandfather would inevitably send all of his employees to look for me, and when they found me, Aunt Barbara would be happy to punish me. If I disappeared, Pillita would get desperate, her spider problem would come back to visit, and my mother would hate her forever. I was thinking about a better plan when all of a sudden the door opened. She stuck out her arms to receive the fritters. She inspected them as though she had taken a bag of rotten fruit.

"Stupid! Moron! Dummy! Look what you did!"

She said a ton of things I did not understand. She grabbed the fritters and threw them against the door. I tried to run to my room, but she grabbed me by the hair. By the door there was a small shoe shelf—women had begun to use very high-heeled shoes, with heels called nail heels, much like stilettos and very sharp. She grabbed the first shoe she could reach and began to hit my head. My hair, neck, back, and white dress were sprayed with blood. I thought I was dying; I'm not sure if it was from the pain or from seeing how the stains on the dress got bigger and bigger. I cried but did not say a word. My tiny, difficult world crumbled once again. I wanted to be with my mother, who lived a few hours from there, but I could not escape, and surely Mother would have sent me back, saying, "Barbara is a good person; she's just a little sad."

When my aunt realized what was happening, she let go of my hair … She was so startled that she began to comfort me. She went looking for towels to try to stop the bleeding and made a makeshift bandage with one of them. She held my head to apply pressure, and all I could manage to say was "It hurts."

She hid me in a storeroom and went to clean the floor downstairs. When she returned, she said to me, "If Pillita asks you, please do not tell her the truth. Tell her that it was an accident."

She was so scared that she began to talk without pausing and continued holding my head.

"It hurts!" I cried. She lowered her head and began to cry.

When I saw her like that, desperate and humiliated, I was happy. *She said she was sorry! For the first time she said she was sorry!* I thought. She did what she did with me, but that night she was kneeling, begging me not to tell the truth. We knew that the wound was deep, because it would not stop bleeding. Barbara went to get more towels and water, and changed my dress. She took her purse from a chair, and we went out in search of a doctor. A few bloodstains remained in the hallway.

"What happened to her?" the doctor asked, bewildered because of the time of night and my head covered in rags.

"She was running around the house and fell," responded Barbara nervously.

"At this time of night? And she hit herself that hard?"

"You see, she hit her head right on the corner of the table," my aunt said.

The doctor cut my hair that surrounded the hole in my head and put in a few stitches. He gave her some boxes for which she gave him some money, and we left. I don't know how much time we spent there, but I felt as though it had been the whole night.

On the way home, Barbara resumed the song she had been singing before: "If Pillita asks you ..." She promised me that if I did not tell anyone what happened, she would soon take me to Pátzcuaro and I would not have to clean the lamps ever again. Trips to Lake Pátzcuaro and freedom from the usual rigorous cleaning that Barbara forced me to do seemed like attractive offers that would significantly improve the conditions of my childhood.

When we arrived at home, she put a cap on my head and sent me to bed. Pillita was in her room. Barbara said, "We're home! Rosa Lilia was jumping on her bed, and she fell. But it wasn't anything serious—just a little bump on her head, nothing to cause any worry."

Neither that night, nor on any other night, did anyone ask me about that bump. Everyone was worried about their own things, so nobody worried about my accident. That night, I lay awake for several hours until I lost myself in a dream that I still remember. The next day, I drew an image of the dream, and years later, I wrote it down for a contest of children's stories:

> *Once upon a time there was a very lonely little girl who had so much energy that she could cross many mountains running, and in one leap could reach the farthest stars. The stars close to the earth were jealous of her energy and her shine. She was such a restless girl that she would look for the truth of things in all the tiny places; when she felt that someone was lying, she insisted on knowing the truth and would look everywhere for it.*
>
> *One day she was jumping through the forest and all of the light there was suddenly disappeared. She was alone and did not know where to go, until she saw a light mixed with yellow and red at the end of a long path. She got close to the light and saw water and fire. Two enormous dragons that were protecting her appeared at the edge of the path.*
>
> *"This path is very dangerous, little one. We should take you to a safe place," said one of them. The girl followed them with the same energy as always and thanked them. When she fell asleep at the foot of an apricot tree, the dragons took her to the room of a large house, where there was a great deal of food. At the moment in which the girl woke up, she looked around and saw neither water nor fire, nor the enormous dragons. She felt strange and began to cry. She cried until her tears had soaked the whole bed.*
>
> *"Why did you bring me here? I was just fine in that forest." When she wiped her face off, she saw an old wooden door, full of spiderwebs. She felt cold and scared. She got down off of the bed, looked at the new clothes that the dragons had put on her, and walked to the door. She turned around to look at the room once more, and examined each corner. She turned again to look at the door, and pushed it. She took a step to cross the threshold and woke up.*

When my aunt Barbara apologized again the next day, I felt with my heart that I should forgive her for all the beatings she had given me. I thought that she had finished the business of mistreating me. I was happy, and thought, *Finally I will go to Pátzcuaro with my cousins without her humiliating me.*

She used to take advantage of the thirteen years that separated us in age and blindly believed in her books that talked about the pure race. She ignored me because I was dark skinned and ugly, as she said, but there was something else behind all that hate. When she would go out with my cousins, she would always say the same thing to me: "You are going to stay here. You have to clean the cat house and those lamps for eight hours."

Nevertheless, I cleaned the lamps, gave food to the cats, and fed them until she would say, "That's good, but try not to look at anyone because you are very ugly." I asked myself what had happened between her and my mother for her to hate me so much.

My mother explained to me that they had no problems as girls. It was when my aunt Barbara grew older and convinced herself that she was better than everyone else. She read about politics and religion and could talk for hours about universal history. For her, the rest of the world was a "bunch of idiots." She became a strange young woman, arrogant and selfish from being the youngest in her family. She was spoiled and treated like a princess in her house. She had never been contradicted or told no by her parents. And her life filled with incessant reading hadn't taught her to interact with others.

My mother told me that her relationship with Barbara became more difficult when Grandfather began to look for a husband for Barbara. My mother tried to reach out to my aunt Barbara, who rejected her. My aunt said the opposite—that it had been my mother who distanced herself because my grandparents gave Barbara too much attention because she was the youngest. I don't know whom to believe; nor is it the time to take sides. However, I believe that the actual pressure from my grandfather made Barbara a cold woman.

When Grandfather yelled, everyone did what he said. And if someone did not agree, he was capable of yelling louder and shaming anyone. My aunt Barbara was one more victim of my grandfather's discipline; he went after her wherever she'd go. Because of this, in her youth she would jump through hoops to go to a party or get together with her friends. She always went around secretly and kept everything under lock and key. She demanded a humanly impossible perfection and accumulated wrath, which she later took out on me. Maybe my grandmother treated me better than she had treated Barbara—I don't know—and maybe that produced more jealousy, especially because my aunt Barbara decided to be with my grandmother at all times.

The traces of pink scars and pits in my head still remain from the night of the fritters. And even though the wound has scarred over, it still hurts.

Morelia
Butterfly in Full Rain

Before going to study at Morelia at the age of eighteen, my life began to change—not like a caterpillar changes into a butterfly, but like a butterfly in full flight in the rain. I took flight to get to know the city and become independent after so much obedience and conspiratorial silence. On this trip I put all my hope into becoming a successful woman. Or that's what I believed. In reality, I was completely lost; I knew that I had to study, but neither cooking nor medicine were in my plans. I don't remember at what time of my childhood or youth that I abandoned that idea. I had the example of my uncle Fermín, who had become a lawyer, but his brief visits weren't enough for me to soak up his intelligence. My grandfather wanted me to follow in his footsteps in business, whereas my grandmother told me to study whatever I wanted. My aunt Barbara said that she wasn't sure I was capable of thinking.

Tere Salinas, my close friend, was the one who opened my eyes. One afternoon she came to my house with some papers from the institute in Morelia. She wanted to study there, which inspired me to settle down in the city with her. The proposal of studying tourism management sounded interesting and came at the right time.

Since I was a girl, I wanted to get married to a nice young man in the Ario church, dressed in white, and to live happy as a clam, but the scandal that ensued when the elderly school director tried to have a relationship with me ruined my reputation even though he was unsuccessful in his pursuits. I saw the church and the white dress slip farther and farther away, at least in that town.

The day I left, I felt relief and the liberty of a freed prisoner on a morning of soft breeze. Life with my grandparents was comfortable, and my aunt had stopped hitting me, but I felt constrained, hidden, and kept like a first love letter. I was determined to find my destiny, forget the gossip about that one man, and find myself, because in reality I didn't know who Rosa Lilia was. In all, my childhood had been normal in some ways, yet full of humiliation and traumas that hadn't allowed me to grow up in peace. My innocence and inherent goodness had backfired, debilitating me when I needed to be tough enough to protect myself. I never had the strength to face my problems and defend myself, which made me the perfect target for bringing some excitement to boring small-town life. As for the allegations of a relationship with the school's director, people made a mountain out of a molehill. Even upon leaving, I couldn't stop feeling hate for the school principal who desired me and the ruthless gossipers who ruined my reputation.

The man's name was Hercilio, and he fell in love with me when I was fifteen years old. He was the principal of Lázaro Cárdenas Middle School and taught chemistry and math classes. My first year I had to walk to the foot of a hill, but my second year the school moved to a bigger, more modern and secure place; it had no weeds and was surrounded by a bunch of trees and had a basketball court. The same year they moved the location, they also rotated the teachers.

That is how I met Hercilio. He was a serious man; some said he seemed like a priest. When he wanted, he could put his eyebrows together, and with that expression he had everyone seated and listening to his lesson. Everyone obeyed him as if the school and the world belonged to him. The first time that he had me close by, he called me forward and asked me where I lived, who my parents were, and if I had any siblings. He touched my head and sighed. From then on, for any kind of nonsense I would be called to his desk. He would sigh again. My classmates realized what was happening and treated the situation like any young person at that age; they teased me relentlessly and called me "the girl with whom the principal is in love."

When we turned in our work, we had to go up one by one to his desk, but he decided the order in which we approached. I felt nervous when he began with that routine. I waited my turn, moving my feet and hands; the more he delayed calling me, the faster my heart would beat. He enjoyed the idea of seeing me seated, waiting for him to say, "Rosa Lilia." That way he assured himself he would have me several days a week close to his heavy breathing. Facing him, I would try to converse with him, responding to his questions, but in reality I would keep my eyes on my notebook so that my classmates would think that he was talking to me about the homework. That was how he planned to get close to me. His fantasies went too far, and he went crazy. I also went crazy, but not from love; his shadow was everywhere. It was truly crazy, because he followed me for years. As he would later say, his heart kept telling him that he was "in love."

During vacations, he asked that I go to school. His image and his voice scared me so much that I had to obey. My grades were good. I was studying for a change, unlike in primary school. I would study at the last minute, but I did it. Even then, I was afraid he would fail me if I didn't do what he asked of me. I was sure that an emphatic refusal of his fantasies would end worse. I never dared to go alone; that's why I came up with a plan called Lupe, Gerarda, y Blanquita, three classmates in whom I could confide the stupid things the old man said to me ...

"My heart is going to stop, Rosa Lili," said the man, who on a whim dropped the *a* off my name. "I don't know what to do to win your love. Touch me here," and he put my hand on his chest. "This is your chance—tell me that you love me. "

Unmindful of the fact that all the other students around could see, he took entire rolls of photos of me, in the classroom, on the patio, during exams, wherever I was. During recess he would look for me so that I would pose, but I grabbed Lupe, Gerarda, and Blanquita and sat them next to me so that they would be in the pictures. He was an old man, almost seventy years old, and had been in love with three female students. We found out because Hercilio's thirty-five-year-old wife came to my house when the rumors about Hercilio's obsession spread beyond the school.

I had left class early that day, and when I came into the house, I saw my grandmother and Hercilio's wife with the intention of having a meeting. The first thing I did was to retreat. I stayed listening; his wife was talking about everything but Hercilio. I decided to greet them from a distance, but Pillita—who had heard the rumors and knew the purpose of the wife's visit—asked me to take a seat. I wanted to die, but instead of going to a better life, I stayed listening to the calm and even affectionate voice of that woman.

"I came to inform you about the matter of Hercilio. I know this family, and I know that your granddaughter is a good girl. You know how gossipers broadcast people's life stories around here—'small town, large hell'—but you two should know what awaits you," the wife said.

"What's awaiting us?" Pillita asked, truly interested in this woman's premonition.

"I was Hercilio's student several years ago. He left his wife, who also had been a student in his class, to be with me. We all fell at his feet, but you have to be strong." She looked at me. "Don't worry about what the people say. The thing is that they don't know Hercilio, but I do. He is not mentally stable, but I am sure this obsession with following you will blow over soon."

Pillita had listened to some strange things before in her life, but hearing from his own wife that this man was crazy left her thinking all afternoon. It calmed me to confirm that the man was ill but I was still worried, because the rumors didn't stop. In the street they looked at me as if I were his lover and said that I was going to marry him. Hercilio continued with his obsessive games; I kept looking for reasons not to play them.

Amanda, his sister-in-law, was working as a secretary for the school, and the poor woman had to do everything he asked her. She gave me messages through the window or took me out of class to take me to his office. "The director wants to meet with you," said the poor woman, embarrassed by his psychopathic missions. In his office he had me seated for almost an hour. He was dedicated to talking on the phone or revising classroom books and paused to tell me something stupid or to examine my life at my grandparents' house. During one of his questionings he asked me if it was true that I was going out with a boy. He didn't stop asking until I told him.

"Yes, and I hope you put your games aside," I said.

He stood next to the window and asked, "Who is he? I want to know; you have to tell me right now." Amanda came in with some folders that required his signature, and I took advantage of the moment to go back to class.

One morning—in the same office as always—he tried to touch me; I spilled a cup of coffee on him that was on his desk and ran to the bathroom.

The rumors about a boyfriend were true. The boy Hercilio asked about was Ramiro; I met him through Blanquita one eventful afternoon of basketball. Blanquita was shooting the ball. I tried to grab it from her and felt her fingertip enter my eye. Ramiro, who was watching from a bench, ran to lend a hand; he took me by the arm and helped me sit down. He sent Blanquita and the other kids to get water. Later he wetted a handkerchief and placed it on my left eye. With my right eye I continued to look at his beauty. He looked like a valiant prince right out of a fairy tale. For the first time I felt an affectionate hand.

When the principal confirmed his suspicion, he forbade playing basketball unless an instructor was present and it was a corresponding class activity. He drove himself crazy trying to figure out how to make me his property, and began drinking and missing classes. He consumed himself in fantasy, imagining that one day I would love him.

They blamed me for taking away his impeccable teaching career and for having turned him into a drunken and suicidal man. A woman I had never seen before in town yelled at me as I left school, "You made him fall in love with you, and now you act like a saint. You want to destroy his life, but we won't leave you alone until you pay for the damage you have done."

Elisa, Eduardo's wife, appeared to take pity on me, but in reality she was jealous of me because my grandparents had me in their house and I lived better than her children. She was a resentful woman who had barely managed to leave childhood when she began facing an alcoholic husband and years producing children. She worried about everything besides her own home, lived others' tragedies as if they were her own, and looked upon happiness suspiciously.

"I know that your grandmother loves you more than she loves my kids. She's always going to protect you and cover up your mistakes," she told me the day that I met the woman who yelled at me as I left school. She was a client at my uncle Eduardo's shoe store. More than anyone else, that woman had taken it upon herself to spread the rumors, and although I could have had the courage to confront her,

I wouldn't have gotten anything more than sad results. Once you throw the feathers in the air, you can't bring them back together.

"Small town … God bless my soul!" Pillita said each time some Christian was a victim of that small-town gossip incited by boredom. She said that life in a place like Ario could be calm and entertaining, but it also could leave you naked in the middle of the forest if everything that happens is public news by lunchtime. That's how I saw myself, abandoned in the middle of the forest full of big trees and gossipers, like what happened to a man named Alfredo.

The story was that Alfredo had escaped from Islas Marías, a group of three islands in the Pacific Ocean off Mexico. On the island Madre was a prison where the accused could live with their families in "freedom." However, they had to work farming and herding. On the island there was a church, many shops, a hospital, and a movie theater. There were no large protection barriers, because if one of the accused decided to escape, the sharks would have him.

Alfredo's supposed mother went to the store often, and my grandmother would give her merchandise. Pillita appreciated her friendliness and gave her good deals. One day Pillita said good-bye to the woman saying, "Say hi to Alfredo for me."

"Who is Alfredo?" I asked her.

"He is a dangerous man who is in prison and is going to get out next week," Pillita said, repeating the old rumor.

Many people got upset upon knowing that his mother was preparing his bedroom. "My son is coming," she said proudly. She was sure that someone had been determined to create a history of vicious attacks about her son. When they saw him around the town, everyone walked around scared to death.

"May God protect us," begged the women from the store. "That man killed and castrated who knows how many men."

During the first week of his supposed liberation—nobody knew his face, but everyone had invented one—the stores closed early, the streets drowned in silence, and only a few food stands remained with the hope of selling a taco or two. Pillita, who had a generous heart, believed in his rehabilitation and eagerly hoped to wait on him. I never saw him but imagined him very well one night.

About a month after Alfredo's release, the neighbors called at one in the morning. We were putting together bags of beans—including my aunts Milla and Lancha, who were visiting—when we jumped at the sound of the telephone. My aunt Milla answered, made a frightened face, and hung up.

Since my grandfather had lost himself in the boxes of paperwork on the second floor and wasn't with us, I managed to speak: "What happened, Aunt Milla?" I asked her, frightened.

"They just informed us that Alfredo attacked your son," she said, looking at Pillita and about to cry.

"Which son?" Pillita asked.

"I don't remember … I think that the person who called only said, 'Alfredo attacked Pillita's son.'"

With the screams Grandfather came to the living room. My aunt Milla repeated the phrase to him, my grandfather grabbed a shotgun, and we all walked around the block to Uncle Eduardo's house. Crouched in the darkness we walked one behind the other looking in every direction with my grandfather in front. When we arrived at Uncle Eduardo's house, no lights were turned on. There were no screams, and there was no blood. We banged desperately on the door, but nobody opened it.

"Alfredo already killed them all!" yelled Aunt Lancha.

"Shut up, woman, stop making me nervous," Pillita said, shaking her.

We went to the police headquarters and filed a complaint. The police accompanied us with a ladder to my uncle's house. The policeman turned on a lantern that reached the second floor. He was trying to open the window when my uncle Eduardo appeared naked with his hair disheveled.

"Are you all right, sir?" the policeman asked.

"Yes, why?" he responded, half drunk and scratching his head. Then he looked at us like we were aliens.

"Keep sleeping," said the policeman.

"Then Alfredo attacked Rodrigo," yelled Aunt Lancha. "There goes Alfredo!" she yelled louder, stretching her arm toward the plaza.

We all ran, but the policeman led the battalion.

"Everyone, calm down! It was just an animal," said the policeman to Aunt Lancha. "The shadow that you saw was a donkey, ma'am."

All the deaths and accidents of those days were attributed to poor Alfredo. Everyone feared him, but nobody could recount an attack. I can't promise that he is innocent, but that night there was more of a mess than a crime.

"They killed Rodrigo!" Pillita said.

After following the donkey through the plaza, we went to my uncle Rodrigo's house. When we entered, we saw him on his bed with a ton of blood running down his body. Nobody else was in the house.

"Don't go in; this is a crime scene," the policeman said.

It was far from a crime scene. Uncle Rodrigo had been attacked by sudden nostalgia for his family. He had drunken a bottle of Charanda that he later threw against the wall. Various pieces of glass got in his feet, and then he drunkenly fell in bed with half his body hanging off the bed.

I was unable to prove the existence of such an Alfredo, but the people ended the story of the criminal by saying that the police of Morelia had captured him and had returned him to the Islas Marías islands forever.

What I did manage to prove was the workings of the Ouija; that terrifying memory makes my hair stand on end. It was a day in which Selene—a classmate from middle school—came to class telling me that there was this new, really fun game and that several of her friends had bought it. It was during the boom of the movie *The Exorcist* in Latin America, and stores sold it as a game.

We bought the board and, just like we did every week—because Pillita kept close tabs on her family—got together at Selene's house to do math homework. That turned into our first session of contact with the dead. Selene invited two of her cousins who became board experts.

What happened with that board was terrible. We had taken it as a game in a way that a fourteen-year-old adolescent can't refuse. We wanted to know how the Ouija worked; if it resulted in some contact with "beyond," it would be much better. Some people said that you could communicate with spirits and aliens, and we wanted to prove it. In the first session, the cousins did everything: read the instructions, moved the pieces, and worked on inventing answers. Seeing as nothing happened, we got together the following week. Math homework was done at home separately because we had become addicted to the dear game. Each one of us read different messages and pretended to talk with whomever we imagined could communicate through the board. After a month, we knew all the Ouija tricks. We experienced a few things, but they were laughs, suggestions, and sounds from Selene's house—nothing from spirits or voices from beyond or nearby.

I started having dark dreams and hearing screams from the grave and voices in my room. I wasn't worried because my aunt Barbara had me convinced—with her completely careless tone—that all noises have an explanation. That's what she had told me on the day that I insinuated that the ghost of the poisoned fiancée was in the house and that she had chains tied around her feet. My aunt Barbara responded: "Idiot! Don't be scandalous. These houses have noises because they are old or because they have rats, cats, or bats in the roof. Don't be stupid, you ugly girl!" I knew that nothing supernatural was going on. My friends and I found much humor in the game because none of us believed in the Ouija's link with the supernatural.

Selena, Teresa, and I took turns taking the game home with us. The most terrible thing happened when it was my turn to keep the game at my house and my grandmother discovered the Ouija hidden inside a box of fine dinnerware and ordered it to be burned. Luckily Aunt Barbara went on a trip to DF and my brother Damián was visiting us in Ario de Rosales. Damián had inherited the kindness of my mother and wanted to become a priest. He had come for a week from Irapuato with a group of young Catholics to visit the town. They wanted to return the lost sheep to the church through prayer. My grandmother told Damián and his friends about the Ouija and asked him to destroy it.

"Tomorrow morning go to the patio and burn it," she said to the young men. "Afterward, do a cleansing on this girl," she requested with anguish.

"No, Damián! Don't burn it. It's a game," I yelled.

"The devil is like that, Lilia," Damián said. That's what they began to call me in my adolescence, and I felt that I was losing a part of the girl called Rosa Lilia. "It starts to destroy your brain through fun. It starts to excite you, to addict you, and later it manipulates you. You have to believe in God and He doesn't like that little game," he explained to me.

The next day, when I got up to go to school, I heard voices on the patio; the Ouija was just a pile of ashes. Pillita saw me and said, "This is not a game." I felt furious, because everything my hands touched ended up destroyed by my grandfather, my aunt, or Pillita. But the rage turned into terror when I saw that from the depths of the ash a string of blood started to emerge and later got lost going toward the street, planting footprints that looked like those of a small animal. We were all left frozen.

"We have to cleanse you," Damián said quickly.

"I'm going to get more Bibles," one of the others said. Even though I didn't believe that I was possessed by any demons, I went along with the fanatical cleansing ritual because I was practically forced to by Damián and Pillita.

In a few short minutes we were seated at the biggest table of the living room, holding hands. Damián read a page that he placed in the center of the table and called upon God to get rid of the evil spirit in my body. I had to repeat the words, and the young men and Damián began to speak in languages I had never heard before. I don't know how long I had my eyes closed listening to the languages, repeating phrases, and feeling heat so intense that I thought the table would catch fire.

When we opened our eyes, Damián said, "What you saw emerge from the ashes were the footprints of a beast. The devil gained power through you, but now you are pure; the devil has left your life.

Upon finishing the cleansing session I felt calmer. I didn't have any more nightmares or hear any noises. Nor did I play again with the board or with anything; destiny wouldn't give me time for those things.

In Mexico one had the option of designating a godmother or a godfather for one's high school graduation; my grandfather said that they were pointless. For my party, my good-natured uncle Fermín (one of my mother's brothers) agreed to be my godfather and came from DF to accompany me. Pillita had bought me a salmon-colored silk dress. Since I had so rarely been that excited to go to a party, I spent all afternoon in the mirror figuring out what makeup would complement the dress. From trying on so many colors, I ended up with about five layers of makeup. Downstairs, Pillita and my uncle Fermín were eagerly waiting. Upon seeing me, he made a strange face, and I didn't know if he was impressed or disappointed.

"Lilia! So much makeup isn't necessary; you look like a clown," said Uncle Fermín. "Your dress is gorgeous and you look pretty without makeup ... No! Please take it off."

I returned upstairs sad, but upon entering the bathroom and looking at myself in the mirror, I understood that my uncle was doing me a favor; I looked like a clown ready for a performance. I always believed Uncle Fermín because his frankness stood above all else, without offending or laughing at others. He didn't like my makeup and told me so; it was as simple as that. I went back down and he said, smiling, "That's better." He offered me his left arm, and we set out with Pillita for Ario's reception hall, where the party would take place.

Upon entering the party, they assigned us a table with pink flowers. A Chilean band, *Ángeles Negros,* or the Black Angels, was playing. On the table next to ours was Selene's family, and a little bit farther away was my boyfriend Ramiro's family. He saw me come in and came over to say hi to Pillita and then shook my uncle's hand. The music started to play, and Ramiro, like a gentleman, put out his hand and offered me the first dance. I looked at Pillita.

"Go on, Lilia, you came to have fun. Go on! Life is short," said my uncle, even more excited than I was.

Ramiro had passed by the outside of the house several times, but as with the other boy, my grandfather ran him off with his screams. He had sent me messages full of love and romantic songs from the Black Angels, the very same group that was playing at the party. The day that my grandfather went to his parents and accused him of spying on the house, he wrote me a letter with the lyrics to the song by that same group: *"Leave me if I'm crying. Not one comfort am I looking for. I want to be alone with my pain. If you see that I've been crying alone, it's that suddenly I am remembering a love which I still can't forget …"*

The theater was full of lights, balloons, and bright confetti. The majority of the town was there at the tables celebrating the graduation of their children, including Hercilio, who didn't have any children but had come as a teacher because he had lost the title of director when he decided to pursue me. Six tables away he sat with his wife, angry because Ramiro took me to the dance. Ramiro knew of the rumors and noticed that the man didn't stop looking at me. We continued dancing until he began to bring his body closer to mine. Without saying anything I subtly pushed him back. He said nothing, and continued dancing as far away as he had in the beginning. In spite of everything, I loved his delicateness, and I was happy to feel that kind of affection, tenderness, and maybe even love that I had never felt before. When the song ended, Ramiro took me close to the table where Hercilio was to show him—I imagine—that I was not alone and that he was in charge of me.

"Hello, sir, is this your wife?" Ramiro asked. The old man shook his hand, nodded, and sat down with a sad face. The woman, smiling and pretending that she had never met me, greeted us and said, "You two look nice." I thanked her and also corresponded to disguise the fact that she had talked with me and Pillita in my house.

I made a gesture to Ramiro so that we would return to the dance floor. The situation was tense, and at any moment the teacher was going to release his rage. We danced one more song, and then we each went back to our families. Uncle Fermín told me about his life in DF, his studies as a lawyer, and that Aunt Mary was pregnant. Pillita immediately showed her happiness.

Hercilio kept watching me between his sips of tequila. The party had been a dream but I came back to reality when the old man, drunk, stood up and tipped over the table, broke bottles, three cups, and an ashtray, and began to scream, "You are mine and nobody else's!" The group kept playing, security guards in green came in, and they took him behind the stage. On the way out he kept screaming, "I'm going to kill myself if you don't love me!"

"Don't listen to him," Pillita said, and we had to tell the story to Uncle Fermín, whose mouth had been gaping after seeing that dramatic scene. When they took the old man away, I felt better.

I danced with my friends with so much eagerness that I wanted to take my shoes off, but I decided not to because Pillita intimidated me with just one look. She had already told me before the party that I had to maintain my elegance until the end. Ramiro joined the group and took me aside, took my hands, and asked me to be his girlfriend.

"I'll think about it," I said nervously while the girls anxiously spied on me.

"Don't think so hard. If you kiss me, it's a yes. If you don't kiss me, then it's ..."

Before finishing the phrase he kissed me.

"We are dating!" he yelled. "Can I tell your grandmother?"

"Don't even think about it."

I accepted. Better said, I took on the role of his girlfriend; however, I never kissed him or held his hand. For me, that type of gesture wasn't dirty, but if I allowed it, he would think I was an easy girl, that I was ordinary, and he would want to take advantage of me.

We silently maintained our relationship. We saw each other when I managed to go out to the plaza or when we played basketball on the school's court. Ramiro—who was a grade below me—asked me to be his godmother for his graduation ceremony. Pillita, who by that time had found out we were dating, helped me lie to my grandfather about having to go to the dance, saying that she had offered me as a volunteer to set up tables. Hercilio was also there with his wife, but unlike the previous year, he stayed seated, talked with different parents for a few hours, and then left.

The day after the party, Ramiro invited me to go on a walk and brought my friend Teresa as a decoy. We talked about school, friends, and the party. We went to a coffee shop, and in the middle of the conversation, he got close to my face to kiss me. I had already lost count of his failed attempts, but one more refusal from me was apparently too much for him and made him lose his romanticism and chivalry.

"I know you aren't as much of a saint as you look, I know you slept with the director," he yelled at me when I didn't want to kiss him. "You pretend to be a big saint, and yet the whole town knows about you."

I felt my stomach boil until the heat reached my head and I thought I was going to burst. That was neither the first nor the last time I would feel such anger. I grabbed the cup of coffee and threw it in his face. I didn't want to see him anymore. I ran home and ripped up all his letters and songs. The gossip had reached such a level that not even the boy who said he loved me could resist the rumors. It wasn't hard to forget him; after three days he tried to ask for forgiveness, but I didn't want to hear it.

"You are in the past!" I yelled out the window.

With a great effort I was the first in my class in the last year of middle school. I studied late to prove to everyone that I was smart. And although I was the best and I was better at math than at literature, nothing could undo my reputation. My classmates—and their friends from other grades—said that my grades were given to me.

At recess they yelled at me, "There goes the shameless girl." How was it possible that the old man had been in love with me and had made my life so miserable? How was it possible that he had wanted to leave his wife on a whim and everyone blamed me for it? How was it possible that they treated me like that without knowing anything about me, how I considered myself a lady, although in reality that's what I would have been if it hadn't have been for my uncle Eduardo.

Hercilio had a sister in Chihuahua who went for a few days to Ario de Rosales on her vacation. Sometime after his debacle at the graduation, he sent her to my house on a mission to persuade me to go out with him. I was with Pillita organizing some boxes in storage when one of the servants entered.

"There is a woman outside asking for you, Rosa Lilia. She says that she's here on behalf of Mr. Hercilio."

"Tell her that Lilia is not here," my grandmother requested, and a little while later the servant returned with some videos and pictures. She explained who the visitor had been: "It was Hercilio's sister. She told me to bring this box and that Hercilio wanted to see her, only see her."

The tapes had videos on them in which he spent hours declaring his love to me and repeating the same foolishness. *"Why are you ignoring me? If you go, my life will have no meaning. I love you so much; if you go, I don't want to live."*

The pictures were the ones he had taken of me at school, alone and with my friends. Pillita was worried that Hercilio's obsession would cause him to kidnap me, so she suggested that I close myself in the house until he thought I had left town. I refrained from going out of the house for two months. Even though I was anxious to leave and felt like I was in prison, I believed that Pillita's plan would keep me safe and help Hercilio forget about me. The plan was complete, and Hercilio's harassment died down.

Two years later, my family experienced the first and only fight between my grandparents. Pillita finally got fed up with the life she had with my grandfather. Although I was sorry about the outcome, the separation fit me like a ring on a finger.

Grandfather, according to the rumors, had become involved with a young woman from Pátzcuaro, the daughter of an investor in decline. But they weren't rumors, because my grandfather had to admit the truth when Pillita put him between a rock and a hard place. "If you don't tell me the truth, I will leave Ario forever and you will never see me ever again, never!" she said.

The girl's father owed my grandfather a lot of money; therefore he offered him his daughter to repay his debts. It seemed like a good idea to my grandfather to revive some habits from the past. In spite of his poor health, he saw the girl several times, and even gave her a store for her to start a bakery she had always wanted. I don't know what he was thinking—whether he was trying to improve the situation or worsen it— when he told Grandmother that he had thought about marrying the young girl but had made a mistake, because he loved my grandmother. Everything was a mess. My uncle Fermín came to intervene, but it was impossible to mediate; my grandmother didn't want to see him anymore. "I want a divorce!" she repeated. She was suffering.

Since she could no longer look my grandfather in the face, she decided to live in Irapuato, with her sisters Lancha and Milla. My mother was living next to them, so I liked the idea even better. Uncle Fermín insisted that I stay with my grandfather to take care of him; symptoms of cancer in his prostate had already started to affect him. He even offered me a car and a monthly installment to take care of Grandfather, but Pillita was my second mother, and in spite of the lack of attention to me, I would remain loyal to her.

Pillita (Elpidia) Negrete.

At the house in Irapuato, they set up a room for me that had been abandoned for many years. They emptied it of boxes and memories that made my aunts cry, not because it hurt them but because they were sentimental. Pillita ordered them to paint it and bought furniture and all that I needed to feel at home. It ended up like a palace. I was happy because I was close to my mother and my sisters, but most of all I rejoiced at the possibility of being even farther away from the gossipy people of the town. *I am going to feel free,* I thought. But everything has its price. Since my grandmother made sure that I had everything, my sisters, who lived off the money that my mother earned cutting hair, started to bother me.

To take advantage of the time, Pillita signed me up for preparatory school. One afternoon, after the second day of class, I went into my room and I thought that a criminal had been there. The bed was backward; my clothes were thrown everywhere, and some items were cut. I didn't want to tell anyone and sat in the bed trying to shake off the suspicion. I decided to sew the clothes that had been cut so that no one would notice and ask how my clothes had been damaged. The same thing happened the following week; my sisters Susana and Ernestina had broken the padlock. Daily, I encountered such surprises, which made me sad. What an illusion of freedom! It was my sisters' turn to humiliate me.

It was hard for me to get used to that city. First it was the heat, then the cockroaches and scorpions that sunbathed outside the door. They not only adorned the patio, but looked for the heat in the sheets. I was traumatized when I had to remove a scorpion from my bed. That day, I grabbed a hammer and killed it. Then Pillita had the place fumigated.

In that city, people were less courteous, especially the men in the street, who yelled at every woman they saw. They seemed like animals recently freed from their cages. And in the middle of adolescence, I didn't escape their swear words.

To make up for lost time, I started to go out with my mother. I accompanied her to the store and on errands for the hair salon. One afternoon when we went to eat pozole, she noticed how the men looked at me with interest and desire, and said, "Men are really awful. When you go out in the street, you need put on a mean face, like this." She made a face. "Wrinkle your forehead, get angry, and never look at them."

"Even better, I should wear a sheet the next time I go out."

"There's no need to exaggerate either. I'm saying this for your benefit."

"What do I wear then?"

"Just do what I tell you and be careful, because there are a lot of marijuana smokers hanging around."

Those were the types of people that scared my mother the most. She said that those depraved men were at every corner looking for drugs or women to ease their troubles. She was terrified of them, and it made me be cautious with them.

"I am going to introduce you to a man if that's all right," my mother said one day. "His name is Horacio."

"What high school does he go to?"

"He graduated already. Now he boxes and is doing very well. He has won several titles."

"A boxer?" I asked, but in reality I wanted to ask, "Are you crazy?"

To please my mother, I agreed to meet this Horacio. On the first date he tried to touch me, his hands full of blotches. I said, "Nice to meet you," and I left. One week later, my mother invited him over to the house for dinner. My sisters felt attracted to him, and while they asked him about his fights, I was thinking about a new boy I had met named Arturo.

To arrive at the preparatory school, I had to take a bus and travel twenty minutes, sometimes seated, sometimes standing. On the way, I didn't know if they were *weed smokers*, but I had to use the technique my mother taught me, because men didn't stop saying stupid remarks to me, sometimes even rude remarks.

I was even more loyal to her advice when they attacked my brother. It was one day after a Mass to which Damián insisted upon taking me; he continued with his desire to be a priest. On the way back, one block away from our house, appeared a car with two men. It braked loudly and the driver yelled to his accomplice: "Grab her!"

"Run, Lilia! Run! I'll take care of it!" said Damián, who believed that with God's help he would be saved. They struggled for a few seconds until another truck appeared. The one man let my brother go and got in the car, and the truck followed them until they were lost. Only God knows what that was.

The next day I wrinkled my forehead, got angry, and took the bus. I didn't look at anyone, except when the same boy got on, like every day, and got off at the same preparatory school. He had short hair and round, very dark eyes, and from far away I could smell the smooth scent of creamy soap. Every day I forgot about my exercise in rudeness to look at him without him realizing it. Bells sounded and birds sang when he got on the bus. Each day it was like a new movie; I imagined that he would fall in love with me, that he would ask me to marry him, that we would have children and live happily ever after. I even imagined the words *The End* on the screen at the movies. Oh, how I liked to dream about the day my Prince Charming would rescue me.

One morning I was profoundly wrapped up in my love dream—flying in the clouds—when I felt someone sit next to me; I came back to earth when I realized it was the young man with round eyes. We looked at each other, but there was a nervous silence until we got to the preparatory. After that episode, I would see his face everywhere: in the bathroom, the patio, the club. Up close he was as handsome as in my dreams. I forgot my sisters, the scorpions, and the whistling in the street. Every place and animal in the world wore Arturo's face.

He was athletic and played for the soccer team. He talked to me for the first time one Monday to invite me to what he called an important game. He wore number 11, and my friends used it for his name.

"Have you seen Eleven?" they asked me.

My mom found out that we were interested in each other because one afternoon, after a game, Arturo walked me home. He immediately wanted to meet my family, but I warned him ahead of time that it was a humble family. They were concerned with me meeting a man with a stable economic situation. My mother never thought that my grandfather would leave me an inheritance, and if he did, her sister Barbara would make sure to take it away from me.

Upon arriving at my home that afternoon, I introduced Arturo to my mother and Pillita. Since I didn't make it a formal introduction, my family didn't think much of it at all, but Arturo regarded it as a significant step in our relationship.

In the meantime, my mother persisted with her thought of Horacio as a suitor. She had a disastrous idea, which she shared with everyone at the table: "You have to marry that man."

Pillita and Lancha didn't trust Horacio. "You want to get rid of your daughters?" Pillita angrily responded. "Do they get in your way? Can't you see that the girl is studying and that young man is too ugly for her? Besides, Lilia doesn't like him—let her decide," she lectured before going to her room.

My mother insisted about the boxer. She bought fruit from the stand that he had inherited from his parents. If she didn't go buy, Horacio had a servant bring the fruit to her. At home there was an abundance of bananas, apples, and strawberries, but the affection was still lacking. I told Arturo about what was happening, and he consoled me by saying, "Go with the flow."

But the boxer's time ran out when he started arguing with a client at the market who owed him money. It wasn't enough for Horacio to just hit the customer directly in the eye; he left the man on the ground, bleeding from a stab wound.

My aunt Lancha started to tell the news with a smile from ear to ear, knowing that it would persuade my mother to stop oppressing me with the idea of marrying Horacio. She often looked out for me and had been waiting patiently for a way to subtly deter my mother from her absurd idea. That day, she came in with the newspaper in her hand, opened to the page that read, "Boxer stabs his client in the middle of the market." He ended up in jail.

It had been almost a year since we left Ario, and Grandfather had spent half the time lying in bed. This was half because of the sadness of Pillita leaving him and half because of the pain from cancer. The young plebeian girl with whom he had cheated on Pillita had left him for a wealthy rancher.

Grandmother—after several tearful insistences—decided to return to Ario for her dear old husband. I had to leave Arturo with the promise that we would meet up soon. We packed our bags and abandoned that hot city. Arturo sent me letters, and as soon as I finished reading them, I wrote back.

One day he came to my town with a friend, and whistled for me to come down to the street. I was still afraid of my grandfather, so I went down secretly and we met up in the square. I started to visit my mother, three hours away in Irapuato, in order to see him, until on a date he told me he was going to study architecture on the other end of Mexico. He proposed that we keep seeing each other on vacations, but the long-distance love soon ended. His departure hurt me, but I kept his letters and his memory for many years.

Having arrived back in Ario, my grandmother resumed her chores at home and tended to my grandfather and his pain. Since I had attended only one year of high school in Irapuato, she also made sure to enroll me in a school in town for my second year. People were still talking about me, my grandfather hadn't changed—worried about business—and the scenery was the same. Nothing had changed.

Jennifer, another one of my uncle Eduardo's daughters, had copied my habit of going on a run. I was fifteen when I started to run, and developed the routine of running up to the top of the San Miguel hill four times per week with some of my cousins at sunrise. She became an exercise fanatic, and therefore every sunrise she went for a run on the San Miguel hill that was half an hour from her house. Sometimes she went with us, and sometimes she went alone.

On that hill there was a cave that seemed enormous; the truth was that I had never been inside. People said that it had hundreds of human skeletons of those who had tried to steal the buried gold. Upon entering, they were devoured by prehistoric animals that took over the cave, primarily giant-headed snakes. Each time I got near caves, I imagined that vipers were looking hungrily at me. I never went all the way up the hill, much less at dawn. Jennifer went alone, going up and down that hill to, according to her, strengthen her muscles and look more attractive.

On one occasion, she realized that a man was watching her. She got scared and began running as fast as she could. It was a man who walked around herding his animals, but when Jennifer saw that there were other men farther down who started to follow her, she ran even faster without stopping until she got to the shoe store, almost out of breath and covered in sweat.

"What happened to you, girl?" her mother demanded.

"I was on the hill and I saw a man who was watching me," she gasped with her hands on her knees. "Then I saw two others and I got scared … They wanted to rape me, I'm sure of it. So I came running back here."

"Are you sure they aren't those old creeps who like to look at young girls?" my aunt Elisa said.

"No. They were young men. They were close," she said, out of breath.

"It's your fault," said her mother. "I told you not to go to that place alone, much less that early. You never do what I say. All for trying to have a lovely figure, you are going to get pregnant. I don't want you to go to that hill anymore!"

Aunt Elisa, as always, made sure to comment on what had happened to Jennifer. With the news about young men lying in wait, five of the older virgins of the town suddenly formed the habit of climbing the hill to "exercise" at sunrise. These women, all more than fifty years old, had never been married and probably never would be. Their decency had prevented them from engaging in extramarital relationships until then, yet the reality of lifelong celibacy made them look to alleviate their desires on the San Miguel hill. Several people said to them, "Go clear out the cobwebs," and when they saw the women climb the hill, they jokingly yelled at them, "Are you on the way to get an oil change?" Of course, they always denied that any encounters had taken place and insisted that their long morning walks were for exercise only.

One year after the episode of suspicious characters on the hill, Teresa Salinas (Tere), my friend since childhood, came to my house with the proposal that we go to study tourism management in Morelia. She had found the perfect profession that allowed her to travel the world, meet many people, and be happy. Pillita was not very convinced. My aunt Barbara was still in DF; therefore her opinion didn't count for much. The proposal became more interesting at the end of the week when my uncle Fermín appeared, with adorable Mary, whose help I enlisted to convince my grandfather.

"Grandfather, tourism is a business," I explained to him. "With that I can practice what you taught me: wait on people, sell tourist packages ..."

"Let her go, Mr. Rafael," interrupted Mary, "She is old enough, and this is what she wants to study."

"No, my little girl, you are going to study to become a doctor, responded my grandfather, ignoring Mary.

"Look ... it's a good idea in order for her to start her studies," she insisted. "Besides, she will be going with the Salinas daughters. From what I know, their family is among the only ones that you respect."

He accepted a minute later. He needed to retain his energy to battle the illness.

With the memory of Arturo, my trip to Irapuato, the nightmare of Hercilio, and the legacy of my aunt Barbara, I left for Morelia, capital of Michoacán. I went to study at the Valladolid Institute, a center of very prestigious Marista priests. It was the year 1981, and I ended up living at a guesthouse, a residence hall with thirty girls, a few blocks from the middle of the city. Pillita dropped me off. It was a large house, baroque-style, with many windows. The house's administrator was Gela, a Spanish woman, with a large nose and a deep voice. She rented single and shared rooms as well as rooms with washing, ironing, and food services. Complete package. I asked for a private room with food, but when I realized that the food pots were used to store things other than food, I stopped eating there. She gave me a room on the first floor. On one side was Gela's half sister Gema, and on the other side lived Marlen. Four girls shared another large room. Tere, Lucy, and Rossie lived upstairs.

Soon after moving in, Tere and Lucy moved to an apartment across the street that their father had bought them. They invited me to live with them, but I told them no. That was another bad decision. I was very unwise; maybe I would have been better off and had another destiny with them, because they were such good girls.

Here my new life started. The room was small, but I decorated it so that it looked more spacious. In the beginning my routine was to go to school and come back home. Later, it would get more exciting, especially because of Gela, who was quite a character and was about as predictable as a gunshot in the dark. I went walking through the streets. I came out on Madero Avenue, which ran through the entire city, and ,entertained myself looking at the shops, the restaurants and the people. It was an avenue filled with lights and life. It also reminded me of my mother's advice, to "make an angry, evil face" each time I saw suspicious-looking men.

Morelia is a big city with a large population and is full of good and bad history. I liked to look at the plazas, the cathedrals, and the seventeenth-century houses and the typical city buildings. It really looked beautiful. I think that for that reason I preferred to walk rather than take the bus to school.

Class had begun, and everything seemed normal until Hercilio showed up. Gela opened the door.

"I'm looking for Rosa Lilia," he said. "I'm her uncle."

Gela already knew the story. I told her that Hercilio wore a gold cuff on his wrist with his name on it, so she immediately knew it was the man from whom I was hiding. Besides, my grandmother filled her in on the situation and humiliation I had suffered back at home. Gela told him that he was mistaken, that I might be somewhere else because there were many boardinghouses in Morelia. And he left. I didn't see him again until three years later at another house.

Since Ario was only about two hours away from Morelia, I went home often to visit my grandparents. On one of my trips home, when I was nineteen years old and in my third year of school, I met Federico. He was a twenty-seven-year-old doctor from Querétaro who was working as a practicing physician for the Mexican Institute of Social Security in a new clinic in Ario. He was one of the many doctors who were sent from different cities all over the country to lend their services to the town.

With my grandfather's illness, Pillita had been put in charge of even more properties in town. On the first floor of one of those properties lived Marta and Lulu. They were young women who lived in the United States but came back on vacations to see their parents in Ario. They were very liberal. They spoke English and Spanish and smoked marijuana. They were fun but a little too crazy for me. I seemed nice to Lulu; therefore she acted in a respectful manner around me. She knew I was a calm girl who couldn't keep up with her craziness and vices. Her mother rented the store to sell American clothes, and upstairs was where Federico, the doctor, lived. Sometimes my grandmother sent me to pick up the rent, and that was how I met him.

He liked me and started to court me. Lulu was a friend of his and helped us exchange messages and go on a few dates. We started seeing each other and sharing more.

I once again desired to get married in a church with a beautiful ceremony and huge celebration of love. That man was my salvation, at first. He made me feel beautiful, but later became a nightmare and one of my great misfortunes.

My grandparents met him and accepted him. My aunt Barbara said he was ugly. Pillita said it didn't matter. "I adore him," she commented. He even came to have dinner with us a few times; I was so happy.

I traveled often to Ario to see my grandparents. One Saturday I arrived late because before that I had met up with Federico and time flew with him. It was nine o'clock in the evening. After entering, the first thing I saw was my uncle Fermín sitting at the table with a bunch of papers in his hands.

"Why are you arriving so late, Lilia?" he asked me angrily. He had never talked to me like that before. "You have to come here early; my father is very sick. You already know that."

"I'm sorry; the bus was late getting here."

"It's all right. Go see my father," he ordered me, and kept looking over the paperwork.

As I walked toward his room, I thought about the fact that my uncle's voice had sounded very strange. He had his head practically hunched over the table and was constantly sighing. Those papers were contracts and invoices. It was even possible that my grandfather's will was there. Fermín had never yelled at me, and my impression was that something was wrong.

I went into the room and saw my grandfather, skinnier and paler than ever. He started to say things that didn't make sense and to make strange noises. *God is coming to get him very soon*, I thought. My grandmother was in the room, my aunt Milla and Susana, my sister who lived in the house since I moved to Morelia because my mother had asked her to come help Pillita. I went closer to my grandfather and he looked like a cadaver. He had only one thin layer of skin stuck to his bones. They had given him blood, something like plasma and a lot of morphine, but the cancer kept spreading throughout his body.

"Is it you?" he babbled. "Tell them to come buy piloncillo."

"Calm down, Grandfather," I said to him, and I touched his head for the first time.

He was doing badly, but he recognized me and his face lighted up, though feebly. A while back I had started to inject him with morphine. He didn't want nurses; he said that they pierced his arm like a colander and left it full of bruises. When I was in preparatory school, I had taken an extracurricular course in first aid. As part of our training, we were taken to elementary schools and rural homes to give immunizations. On those field trips, children made long lines to get shots from me, passing along a tip: "It doesn't hurt with that doctor," they said. My aunt Milla had also shown me how to place my hands, how much pressure to apply, and all the techniques that had been passed down from generation to generation. That night,

I had my hand on my grandfather's head when he began to make strange gestures and started to bleed from his mouth. I tried to help him, but they quickly removed me from the room. I left his room but remained uneasy about what was happening. My uncle Fermín was still looking over the documents.

My grandfather died at midnight. I found out when I heard Pillita scream and cry. Susana, who also was asleep, woke up.

"Rafael died," screamed my grandmother.

"Why are you crying, Pillita? He was so bad to you," Susana said. My aunt Milla stayed still and sat thinking; she wasn't crying. We all went to his room, except my uncle Fermín, who was talking with the doctor and later with the priest. Then he went to take a shower, and everyone looked at him strangely. Nobody understood why he would take a shower right at that moment. I understood him; I was imagining that he was so affected that he wanted to wash away the pain with water. Everyone was doing different things. They entered and left his room, until I was left alone with my grandfather. There was a dead man in front of me but I wasn't scared of him. I looked at him carefully and asked myself, *Is he dead?*

"Grandpa, Grandpa," I said, without a response. "Well, I guess you are dead. Where do I start to dress you? I forgive you for the times you hit me, the stress you caused me, your yelling, and the way you mistreated Pillita. I forgive you, Grandpa. Go in peace. If it's true that the last organ to go is your hearing, then I want you to know that I forgive you, and I am sure my mother does too."

From his room I could hear the conversations about the coffin, whether it should be wooden or metal; they argued.

"How are we going to bury him in a wooden coffin? The whole town will criticize us," said Uncle Fermín. I even heard the voice of my aunt Elisa's, who had arrived with my uncle Eduardo. She said that Grandfather had admitted to her he wanted a wooden coffin. With so much going on, I locked myself in my own world. I let them converse about all the trivial things and uncovered my grandfather. I wanted to see his body; most of all what it was to have prostate cancer. He had suffered so much that I imagined that there was something visible there. My grandmother always kept a tight rein on my grandfather when it came to women who surrounded him—years before he had gotten with one of the servants. A baby had been born out of that relationship, and my grandparents paid the servant to go far away.

"Is it true that you sinned so much with that thing?" I asked him. I looked one last time at his dead stomach and covered him up to his waist. "Take care, Grandfather. I forgive you and hope your soul is at peace," I said before getting to work. I never believed that souls go to heaven, never, but I was so touched by seeing him dead that I confessed to him, "If your soul is still walking around here, like how you believed Uncle Rodrigo's soul had stayed in the cat, I hope that you become my chicken and bring her back to me," I said with a smile because I thought it was funny what I was asking him.

Downstairs the heated discussion continued.

After clearing my head, I put in his teeth, put on his best suit and a tie, and took my makeup box out of my purse to do his makeup. I put cotton in his nose and gel in his hair, and even put on his hat that he wore for important meetings. I stepped back to look at him and he seemed like an artist. The voices died down and I heard footsteps. It was Uncle Fermín.

"Is that my father?" he said, surprised. "You did his makeup? Oh my God! It seems as if he were alive."

When the coffin arrived—ultimately they chose a metal one— it was Sunday morning. We held a wake all day for him. As the hours passed, family and friends from Morelia and DF, a large number of neighbors from in town, and my aunt Barbara had all been arriving. Inside the coffin, I placed an onion for the smell and a lemon to keep the mosquitoes at bay. The house was full of people in every nook and cranny. Nobody cried, only Pillita. I patrolled the hallways to listen to the people's conversations; someone said that my grandfather was a great man who had dedicated his life to his businesses. I would have like to have heard that he was a humble man dedicated to his family.

I cried for him days later when I began to remember the moments in which he would ask me to cook for him. We never had an affectionate relationship, but he showed his affection by praising the meals that I prepared when Pillita was traveling for her medical checkups. The next week at the funeral I felt that I missed him, that he was an important man in my life. To remember him I sat in the chair in which he always sat to relax and make numbered lists. I cried. One day Aunt Barbara saw me and told my grandmother. She said that I was upset and depressed, and that I had gone mad because I went to sit in my grandfather's chair and talked to myself.

My grandfather's corpse was in the only cemetery in town. Many years later he would be reunited with Pillita when the family— without a majority consensus— would decide to place her bones in the same coffin.

I didn't call Federico to tell him that my grandfather died. He surely could not have attended the funeral because he also was providing medical services in the state of Coahuila. One week later we met up in Morelia and I gave him a summary, although he insisted on having the details. He was surprised and asked me specific questions about my grandmother's future, my aunt's, and my own.

Between his trips, we met in Ario, in Morelia, or at his parents' house in Querétaro. He told me about his patients, illnesses, and new medicine I always listened to him attentively. I found it interesting that he was always drinking alcohol but never got drunk; on the contrary, it made him happy and in love. He offered me a drink, and I rejected it several times until one day we went out to eat and he convinced me that you had to know how to handle your alcohol.

Federico arrived at the boardinghouse with flowers, but I was out buying books with Tere. Upon returning, Gela gave me the flowers with lovestruck eyes; they were gorgeous flowers, filled with bright yellows, reds and blues.

"The doctor is in love with you ... Look at how lovely these flowers are ... When are you two going to get married?" Gela asked.

Gela was as happy as if she were talking about her own wedding.

"Very soon," I responded. Federico had asked me a few questions about marriage.

I took the flowers to my room. Not even five minutes had gone by when Gela knocked on the door. "The doctor's on the phone; run, girl," she said. Federico told me that the flowers were the first part of a surprise; the second was an invitation to eat roasted goat. It was at a restaurant where they prepared the baby goat just like in Monterrey, which was why the name of the restaurant had the same name as that city in the state of Nuevo León.

Upon arriving, he opened the car door for me, took my hand to help me out of the car, and then offered me his arm while we walked. The restaurant had wide-open spaces and old wooden furniture. The ancestors of the owner had lived there and he wanted to transform it into a place to eat and feel like you were on a ranch. The baby goat was opened and placed over an enormous wood fire. Then they brought portions of it to each table, with onion, salad, tortillas, and salsa. It was an elegant ranch; the dishes were from an antique collection that the first owners had bought in China. In spite of the fact that there was a waiter standing next to our table all the time, others came by one after the other to ask us if we needed anything else. It was a great deal of courtesy to which I was not accustomed. Federico asked for tequila: "The baby goat tastes better if you eat it while drinking tequila," he said to me. He didn't hide a ring in the cup, but that night he asked me to marry him. We toasted to that.

"When we leave here, I will take you to my friend's apartment. He is studying here in Morelia but comes from Oaxaca," he said as he took my hand. "I want you to meet him and see the special kind of liquor that he brought; it's a liquor that has a worm inside. Do you know that kind?"

"I don't know anything about alcohol, only about drunkards when I was a girl but I didn't know the difference between the bottles."

He served me more tequila. I wasn't at all used to the effects of alcohol because it was the first time in years that I had even tasted it. That night I enjoyed its mellowing effect; I was relaxed, content, and had forgotten all my worries. The night seemed perfect, and the food was delicious. The invitation to go to his friend's place seemed strange to me because we had never spent time with anyone else, but he was going to be my husband, so I could trust him. During dinner he talked to me about the wedding. He asked about whom I would invite; he even drew up a list on the napkin. I felt like an important woman and so fortunate for living that moment.

"Have another tequila!" I heard him repeat about four times. "Look, grab the lemon, and put some salt on it and … down it goes!"

With my stomach full and my heart content we went to his friend's apartment. He opened the door for us as if it were New Year's; he hugged Federico and then clapped him heartily on the back. Then he took my hand, amusingly made a courtly gesture, and kissed it. I felt uncomfortable. The apartment was on the sixth floor of a building in the middle of the city. It had large windows that ended in some kind of loft where his bed was. He had an American kitchen and a large space for a living room, where there was a white sofa and a few cushions that went with the rug. That's where I sat while Federico and his friend talked, looking at the bottle. They were talking about mescal, liquor made from agave. Federico sat down next to me, and his friend sat down on the rug to chat. "A lot of people say that the worm inside has an amino acid that is curative, and I believe them …," his friend started off saying. "Have a glass," he offered. "You are going to feel great."

"Forgive me, but I am appalled seeing that thing floating."

"It is an innocent worm …," Federico said. "Think of it as a piece of fruit."

"No thank you, I really don't want any of that."

With that response the conversation ended, not because his friend got angry but because he said, "I have to go, but make yourselves at home … There is beer in the fridge, and in this cabinet there is brandy." He took his wallet from on top of the television and left. There was silence.

Federico took me to the second floor to show the pictures that lined one of the walls. His friend was an adventurous yet organized man; he had organized the pictures by year and location. While

Federico went to the kitchen, I stayed looking at the pictures that said Oaxaca, pictures of beautiful beaches, the Monte Alban ruins, and one of the Lacandona jungles where the adventurer was hugging two Zapatista warriors. Federico appeared with two glasses.

"Since you aren't going to have a cup of mescal, I brought you this."

I took the glass not focusing because of the pictures. I didn't even ask what it was and took a big sip. I kept looking at the pictures of Acapulco and Veracruz until I had the urge to use the bathroom. In the mirror I saw my red face and puffy eyes—as if I had been crying for hours—and I felt hot. I was sweating and had to sit down for a minute because my vision became clouded for a few seconds. Feeling dizzy, I left the bathroom. The last thing I remember is Federico sitting in the bed, laughing. I sat next to him, and I don't remember anything else until I woke up naked. I got up quickly and saw that the sheets had blood on them. I was not sure what he had done with me, but I felt a burning between my legs and couldn't walk normally. I woke him up.

"What happened?" I asked him, scared.

"You don't remember?" he said to me. "You asked me to."

"What? But I was in the bathroom and started to feel dizzy, and ... What happened?" I said, throwing a pillow at his head.

"Nothing bad happened. Everything is fine; don't worry, because we will be married soon ..."

Before then we had not even kissed, let alone been sexually involved. Until then, our affection was expressed only with hugs and holding hands.

I should have left him at that moment. I felt like trash, but he explained to me that it was normal to have relations before our wedding. And besides, he said, I had insisted that we do it there at his friend's place. When I remember this, I feel hate, because he was a liar, not only because of that night but for what came afterward. I had always guarded what I considered my virginity, despite the tragic abuse by my uncle Eduardo. Yet that night Federico had violated me in many ways. The blood and the pain indicated that he had done what he wanted to without any consciousness or correspondence from me, and so had been forceful and violent with my body. And since I had been unconscious for many hours, I suspected that he had had sex more than once, maybe even several times.

My dream had been to get married in the church, following traditions and all that goes along with those beliefs. Federico was a tricky man raised in a big city. I saw that he had succeeded in duping me, using alcohol as the tool to rob me of my consciousness. Yet he told me not to worry, that couples had sex before getting married, and that it was better for the future of the marriage. Days later he gave me contraceptive pills, and having sex turned into a routine. In love, I played his game.

I even met his parents. That day, Federico was cheerful and his parents were friendly with me. After I got a tour of his house and had tea with him and his parents, he told them that we wouldn't be eating dinner at the house because we had reservations at a restaurant. Even though I thought that was strange because formally meeting one's fiancé usually involved having a long dinner at the parents' house, his parents said, "Okay, enjoy your dinner!" So I thought nothing of the lapse in formality.

Federico had me blinded, following his every order. I was capable of waking up at dawn, taking the bus two hours from Morelia to Querétaro, and returning, all in the same morning. One day I arrived at the bus terminal and talked to him on the phone so he would come get me in his car. He responded that I should take a taxi because he was busy preparing for an exam to get a job at the hospital in DF. On that occasion I called my adopted sister Nataly—my older sister who had moved to Querétaro with her husband—to ask her to pick me up.

"When are you two getting married?" she asked me after I updated her about my life.

"Soon," I said, looking at the floor. "We haven't talked about it because he has an important exam to take and I don't want to bother him."

"Well, don't forget to put my name on your guest list," she joked.

Almost all of Federico's family lived in Querétaro, yet I knew very few of his relatives, because each time we arrived at his house,

Federico took me straight to his room at the back. I wanted to walk around the grounds and talk with his sisters, but he locked me in his room to have sex. If it wasn't in his house, it was in a cheap hotel. Going out to restaurants and elegant places had ended along with the disappearance of his chivalry. During the last three times we went to a hotel, it came time to pay and he would stand idly, pretending to look for his card in all his pockets. On those three occasions he took so long that I took out my money and paid.

We had been together a little less than a year, and something strange was happening. My brain began to react. "Hello, wake up!" I said to myself one time on the bus going back to Morelia. When I arrived, Rossie was moving her things to another room because Gela had ordered that they fumigate the whole house. "Go get your things; you are going to have to bring them to my room this week," Rossie said.

Rossie was studying nursing. She was a girl to whom I only said hi, but I always saw her happy in the arms of her boyfriend, who was studying to be a doctor. That week we managed to talk, and I told her about my unsettling observations of Federico's behavior. She dared say to me that maybe he was hiding something.

"Open your eyes," she advised me.

I decided to open my eyes and went to Querétaro one day without telling Federico. I called Nataly from the bus terminal so she would take me to his house. She didn't answer. The plan to take him by surprise ended when I couldn't even find a taxi. It was five in the afternoon and I began to get desperate, so I had to call Federico. His mother answered the phone.

"Federico isn't here. Who's calling?"

"I am a friend. I am calling him from the town of Ario de Rosales," I lied to her.

"Of course, yes, he told me he had gone to that town to work. You must be a nurse, right?"

"Yes, I am …"

Without letting me finish the phrase she told me that Federico had left with his fiancée to buy some things for their wedding.

"What fiancée?" I asked her.

"Isabella is his fiancée. Didn't he invite you to the wedding?" she asked. And by her tone I managed to imagine the happy face she had on.

For the second time I felt my stomach boil, and before my head exploded, I hung up the phone and began to pace around the bus terminal. Federico, without a doubt, didn't have economic problems, but he wanted a job as a doctor at a public hospital in DF, and for that he needed influence. Isabella, whom he had met during his visits to the hospital in Coahuila, was the daughter of a well-known politician in Querétaro, and I can attest that he used her too. One hour went by, two hours, and I didn't know if I should go to his house to confront him or wait for him at my house a few days and humiliate him.

I didn't go through with either plan, because I was ashamed and preferred to be alone. I asked for a hotel, and before that I went to buy a bottle of tequila. I don't remember if the bottle was big or small, or what color it was. As soon as I got in the room, I drank about half the bottle and knelt down on the floor and cried. I went over the story again and again, not wanting to believe Federico had taken advantage of me so ruthlessly. I yelled with all my strength, "Damn you!"

In the midst of my rage, I cut my forearms with a knife that I always kept in my purse. People kept hearing the screams until one of the hotel employees came, opened the door, and found me banging my head against the wall. I wanted to die. The same young man who found me took me in his car to the hospital. He left me at the entrance and I never saw him again. The police arrived, and after the treatment they asked me what had happened.

"What man were you referring to when you were yelling in the hotel?" one of the policemen asked.

"My boyfriend," I confessed to him.

"And what do you have against the man?" the policeman asked, looking at my hands. "Did that man leave you like this?"

"He did this to me," I answered him without thinking about what I was saying.

The police took me to Federico's home. I waited in the car until I saw him come out—followed by his mother—and they put him in the other police car and took him away. His mother came to my window.

"What did you do? Don't you realize this is detrimental to his career?"

"You knew I was his fiancée!" I screamed. "Federico had been the only man in my life, the man that I loved and the one with whom I wanted to have a family."

"Stupid girl, why did you think my son was going to marry you if he already had a girlfriend?" she said, looking at me from head to toe.

"He has to pay for all that he did to me! I have to get rid of this anger, ma'am. He has to pay!"

"Of course he has to pay you, and you know why … because you are a prostitute," she said, and she threw some coins at me.

I missed my grandfather and thought about the day he died. I combined the inexplicable love for a coldhearted old man with my hate for that wretched man who said he loved me. Without wanting to, I had related loving Federico to my grandfather's death because several times he insisted on asking me about my inheritance and the properties. One day I told him everything that Pillita had told me on a regular afternoon: "When I die, all my money is going to Barbara, your mother, and you. Your grandfather Rafael took responsibility for leaving an inheritance for the men." Instead of feeling grateful to Pillita, I had the urge to cry. Therefore I made a memory of the conversation with Federico. I asked him where we would live when we got married. He answered, "What? Your grandfather left you nothing?"

I went to Nataly's house for two days and then returned to Morelia as a loser. An idiot, I had believed in a dream of marriage with a doctor that finally ended as a nightmare. I tried to forget him, but the effort turned into a profound hate toward him and disdain for all men.

⟋♥⟍

It was June and I had begun my last year at the institute. I felt like I hadn't learned anything. I was there because Tere had taken me, but I didn't have any desire to do anything with my life. After I left the town, everything had been ruined by the circumstances, except Federico, when he became my reason to live. Since I wasn't able to construct my own destiny I clung to Gema in order to see if some of her happiness would rub off on me—her sister Gela said that she would infect me with evil. Gema was six years younger than Gela and was working as a secretary for a government office; for that reason she had contacts and parties throughout the city.

Two years before, she had gotten me a part-time job at a construction company, where there was an architect, a civil engineer and a geologist. I answered the phone, wrote letters, made coffee, and resolved domestic problems. They were nice men and were happy with my work, except for the days that I disappeared to go look for Federico. But they forgave me because I hadn't missed any other day and they liked me; they said that I made a big effort to come to work every morning and then go to classes in the afternoon. Even though I had money, Pillita continued to pay for my studies, books, and the boardinghouse. Since I never wanted to abuse her kindness, I used the money I was earning at the office for the bus and to buy clothes and whims. The men at work were the only ones I didn't hate. I was thankful to them for giving me the opportunity to learn.

I had a good friendship with the geologist, whom I called Uncle Alfonso; I even introduced him to my aunt Barbara one day when we went to Ario in his shabby, smoky car. My grandmother loved that man. Barbara talked with him, but later told me, "He's ugly. He has thin lips, which means he's a bad man." I'm sure she also didn't like his car.

Uncle Alfonso was offered a job as sub-secretary to the governor—at that time Cuauhtémoc Cárdenas, son of general Lázaro Cárdenas—and as soon as he accepted, he took me to help him with the correspondence dispatch.

I worked there for one more year, carrying letters and documents; I would go around the whole day, running from one office to another, through the hallways of the governor's palace.

I had finished my classes and exams at the institute. I had a diploma, yet I did not know what to do with it. But at that time I was more concerned with working on what was available. I needed to have contacts and to stop hating Federico. There was so much to do that I barely had time to go to the restroom. Uncle Alfonso went out to plots of land, visited the countryside, and analyzed the governor's projects. On some days, like Tuesdays, everything was twice as intense. Cuauhtémoc—following in his father's footsteps by helping the working class—would meet with the country dwellers to hear their needs and later find them loans to improve their businesses. People would line up early—and some would even start the line the night before—to attend the meetings. Even though it was stressful, I liked it. I was learning, and everything was going better than I had imagined. But it wouldn't last.

Gema was one of the planners of the government parties. I accompanied her a couple of times, but I never agreed to participate in the group of young women whom people called "escorts." At the first party, Gema introduced me to what we could say was a very special man: a public accountant. He was a dark-skinned man, with large hands and short legs. He used eyeglasses from a different period and spoke so quickly that I understood only half of what he said. He seemed like a good person, but I did not like his appearance. I was disgusted by many things since I was a little girl; the saliva that flowed from his mouth and collected at his lips made me want to vomit. By bad luck, the gentleman was smitten with me. He asked Gema if I lived with her at the boardinghouse and began to visit us.

One day he arrived in his new Volkswagen and invited us to eat ice cream. When we arrived at the shopping mall parking lot, he got out to buy the ice cream. Gema, who was five months pregnant, said, "It will be better if we wait for you here because I am feeling tired."

The accountant responded, "No problem!"

When he had gone, Gema rubbed her hands together and got into the front seat.

"Let's go, Lilia! Let's take a ride in the car," she said with a smile that was difficult to replicate.

"Are you crazy? That old guy will call the police."

"I'm sure he won't. Let's go!"

We went down Madero Avenue, making laps a couple of times, and stopped to buy ice cream. Gema couldn't stop laughing when she imagined the facial expression the accountant probably had when he realized that his car wasn't there. She had such a contagious laugh that I laughed along with her, even though I didn't like her joke. We went to the boardinghouse, where we imagined that the accountant would go. He was already there, speaking with Gela, who saw us as soon as we arrived. We got out, left the keys on top of the car, and escaped running. When we returned to the house, Gela told Gema, "You are causing me many problems. You cannot take other girls along with you … Look, Gema, besides, you are pregnant. What are you thinking, running like that?"

Yet the accountant came back around to the boardinghouse more than once. He would bring me flowers and leave messages with Gela, who would always come to tell me, "You can come out now. The old guy left."

That went on until one day I saw the accountant on the street, the same rainy day on which my paternal grandfather, Vincent, died. I was walking with Esperanza, Gema's friend, who had offered to accompany me.

"Where are you headed?" he asked me.

"To a party," I thought to say. "Will you take us?"

"Of course. Where is it?"

"Around here, quite close," I said.

He drove, asking constantly where the party was. Esperanza and I kept saying that we were getting close. When we arrived at my paternal grandmother Trina's house, I remembered the days of my childhood, when I would go out to visit her, and the fruit she would give me. But I concentrated more on all the times she told me I was beautiful and that she liked my nose; it was like a breeze of self-esteem.

There were a couple of neighbors in the street, taking shelter from the rain, with coffees in their hands. We got out of the car, I greeted someone, and we entered through a long hall filled with small tables with bottles of wine. The accountant sat down in a corner, and I handed him a glass of punch. I went to greet my father's family, even though I had not been close with them. My aunt Barbara had been very clear when she warned me, "Maintain distance from that family—they are not good for you. Greet your grandmother Trina, and maybe your aunt Estela, but no one else."

I felt sadness, but did not know whether it was because Grandfather Vincent had died or because he reminded me of my father. They had the same eyes and the same flaw.

"Don't cry; we need to be happy," my aunt Estela said. "Your grandfather didn't want crying at his wake."

The music of Pedro Infante—my grandfather's favorite—started to play, and I realized that no one was crying. Instead, they were conversing with full beverage glasses, as though they were in the middle of a party. Even Panchito, who went from wake to wake, had a drink. He was not a priest, but he lived on the street, and where there was a dead person, he would go to the wake in search of food and alcohol. An hour later, my mother and Pillita arrived. They greeted everyone and left.

I did not stay for the funeral, because the next day I would have to run with the governor's papers. I hugged Grandmother Trina. She touched my nose and gave me a kiss. We grabbed the accountant, who was mounting a tutorial for some elderly men from the countryside, and set out for Morelia a little before evening. The accountant, either because of compassion because we had left my grandfather's funeral, or because he had drunk a lot, remained quiet. That was a miracle. We arrived at home early in the morning. Esperanza got out with me so that the accountant wouldn't bother me with his boring conversations. We said good-bye and entered the house.

The man thought he could conquer me with that favor, and began again with the calls and futile waiting. One day, he was leaning on his car waiting for me. It occurred to Gema to go up to the roof to throw water down on him from a bucket.

"I am going to call the police!" he yelled when he felt the three liters of water fall on his head.

I never saw him again.

⌒♭⌒

That Christmas, all of the girls in the boardinghouse had decided to spend the holidays with their families. Instead of going to Ario de Rosales, I accepted Gema's invitation. Carlos, the manager of one of Morelia's soccer teams, had younger sisters who had invited Gema to Christmas dinner. Gema had met them before Carlos's good luck and his brothers' businesses had rescued the family from poverty. Carlos was about forty years old, short and stout with traces of Indian. He traveled every month for business matters. In fact, that night he had arrived from a trip to New York. At dinner, we conversed casually until he asked what my last name was.

"What?" he asked. "You are part of the Negrete family? The Negretes from Ario de Rosales? Don't tell me that you are Don Rafael Negrete's granddaughter!"

"Yes, he was my grandfather, but he died a couple of years ago."

"I give my condolences," he said, standing up from the table. "Don Rafael was a great master of mine. Almost all the money I have earned is thanks to his advice. He was truly my master."

After learning of the coincidence, he shared his memories of poverty, of how he had met my grandfather and how he had transformed his family members' lives. We all listened attentively to the story about his eight siblings. His father had been a gardener in a very wealthy house, the owners of which allowed him to live in a tiny house in the corner of the estate. Carlos told of how, as a child, he sold gum at the movie theaters and, as a young man, met my grandfather through his friend Nicandro, who had a store in Morelia for which my grandfather supplied merchandise.

"Of course," I interrupted. "If my grandfather traveled frequently to Morelia, it was because his brother Antonio lived there and because he had many clients, one of whom was a man named Nicandro. I even played with Nicandro's daughters while Grandfather exchanged merchandise and talked about piloncillo," I said, impressed with the sudden recollection.

"Don Rafael was the only man who believed in Nicandro's store," Carlos said. "He supported Nicandro until he got his feet on the ground. Then, he lent me money so that I could set up my first business, which I later turned into a supermarket."

I remembered those days in which Grandfather would wake up in a good mood and take me to Morelia. The truth was that Pillita persuaded him to take me so that Barbara wouldn't get so annoyed with my presence at home. I had forgotten the memory of the trips to Morelia, just as I had forgotten something of which Carlos reminded me.

"Were you the girl who would urinate?" he asked me. "Don Rafael said that the piloncillo had a strange odor, which is why he sold it to Nicandro at a cheaper price.

I stayed silent.

"Of course … You were the pipsqueak who went around with him," he said happily, celebrating his discovery.

Just remembering why I used to urinate made me need to go to the bathroom. "Excuse me," I said.

When I returned, Gema whispered in my ear, "You caught his eye." She insisted that Carlos had been charmed by me, and that I was very lucky, because he had a great deal of money and was going to make me happy.

"Shut up," I said to her. "Did you invite me here to spend Christmas peacefully, or did you bring me as bait for Carlos?"

The conversation had been entertaining, but two hours later, the guy was still telling stories about my grandfather and businesses. He was acting like a total gentleman, but the truth was that he began to bore me when he began telling the life stories of his own grandparents.

After that night, he invited me out to eat several times, and gave me tickets to soccer games. Gema would accept the tickets and took all of the girls in the boardinghouse to the stadium.

There was still piloncillo in Grandfather's storerooms. I asked Carlos if he wanted to buy it, and he accepted. I took Carlos to my house and introduced him to Pillita and my aunt. He told them his story for three hours, and both of them seemed to fall at his feet. I did not notice the moment at which, in the middle of all the dates, I turned into one of the many women with whom he would go out. Having a twenty-year-old as a lover was a great source of pride for him.

Every Friday there was a government party. For one of them, Gema fixed my hair and put me in one of the dresses she had saved for sentimental purposes since her pregnancy. We left Ernesto, her baby of just a few months, with Gela and went to the party, not before picking up Esperanza. She came out of her house with her high heels in her hands. Gema was an unstoppable young woman who enjoyed life and all the conversations at parties. I never saw her use drugs, and she drank alcohol with such grace that it was as though she enjoyed holding a glass more than drinking it.

I met many people: one man who rented seats for events, a woman who took care of the governor's dinners, and another who wrote speeches for another politician whose name she preferred not to share. Esperanza and I laughed at the anecdotes. Gema took on her public relations role in all of the groups until two in the morning. When we tried to return home, we got stuck halfway there with the motor smoking up. Gema, with her characteristic daring, made the first car that passed stop to help us.

That night I met Leandro. "Let's leave your car here," he said. "I will leave you ladies at your house," he proposed. Esperanza and I sat down in the back of the car. Gema took it upon herself to introduce us, and kept asking Leandro questions until he finally answered. "I am going to a party, and I'm sure you want to go along," he said.

"I can't," said Gema. "You girls should go."

"If you don't go, I won't go either," I told Gema.

"Rosa Lilia has spoken!" said Leandro, simultaneously celebrating my utterance and making fun of my permanent silence.

"I'll go!" said Esperanza.

When we arrived at our house, Leandro insisted on convincing Gema but had no luck. Gema thanked him and quickly went inside. Leandro told us that we had to pick up a few bottles of alcohol, and in fifteen minutes would be at the party—it was at his own house. Esperanza was regretting her acceptance of the invitation, and asked Leandro to excuse us because she was very tired. Leandro offered to take her to her house, and soon just the two of us were in his car, with a large bottle of rum.

We talked about his work at the hospital, our parents, and music. Without realizing it, I relaxed, but I did not stop thinking about Federico even though several months had gone by since the end of our relationship. For some reason, any man I spent time with reminded me of the hate I felt for Federico. I had promised myself not to fall back into the same trap, and I had decided not to let my feelings get involved and not to trust any man. *If they can be so bad, then I can too,* I had thought.

We had drunk nearly all of the rum when I impulsively asked Leandro to take me to Nataly's house in Querétaro, three and a half hours away. There was no reason in particular—only to travel.

"No problem," said Leandro. All the way there—with curvy roads—we continued enjoying the conversation and some sips of tequila. We arrived at Querétaro around seven in the morning, so Nataly was surprised by my visit and offered us coffee. I drank the coffee alone because Leandro said, "I am going to wash the car, and then I'll be back."

"Who is that?" asked Nataly. "You are reeking of alcohol."

"I met him last night at a party," I responded sleepily.

"And you are alone with him? He doesn't scare you?"

"He is a good person, don't worry," I said as I leaned over the table, on the verge of fainting.

"Don't go back with him, please. Let him go alone. I'll take you to the bus terminal in the afternoon. How did you get the idea to come here with that guy? Really, you're ..."

Nataly didn't finish her speech, because she realized I was sleeping. She took me to her bed and didn't wake me up until three hours later, when Leandro came back. I remembered Nataly advising me not to return with Leandro, but I didn't have any money with me. The bus ticket would take me only to the terminal in Morelia; then I would have to pay even more for a taxi home. Furthermore, I had drunk half a bottle of rum and thought I would vomit on the bumpy bus ride. So I decided to go back with Leandro.

When we arrived back in Morelia, he invited me to meet his grandmother Teodora. Leandro's clothing and way of speaking were so simple that I imagined that he lived in humble accommodations. We arrived at the outskirts of the Chapultepec colony, and when I saw the house, I was surprised by the gardens, water fountains, and enormous trees. Teodora immediately came out to greet me.

"I'd like you to meet Lilia, a friend," said Leandro.

"What a beautiful name!" said the woman.

"Actually, it's Rosa Lilia," I responded, shaking her hand.

"Even better!" said the grandmother.

The kind lady led me by the arm and sat me down on one of the benches. Leandro went into the house. Teodora received me with so much affection that I loved her from the minute I met her. She had long, black hair that reached her waist and was tied with a red ribbon. She took out a couple of glasses from a wooden box and served me something pink.

She had taken a couple of drinks when she began to tell me about her life. She cried as she always did when she remembered things from her childhood, as Leandro told me. She moved all of the visitors with her stories of a poor young girl. She told me that her parents had hens that were dying because there was not enough to feed them. To buy books for school, Teodora would grab the chickens, put alcohol on their necks to awaken them, and sell them on ranches. She had been an instructor and the principal of a school, where she met Leandro's grandfather. I did not understand very well, but she was trying to tell me that her husband was very bad. He did not hit her, but he cheated on her with several women whom he caught off guard.

Teodora had raised four children: Leandro, Miguel, Javier, and Lourdes. She lamented the fact that Lourdes became pregnant at fourteen years old.

With every sigh she took a drink from her glass. She sighed so much that I had a hard time believing she was still lucid. The way she spoke with pauses and her languid gestures were characteristic of someone calm and patient; she transmitted her suffering yet her strength as well. She reminded me of my mother, who at moments I imagined was sitting with us on that very bench, speaking to me of her past, explaining why stories repeat themselves. Teodora would receive me at her house many times; the bench would be a different one and she would continue serving me glasses of pink liquid while Leandro and his uncles conversed at length inside the house.

When Teodora said good-bye to us on the first day I met her, she extended an invitation to Leandro: "Your mother is going to have a party in her house today. Why don't you go with Rosa Lilia? I won't be going because I am very tired."

To Leandro, parties were like nectar to a hummingbird, so we went to the downtown of Chapultepec colony. I thought the day would never end.

I was surprised when Leandro pointed out his mother while we were still in the car. "That's her," he said, pointing his finger. María Elena, his mother, was at the door in an elegant blue chiffon dress, greeting guests. She was wearing high heels and her hair was almost red, having recently been styled at the salon.

When I saw her, I turned back to look at Leandro to see if he had inherited any of his mother's beauty. It was in vain; he had missed that chromosome. I was even more surprised when María Elena got close to the car and asked, "Who did you bring in the car with you?"

"It's Lilia, a friend," answered Leandro.

His mother retorted. "And your wife?" she asked with her hand on her hip. "Go get her. What do you think you are doing with this woman? Bring Maria."

I got out of the car and slammed the door so forcefully that several people jumped from fright. I began to walk without a destination but with a determined stride. Leandro caught up to me in his car, got out, and took my hands in his.

"I want to explain," he said, embarrassed.

"You have nothing to explain. You and I have nothing. I don't want to see you again … I don't want problems."

"It's true that I'm married but we are getting a divorce."

"I'm not interested in your life; I barely know you … You really don't have to give me any explanation."

"Why do you think I'm going around to parties?" he said. "I don't have any feeling for her. I don't love her; I'm just waiting for her to sign the divorce papers."

"Please shut up! Your mother humiliated me, and it was your fault."

"If I don't show you my divorce papers by next week, you don't have to talk to me ever again, okay?" he said.

I got into the car. On the way, he told me that he and his wife had gotten married one year before. They didn't have children, and even though they were in the process of a divorce, they were still living in the same house. It was a property that Leandro had received from the government, and for which his salary was discounted every month. I heard only half of his story, because the other half got lost amid my thoughts and the people I saw parading in front of the windshield. Upon arriving at the boardinghouse, I thanked him for the pleasant moments that I had spent with him, except for the occurrence with his mother.

"Please don't come looking for me. I don't want to be responsible for ruining your marriage," I told him. And I closed the car door. We said good-bye without plans to see each other again.

I entered my room and threw myself on the bed in an attempt to recover the lost sleep. Before sleeping, I thought over the party, the trip to Querétaro, Grandmother Teodora, and the woman with nearly red hair, yelling through the car window. Leandro seemed attractive, but he was not my type. And although I thought for a moment that I could fall in love, I said, "He's an idiot."

I had gotten used to seeing more intelligent and elegant men in the governor's office. Even Carlos had more style, and in a certain way, he had become my suitor. The truth was that we had gone out a few times, and even though he had not declared his love to me, it was visible in his eyes that he wanted something with me. He was a man with a lot of experience but no responsibility. His interests were focused on his businesses and on enjoying life; he spent his money on dinners and hotels with his female friends.

Leandro returned one week later. He was outside my house, leaning against a tree. As soon as he saw me, he walked back to his car to open the door for me.

"Get in, please. I want to talk with you. I feel bad about what happened the other day, and I want to invite you to a party."

"To a party? Like the one where you took me last time? You're crazy!" I said, agitated. "I already told you that I don't want you to come looking for me."

That day, as though prophesying the future, he said, "Maybe you'll make me work to get you, but you won't get away."

He came back the next week, and the next. Angelita, the woman who helped Gela with the chores, was Leandro's messenger. "The chubby guy came again," she'd say.

He insisted every day, until one morning, on the way to work, he found me and asked to drop me off at work. I was embarrassed by his insistence in the middle of the street, so I got into his car on the condition that he let me out one block from my work because I didn't want anyone to see me with him. We talked about unimportant things.

Carlos, who came and went on with his busy life, called me on the telephone on some days. On others, he passed by the boardinghouse and joked with Gema. We would all laugh for a couple of hours, and then he would disappear. On occasion, he ordered his chauffer and we would take a ride around downtown.

One Friday, around seven in the evening, he invited me to Acapulco. The next day, we left in his jet plane with two of his partners. Carlos played cards with them and laughed. He treated me with respect; maybe that was exactly how he treated all of his women.

"Here, take this money and buy yourself some clothes, if you want," he said as he was winning the game. Upon returning from the romantic trip to Acapulco, I was met with unpleasant news. When I arrived at the boardinghouse, I found out that Gela had to travel to Spain for three months. Gema would stay in her room, but the remaining thirty young women, including me, had to look for another place to live. We had one month to move out.

Leandro showed up with his best face, mimicking an innocent boy, to show me that his wife had signed the divorce papers.

"Now do you see that I wasn't lying?" he said, smiling as he handed me the folder.

"Wait, Leandro. You don't understand," I responded impatiently. "I don't want to be with you. I never saw you as a man. I thank you for the pleasant moment we spent together, the trip, the music, and everything that you offered me, but that does not mean I want to be with you."

"That's fine, but I wanted you to know that I am a free man," he said sadly, and he seemed to wear the face of a shamed boy.

"Maybe we'll see each other another day," I responded, tired. "But, really, don't think that I want anything more than a friendship."

He went away calmly.

I thought that moving from the boardinghouse would be the perfect chance to not see Leandro anymore.

When the month was over and it was time to move out, Noelia—a friend at the institute—offered to share her room with me for a few days while I found a permanent place to live. Noelia lived downtown with her mother and two brothers. Her father had killed one of his nieces and then committed suicide in an armchair. I found out because one day I asked why the armchair had such ugly stains; according to Noelia, there had been an accident. Her mother, infuriated, almost hit me and told Noelia to take me out of there.

During the following days, I came out only to go to the bathroom, and when I came home from work, the woman would not open the door for me, not even on a rainy Friday when I had to wait for four hours for Noelia. But the biggest problem happened when I vomited in the bed. I couldn't make it to the bathroom, and Noelia's mother noticed. She created a tremendous scandal; she made me clean the mattress and left me sleeping in a small room that she used as a pantry.

Noelia went with me to the doctor because my suspicion was practically a fact. I was pregnant from Carlos and was already two months along. Noelia's mother gave me until the end of the week to find another house. I thought about Federico, and how different everything would be if he had loved me. I felt anger toward the world and myself. I couldn't believe what was happening. Me, with a child! And with Carlos.

I went to Ario, but I didn't tell Pillita, much less Aunt Barbara, what had happened. She would have locked me in a room out of fear for the gossiping of the town. Visiting Pillita was like a silent confession that gave me a fleeting sense of protection. I couldn't tell her what was happening because I was scared. But I imagined that being close to her would make her somehow find out. I wanted her to know without having to tell her. The fleeting protection I felt was imaginary, because Pillita didn't know that I was pregnant, yet I still felt safer just by being near her. I desperately wanted protection from my uncertainty and fear.

On the way back, I ran into my cousin Jennifer at the bus terminal. She was an intelligent and liberal young lady, very different from her twelve siblings. Seeing her reminded me of her runs through the hills, the busybody that her mother, Elisa, was, and the hate I felt for her father, Eduardo. I also remembered that Hercilio had been her teacher and that the two had had the habit of talking in the schoolyard. Jennifer told me about the fight she had had with her mother and said it would be the last, because Jennifer would never again return to Ario. Aunt Elisa had called her a prostitute, and Jennifer couldn't take any more of her shameless reproaches. She retorted, "Whom are you calling a prostitute? All you have done in your life is open your legs and have more and more children you didn't know how to care for. My father molested almost all of your daughters, and you accepted it. And you call *me* a prostitute? You didn't protect me from your husband! From my own father!"

I imagined Aunt Elisa's face as she listened to those sharp-edged words aimed straight at her heart. To change the subject, I summarized for Jennifer the details of my life: the boardinghouse, Noelia's house, Carlos. I even dared to tell her about my pregnancy. She told me that she was living in Morelia and offered to share her apartment and its expenses with me. I could then breathe more easily.

Jennifer's apartment was on the first floor of an old building. It was small, disorganized, and cold, and barely had furniture. I slept on the floor, but the apartment served as a refuge for me to think. It didn't work, because everything was still obscure a month later as I awaited the child of a man who was more than twenty years my senior and showed no signs of wanting to settle down. I continued working and hiding my belly.

One day, Hercilio sent me some telegrams with declarations of eternal love; he promised to pursue me until death. Crazy old man! How could he think that I would fall in love with him? I don't know exactly how he found me in Morelia, but I suspect that Jennifer told someone who leaked the information to Hercilio. Or maybe he found her and persuaded or paid her to keep him abreast of my activities. I knew that they were friends from the days that she attended the high school where he worked.

Several days later, he showed up one afternoon. I was in my room when Jennifer opened the door and had him enter. I was scared, because that man was there and because Jennifer had allowed him to enter. I escaped through the window and begged a young man from the butcher's shop on the corner to hide me. I stayed there for three hours until I saw Hercilio get into his car. Jennifer said good-bye to him. On returning, she asked me why I didn't want to see him if he was such a good man. I told her about the times he had harassed me, although she knew the story perfectly well. It's just that in her crazy little head she had the idea that I could have a relationship with that man.

The intelligent young woman whom I had met in the town had disappeared; Jennifer had dropped out of college, dedicated her time to smoking marijuana, and shared her apartment for parties. She had been the only daughter to show her true self, but on the way, she lost sight of her objective. She was just a kid, devouring scientific books and modern novels and even psychological trends, which she later applied to her siblings. Yet no book could help her escape from drugs and the environment in which she was trapped.

I had barely been in her house for two months and already wanted to flee, but the money I earned at the government office was not sufficient to support myself alone. I had no other alternative but to wait "until something changes my destiny," as I would say. I was lost without any clue about how I could improve things. If at Grandfather's house I had had no orientation with which to guide my life, I had even less at that moment. I felt empty and with no direction.

One afternoon, Leandro appeared outside the office; it had been a long day, and the symptoms of the pregnancy had me pale and weak. Leandro took me to my apartment and met Jennifer, who immediately invited him to the next day's party at her house. They became friends, and during the party they talked without stopping. Leandro even commented to me that Jennifer seemed very attractive to him. With that declaration, I thought he would leave me in peace. On the contrary, that was the excuse he needed to see me more frequently.

Everything was messed up; none of the puzzle pieces were where I wanted them to be. The parties made me nervous, the drunk men disgusted me, the drug users went around and around the house, and the music boomed like a bass drum in my head. Leandro, who insisted that I participate in the parties, offered me pills for my nerves. Those tranquilizing pills have different side effects in everyone, and mine was to lose control of my emotions. I had to miss a whole week of work because I couldn't stop crying, had no energy, and wanted only to lie down. Jennifer tried to comfort me, saying that I had the solution right in front of me.

I decided to have an abortion, and since I hadn't come to tell Carlos the truth, Jennifer went to get him. I just wanted to die. She asked him for money to take me to a safe place, and he responded, "Who knows if that child is mine?"

He was suspicious because he had heard about Leandro, who had been visiting us in the past few months, and proved it for himself one day when he came to get me from my apartment to take me to the movies. After insisting, Carlos gave Jennifer the money.

She took me to a retired nurse, a woman with a soft voice and a face that did not correspond to the slowness of her movements. The house was dark and cluttered, with so many pictures that the walls were barely visible. I walked through a long hall with more pictures on the walls. At the end, there was a white room with an old stretcher and a table covered with metallic devices. She told me where to lie, gave me a couple of minuscule pills, and went out saying, "I will be back in ten minutes."

When she came back, she put on some gloves that were too big for her hands and asked me a couple of questions. She told me what she would do, and inserted a small hose in me. I closed my eyes and prayed to come out alive. I didn't know anything about abortions, but my cousin had already had ten; the last four had been with this woman. Her method was to initiate the abortion by detaching the fetus from my uterus and making me take a drug that would make me birth the dead fetus.

While the woman did her business, I thought about so many things that I don't even remember if the procedure was painful. After two hours I got up, nauseated, and could feel discomfort in my abdomen. She sat me down in a chair while she spoke with Jennifer.

"Don't leave her alone," she said. "She will definitely expel the aborted fetus this evening. If she begins to hemorrhage heavily, you have to inject her with what's in this bag."

Sleeping on the floor would be worse, so Jennifer lent me her room. She left a cup of tea on top of the night table and left with her friends as soon as they rang the doorbell.

A half hour later the fever started, and unbearable pains mixed with guilt and agony. My pants became drenched in blood, so I tried to get up, but my legs barely worked. I looked for the injection that the nurse had given me, but I could only find the bag. I grabbed a towel and went to the bathroom, where I fainted.

I didn't stir until, between lights, I saw Leandro's face. I was in the hospital, connected to a sack of blood and a machine that didn't stop beeping. I asked the nurse not to tell Leandro what had happened.

"Don't worry about that now. He was the one who brought you," she said.

Leandro had arrived at the right moment, as never before. He found me on the floor, covered in blood, two hours after my cousin had left. He knew that I was in the apartment because Jennifer had called to tell him I was sick and needed someone to take care of me. Leandro pounded on the door three times, and when no one responded, he pushed it in. He saw blood and followed it to the bathroom. That was where I was, collapsed on the floor and nearly dead. Leandro paid for the hospital and visited me each of the five days I was there, as did Jennifer and Alejandro, Leandro's best friend. Together, they made a party trio. They would spend the whole afternoon in the hospital room talking and even drinking from bottles that they hid inside the white furniture.

From then on I felt tied to Leandro. I did not feel love, but my gratitude was infinite. When I returned to the apartment, Jennifer had saved the fetus to show to me.

"You're crazy!" I told her. It was nothing new for her; she never wanted to have children because she said they reminded her of her childhood and came into the world only to suffer. With each abortion she had placed the creature in a container and later buried it at the base of a tree. How was she capable of doing such a thing? Later, she explained to me why. She could have placed them in the trash, but she had a little heart. So she buried them—in spite of the horrible ordeal—as an act of kindness.

Three days after the abortion, while I was still recovering, Carlos appeared with news about the death of Jimmy, his younger brother. Months before, their other brother Max had been run over by a train. But Jimmy died in a robbery of one of the storage houses of the family's stores. He confronted the robbers and received more than ten gunshots in the head.

It was a hard blow to Jennifer because Jimmy had been her faithful fiancé; they had loved each other and even used drugs together. And ever since she had begun going out with him, she had stopped sleeping with her other friends. He was killed on the same day of my abortion; that's why Carlos was affected doubly. With a hanging head, he asked me to forgive him for having left me alone and for doubting that the child had been his. He was remorseful for acting too late and wanted to make up for it. He sat on the ground and said, "Let me take care of you."

I had the urge to insult him, but I saw that he was depressed so I decided to listen patiently. From that day on he began to visit me.

The room was cold, colder than the middle of winter, which made my recovery slower. At work everybody thought I had had an operation as a consequence of appendicitis and couldn't be visited. Jennifer came in and left with her secret activities in Ario de Rosales, secretly robbing her parents' shoe store, buying and using drugs, and having sex with many different men. She already had syphilis and gonorrhea.

In the meantime, Leandro came by twice a day to ask me if I needed anything. Those men concerned with my health made me feel protected but also nervous, because they would run into each other at my door and argue.

I slept on the floor of my apartment, on top of a *petate*, a type of artisan mat that is used to sleep outdoors. I don't know how I slept there; my back was full of pain. Carlos bought me a bed, ordered the room to be carpeted, and painted the walls light blue.

I felt worse and worse every day, from the infection and from my soul. I asked myself what had happened to my life. I was only twenty-one years old ... Where had dreams gone? If I wanted to go in one direction in life, why would destiny take me the other way?

Those were terrifying days: a nightmare each night and a torment each day, especially when I was alone at home, because I would drink what was left in the bottles that Jennifer's friends had left from the party the night before. I cried and yelled and banged my head against the wall, punishing myself for killing my child and for being where I didn't want to be. I remembered Federico and once again blamed him for my disgrace.

One day, in the middle of a crisis, Leandro arrived, and five minutes later, so did Carlos. They began to argue and ended up with punches swinging through the hallway. I closed the door on them and continued drinking. Leandro didn't want me to continue seeing Carlos, whom he said was an old womanizer who didn't care about anything besides money. Carlos would say that Leandro was an alcoholic who wasn't worth a damn and that he himself was the only one who could offer me a new life in a comfortable place and maybe marriage; he was still thinking about that last term.

I felt helpless, confused, and nostalgic for the past. Despite not having the best childhood and teenage years, I would have liked to freeze my life back there and not continue to grow up. On those days I yearned to live in Pillita's house, clean the cats and help in the store, run away from Grandfather's belt, and take care of Uncle Rodrigo.

I stopped eating, and each day the infection became more acute. Jennifer became desperate and didn't have any better idea than to ask for Federico's help. I didn't find out about her plans until I saw that man standing in my bedroom door. He seemed older, tired, and a little bit bald. Had it not been for my fever, I would have jumped on top of him and ripped out his eyes.

There was silence until he sat on the bed and said, "I'm sorry." I didn't know what to do besides remember the day I found out about his wedding and his mother calling me a prostitute. Then I forgot about the fever and the pain.

"Ever since you cheated me, I have done nothing but make mistakes. I have lost myself in life and it's your fault," I yelled at him. "I wanted a wedding in the church, children, and a family. I had hope with you, the hope to become a happy woman."

Federico cried, covered his face, and hung his head. I continued with my speech until he tried to talk …

"I …"

"I don't care about what happened to you!" I interrupted. "Whether you got married, whether you had kids, I don't want to know," I said, crying.

"At least let me examine you. You look very ill."

"Get out!" I yelled furiously. "I don't want to see you ever again!" I felt great hate toward Federico for having provoked me into such destructive behaviors. It was cathartic to blurt out how I felt about him and helped me to begin moving on.

I recovered little by little. I got out of bed and began to eat. I returned to work. Life with Jennifer became less and less bearable. There were parties almost every day, and friends would come on the weekends to play guitar. The worst of all this was that, when she was completely drunk, she would end up going to my bed to sleep with men from the parties. She chose my room because Carlos's remodeling had made it much more comfortable than hers. She was messy, not just with her own things.

On the day I moved into her apartment, I asked Angelita to clean it. It took her three days to work on that pigsty. Angelita said that she didn't understand where Jennifer got so much energy for so many men.

"That little girl doesn't stop to move her buttocks," she would say when she'd find Jennifer's underwear. Angelita was a lovely woman who was always in a good mood; her presence was synonymous to happiness. I asked her to continue helping me clean the apartment. She even prepared us pots of pozole, but one day she left when Jennifer arrived high and began to insult her.

Carlos became distant for a time, which he explained was because of his traveling, yet he continued to show concern for my health. Leandro began saying again, "You'll give me a hard time, but you won't get away."

When I felt better, I accepted his invitation to dance. First we went to a restaurant, and then to a bar on Madero Street. Leandro was the kind of man who could spend the entire night talking and didn't need to take a break from drinking. We had such a good time that I didn't realize that I *did* need a break.

We went to his house at five in the morning. I lay down in his bed and said I would stay there. That night we made love. I didn't like him, but I was grateful to him for saving me the night I collapsed. I paid a high price for that feeling of gratitude. As a child, I had lived with the notion that favors had to be remunerated and that affection wasn't free. If someone did something nice for me, I would have to tolerate whatever was necessary to repay the debt, even if it was being hit. That was what Aunt Barbara did; she took me to Pátzcuaro in exchange for humiliating me.

I had thought I could change all of that with Federico's love; I convinced myself that it was possible to flee from a past of alcohol, abuse, and violence and arrive at a promising future. But his treachery crumbled that conviction of mine; I stepped into murky waters and sank.

I came to love Federico; that was a unique feeling in my life, which was why I knew that it wasn't the same with Leandro. But I let Leandro take care of me; he didn't obligate me to have sex, and that was a point in his favor. I wanted his company, and he wanted mine. We continued to get together, talk, and listen to music in his car as we had the night that we met. I liked that, despite the fact that in the beginning I saw him as an idiot; the music that we listened to made me modify my opinion. His car was stocked with a good type of music; he made an effort with this, and we enjoyed the artists that were popular in the world, like the Australian group Men at Work. Many North American artists sounded like the group at that time; finally we had found a subject that we could share. We became a bit closer, and he went as far as offering me his house. He even asked me to quit my job because it wasn't necessary and because I deserved to rest.

"I'll think about it," I told him. The surroundings became clear and a miracle had fallen from the sky; that's what I thought.

Carlos visited me one day before I moved. I told him I was about to begin a life with Leandro.

"Don't go, Lilia, please," he begged me.

"I already made the decision, and it will be good for me. I cannot continue to live here."

"But if I offered you a house … Look, give me a chance. If it doesn't work, you can come back."

"Carlos … look at you," I said to him seriously. "You are much older than I am, and you have never had a stable relationship. On the contrary, you prefer to be surrounded by women."

"Give me a chance, and if you don't like it, you can leave me. It's that simple," he told me. "You are going to suffer with that man."

It was 1985, and I was twenty-three years old. I packed my clothing, got together the few pieces of furniture from the room that had been remodeled during the last few months, and went to the same house Leandro had shared with his wife. It was a large house, with two floors, three rooms, and a bathroom upstairs. On the first floor was the living room, a dining room, and a kitchen with a door leading to the patio. It had an abandoned garden, which I soon turned into a happy space. When I entered, I felt a sadness so acute that I could taste it, the same bitterness that I had felt when I found out that Federico was getting married to another woman. It was a strange sensation; my legs felt like strings, and my stomach was in knots at the same time. I didn't pay attention. Instead, I told myself, *This must be from nervousness about living with a man.*

During the first weeks, everything was normal. Leandro worked his shifts at the hospital, sometimes during the day and sometimes at night. All the while, I continued carrying papers from one office to another. In the evenings, I took care of cooking, cleaning, and attending to Leandro. I worked on his clothes, the garden, and errands; I was a complete housewife, something I could do very well. Aunt Barbara had taught me to keep everything clean and shiny. Leandro repeated that he did not want to have me working outside the house.

The neighbor women commented on my presence in the house. They even ventured to tell me, "Be careful. Leandro used to beat Maria, but luckily Leandro granted her a divorce."

I started to feel the knots in my stomach again, but there was no sign of violence in Leandro. Maria lived with her mother close by, and Leandro had waved and said hello to his ex-wife a couple of times on the street. One day I ran into her in the neighborhood. I got nervous; I was sure she thought I had taken away her husband. She greeted me as though I were her favorite neighbor. I lowered my eyes, curved my shoulders, and continued walking hurriedly. At first, I felt embarrassment and humiliation. Then, I felt anger and the desire to return and confront her. How did she dare to greet me, to mock me by being friendly when she probably hated me. I did nothing and just kept walking.

At a later time, when I told Pillita about that encounter, I understood that the woman wanted to express something to me through eye contact, some kind of compassion. Maybe she was trying to start a conversation so that she could tell me about Leandro.

It was something that would take time.

Three months later, Jennifer came to live with us because she had lost her job and didn't have money to pay her rent. I spoke with Leandro, and he offered her the only available room in the house.

Along with her arrival, some of Leandro's first signs of illness became more visible.

I discovered that he used drugs daily and had started when he was twelve years old. He kept medications and syringes in a box that he forgot to close. He missed work and disappeared every night. He said that his work shifts were irregular.

Jennifer did not last very long; she went back to her messiness, parties, and vices, and since she lived with us, she sometimes included Leandro and his group of friends. I didn't miss the first parties; Leandro said he wanted to share them with me. For that reason, he served me a glass of brandy and two pills, saying I could avoid having a headache the next day. Those pills produced a sensation of sleepiness that made me sleep until noon.

What made Leandro furious was when, three months after she had moved in with us, Jennifer brought Carlos to the house one day.

"He is waiting outside in a pickup truck," she said.

"Why did you bring him here?" I complained. "I don't want to speak with him. Don't you realize that you are creating a big problem for me?"

"Don't make him wait. He said it would take only a moment, and would be the last conversation."

"Surely he paid you to bring him here; you always do these things," I told her.

"We will be waiting outside," she told me, and left the house.

It was true; Carlos and Jennifer were in the truck. I crossed the street, began to step into the pickup truck, and saw that Leandro was arriving home. I got so scared that I told Carlos to go away and return no more.

Jennifer returned three days later, saying that she was going to live with a friend, but I am sure Leandro realized what had happened and kicked her out. He did not comment on anything, but that night he drank half a bottle of tequila, took out his boxes of pills, and forced me to take several. He threw me on the bed and hit me, and I woke up the next morning, naked. That very day, Leandro forced me to quit my job. His explanation was that I needed to attend to him and his guests, cook, clean, and iron, and shouldn't be wasting my time working outside the house.

The next few days were even worse. We argued in the midst of unplanned parties. Undoubtedly, I had lost importance for him. It became clear to me one night when he yelled at me in front of his friends, "Murderer! I hate you … You were capable of killing your own child."

He tormented me, saying I was worse than the devil and that God would punish me. When he got like that, nothing could calm him down. We would end up in arguments full of insults and hate. Alcohol was a release valve for me; I could only defend myself against his aggressions while drunk. In the middle of an argument, I would cry and yell until I fell asleep in any part of the house. Every morning I felt guilty and promised myself I wouldn't go through that again. But the problems were far from over.

Leandro's company was like kindling on fire. His beatings became more and more severe, especially when he arrived with women. I don't know if they were prostitutes or friends, but he liked to hit me after rolling around with them.

"When you sleep, I am going to kill you," he would threaten. I didn't want to ask for help; my aunt Barbara would be ashamed, and Pillita had plenty of problems with which to occupy herself after my grandfather's death. I was in hell once again. I spent all of the day without the capability to think, without being able to realize what was happening. I became addicted to calming drugs and alcohol. When Leandro went to work, I would look all over the house for leftover alcohol and pills.

Things couldn't be worse, unless I were to become pregnant, which was definitely what he wanted. When I was sure that I was pregnant, I told him. He was happy and informed his family. But I didn't want to stay with him anymore; I wanted so much to escape to Ario and start things anew. I desired to run away, but the days passed and I didn't gather the courage to leave him. I was not going to have another abortion, nor was I going to return to Pillita's house as a single mother.

I didn't escape; on the contrary, I asked Leandro for more calming medications and stole the alcohol that he stored under the armchair. The house had not been cleaned, and I spent the whole day sitting on the ground without eating or thinking about anything, just looking out the window. Leandro was either in the hospital or in some bar looking for prostitutes. Sometimes he stayed at home but ignored me; he opened his mysterious boxes, administered injections, left the house, and wouldn't come back until late or sometimes the next day.

Four months later, the routine was the same. Pillita found out that I was pregnant, was pleased, and asked me to visit her for a weekend. That was when she saw my beaten face.

"Don't worry. I hit my face on the window, and it was a while ago," I told her. I don't think she believed me, but she didn't say anything to challenge my explanation.

I returned to Morelia desperate for the pills and a bottle of anything. On a night that he was sober, Leandro asked me to abort the baby. "I'm sure you are going to give birth to a monster," he told me. He succeeded in calling my brother Damián on the phone and asked him to travel to Morelia to take care of me.

Damián arrived a few days later. As soon as he saw me, he wanted to take me to the hospital, but Leandro wouldn't allow it and turned away to get a glass of milk from the kitchen. Then, he said, "Try this to see if you can vomit." Nothing.

Damián took me to the bathroom and even slapped my face a couple of times to see if I could wake up. When I was able to open my eyes, I said, "Who are you?"

"Let's go, Lilia; gather your strength. Do this for your child," he said. After a couple of minutes he made me vomit, and then laid me down in bed while Leandro emptied a couple of bags of saline that he had stolen from the hospital. I slept for an hour.

Upon awakening, I saw my brother and hugged him. I cried on his shoulder without being able to tell him that Leandro was to blame for everything. Damián took care of me all day and offered to take me to Ario, where I would receive more attention. He didn't dare to ask Leandro about the marks on my arms and around my neck, but he was sure they were marks from Leandro's alcoholic hands.

"You have to protect your baby," said Damián.

"It's the same thing I have been saying all this time," said Leandro without moving an inch from the bed. "She doesn't want to listen."

"You are going to have to take better care of her," said Damián in a defiant tone. "If not, I am going to take her away."

"I have taken care of her, but she won't stop crying. She spends the whole day lying here or on the floor. She doesn't want to eat anything, but just takes tranquilizers."

"And where did she get those tranquilizers?"

"She took them out of some of my medical supplies from the hospital," he lied.

Damián left at 8:00 p.m.

We spent a couple of days in peace. We celebrated the five-month mark of my pregnancy. I didn't see Leandro drink or even open that box. I could sleep without nightmares or tranquilizers, and we even talked about the baby. He told me that his family was happy and wanted to organize the baby's baptism. During the day, I cooked food and we went out to walk. On the third night, he got up to watch television in the living room. A few hours later, he came into the room and approached the bed, furious. He began to push me, saying, "You have to abort that monster."

We began to argue, until he got close to my stomach and said, "Get out of here and get rid of this monster. If you don't get an abortion, I am going to put a knife into you." I left the house running.

A few blocks away, I found a neighborhood pharmacy. The young man at the counter immediately passed me a telephone. For a moment I thought about calling Damián, but I knew that he wouldn't be able to help me the way I needed. He was studying in college, was poor, and didn't have a house of his own. On the occasions that he had visited me, I sneaked money into his pocket because I knew that he struggled to pay for books and bus fare. My mother wasn't stable enough to help me either. My best alternative to get out of Leandro's house would be Pillita, so I dialed her number.

"Grandmother, he wants to kill me. Leandro wants to open my stomach and kill my child. I don't want to go back to that house anymore."

"Wait, talk with your aunt Barbara," she said in an unconcerned tone. "Let's see what she says."

"Aunt, I don't have anyone else except for you two," I begged her. "I don't want to go to my mother's house. She has too many problems."

"Where are you?" she asked calmly. "I'll tell Uncle Antonio to go look for you. Don't go anywhere."

The young man at the pharmacy got me a chair and gave me a blanket. I cried silently, hugging my belly for half an hour. Truck lights appeared and made me stand up. Uncle Antonio had come with his two children, and before taking me to Ario de Rosales, we stopped by the house to pick up a few of my things. Antonio spoke with Leandro, and we took out the refrigerator I had bought, a few pieces of furniture, and my clothes. Leandro seemed paralyzed. Besides, he couldn't do much, considering how drunk he was. As always, he surely thought that I wouldn't ask for help.

We arrived in Ario de Rosales and went into my grandparents' house with a certain normality. No one asked for more details that night. I rested and slept peacefully.

Three weeks later, Leandro had cried and sobbed so much to Damián that he persuaded him to deliver a letter to me.

"He came looking for me in Irapuato," said my brother. "He is sorry; we spoke for several hours, and he asked me to please have you read this letter." I took the letter and, hidden away from my aunt and grandmother, read what Damián had summarized for me.

The letter had caring words and regret that Leandro uttered for the first time. He promised to change, to stop the drugs, alcohol, and mistreatment. He promised to love me, and above all, he regretted having asked me to have an abortion.

"If you want, I will ask you on my knees, crying: 'Forgive me and marry me,'" he wrote. I decided to show the letter to my grandmother. She shared it with my aunt Barbaram who said the very phrase my mother used to say: "That man will never change; he was born crazy and he'll die that way."

No one in the town knew that I was pregnant, and neither my grandmother nor my aunt wanted the townspeople to see me that way.

Those three months I spent with Pillita and Barbara were sad; it was just like being in prison. Leandro's letter was convincing. I believed him, but I would feel like a hypocrite if I went back to him, since I was the very person who had denounced him as a violent man and had asked for help to get out of his house.

A few days after receiving the letter, Leandro arrived with his mother and Grandmother Teodora to ask me to go back to him. My aunt Barbara wasn't at home, so my grandmother greeted them and spoke with them. I waited on the second floor. Leandro confirmed what had happened the night I left, and asked for forgiveness and for my hand in marriage. Pillita came upstairs with the news.

"Don't pay attention to Barbara; if you want to get married, then do it. Maybe Leandro has changed, and that works so that your baby won't be born outside of marriage," she said happily. "But don't tell your aunt that I said this to you."

I went downstairs, listened to Leandro for a few minutes, and agreed to marry him. In the same conversation, we arranged a civil ceremony for the next week. My aunt Barbara listened, unconvinced.

At the quick and simple ceremony were Leandro's mother, Teodora, Barbara, Pillita, my sister Mili and friends Lucy and Tere Salinas. Leandro was happy and affectionate, and I was six months pregnant. We stayed that night in Ario and went to Morelia the next day. My mother couldn't travel to the wedding but sent her message: "If you don't get married in the church, you will be condemned."

When I left the town, I understood why I was leaving. I did not want to be the object of gossip and didn't want to be seen as the poor victim. I didn't want to give anybody more reasons to speak of my failures, or have anybody find out that I was pregnant, abandoned, and failed. I wouldn't give them that satisfaction. They had already made fun of me enough because of the story with Hercilio.

When we returned home, Leandro continued to be affectionate. He hung around me, was concerned about what I ate, and hid away his pills and bottles of alcohol. I watched him suspiciously, because it was hard for me to believe in his new pattern of behavior and I was alert to the possibility of something bad happening.

With the passage of the days, his enthusiasm in taking care of me declined, until he started feeling like a used man whose liberty was restricted. He missed his friends, the parties, and the women. I was more stable and level headed; I fed myself and tried to continue to take care of my pregnancy. There were only two months left before I would meet my child; Leandro was sure it would be a boy. My belly was so large that walking was a challenge. I spent entire days resting on the second floor.

One day, Leandro rang the doorbell on the first floor, but I couldn't get to the first floor to open the door for him. When he entered through the kitchen, I was halfway down the stairs. He began yelling at me, saying I was lazy and spent the whole day in bed, and was incapable of even taking care of him. In the midst of his anger, he pushed me. I fell down several steps, trying to protect my belly. Nothing happened to the baby, but I broke my ankle. If it was hard to walk before, it was impossible after that fall. Leandro called his brother Miguel to help him take me to the hospital. Of course he didn't tell his brother that he had pushed me, and I didn't tell anybody. In everyone's eyes, what happened to me had been an accident. I couldn't go to Ario again, crying and asking for help, since I had decided to get back with him. Yet my grandmother and aunt asked me one day, "Leandro pushed you, didn't he?"

I went through several examinations in the hospital. Miraculously, everything was in the right place, except for the bone in my foot. They put a cast on my foot and sent me home. I had to use crutches until the day I gave birth.

On a day in October, with a few weeks left until the due date, Leandro took me to Ario. We were having an afternoon snack when I heard a great deal of noise in the street. Pillita and Leandro helped me out to the street to see. It was a group of men carrying a religious image and followed by a multitude. It was the Virgin of the Rosary. *I don't know what miracles you grant, but I can see that all of these people have faith in you,* I thought. *I want you to give me a miracle.*

Every October 7, the whole town celebrated the *Buenaventura de la Virgen María del Santísimo Rosario,* or the Festival of Good Fortune of the Virgin Mary of the Rosary and Holy Sacrament. It is said that, many centuries ago, a Virgin appeared to a man named Domingo de Guzmán in a chapel in France. The Virgin was holding a rosary in her hands, and taught the man how to pray the rosary. She also asked him to preach to other men, especially to those who were preparing for a political or religious war. Domingo taught the soldiers of the Christian army how to pray the rosary, and they triumphed in the battle of Muret. Since then, the victories of many historic battles have been attributed to the Virgin. With my own battle almost lost, I asked the Virgin to take care of my baby. "I want my son or daughter to be born well, and if it is a girl, I promise I will name her Rosario," I prayed as the image passed in front of us. A second miracle would be asked for years later.

A couple of days later, the signs that the birth was near began to appear around midnight. Leandro called an ambulance, and they took me out on a stretcher. The crutches with which I had walked for almost two months stayed at home. I felt so much pain that I didn't even think about my ankle. The doctor told a nurse, "Watch out for her foot."

I replied, "I don't care about my foot, doctor. Get my baby out of me."

I was eager to find out if it was a boy or a girl and to see whether my requests to the Virgin of the Rosary had been granted. Leandro left the hospital, saying that he had something to do and would return in the morning.

The next day I had a normal birth, and my daughter was born without problems. Leandro arrived drunk with a bouquet of flowers and accompanied by his friend Alejandro. He touched my face, kissed our little girl, and left. His mother arrived with minuscule gold earrings and with the idea of naming the baby Jessica, Christianne, or Daisy. When I told her that I wanted to name the baby Rosario, she responded that it was an old woman's name. However, I explained my reasoning, and there was no further discussion. She was a miracle, and no one would change her destiny.

Even though my daughter decided a few years ago to change her name to Rosie (she said that she needed something more appropriate for living in the United States), I had made a promise to the Virgin and I kept it; we named her Rosario, and later would call her Charito with affection. The second miracle I asked for from the Virgin a few years ago was to write down my story in a book.

The next day, I was back home. I still had the cast. We did Charito's baptism at Grandmother Teodora's house. It was a colossal party, with elegant guests, a mariachi band, and several different dishes served; it was the most extravagant baptism I have seen in my life. At first I wanted Pillita to be Charito's godmother, but she said that she was too old and that Barbara would be a better choice. Then I wanted to designate Charito's godmother as María Jesús, a friend who had helped me escape from Leandro several times, but Leandro said that she was not important enough. My aunt Barbara accepted being the godmother, but when we asked her to take Charito, she wouldn't; she said that babies made her nervous and she might be inclined to throw her out. Leandro was well behaved at the baptism, probably because his uncle Miguel, whom he respected greatly, was present at the celebration. We chose Miguel to be Charito's godfather.

Pillita paid Consuelo, one of the youngest servants, to help me with Charito. She was a timid girl but had a heart of gold. With her support, and when I took my cast off, I was able to change my life into something more normal, and Leandro helped me with this endeavor. His mother had important contacts in Morelia, so she helped me get a job in the Department of Education. Charito was already three months old, so I felt ready to go to work full time and leave her alone with Consuelo during the day. The parties that Leandro's mother put on in her house were full of so many important people that she wasn't surprised when I left my job interview and told her that I would start working in three days. Leandro didn't object.

I had to take papers from office to office and manage the book where the employees signed upon entering and leaving, giving explanations for late arrivals in the morning. I found out about the problem a man had with his wife, or that another man's son had been transferred to another school, and other less believable stories. I knew all of the people in the building, shared with them, and felt productive and happy to earn my own money and use it at home.

To take advantage of my time and increase my income, I began to sell American clothing. I entered into contact with Elia Mares, the owner of the clothing store in Ario de Rosales, and asked her to sell me merchandise. Besides taking correspondences from office to office, I would go with bags of clothing over which the women fought. They all began to talk, and I soon became famous in the building. I also organized *cundinas*, a type of lottery in which each person could win at any time. Teachers, engineers, and all kinds of people began coming to me, interested in what I could offer. I would take the money I earned to buy more clothing to sell, or I would make empanadas, a kind of pastry filled with chicken or beef; I barely had time to do everything. At that time we continued to pay Consuelo to live with us and take care of Charito. She traveled home for a weekend twice a month, so her constant presence in my house was very helpful.

Life with Leandro went on normally; he continued taking drugs and drinking, but he did it discretely, alone at home. With the money I earned, I was able to buy wicker furniture and rugs for the entire house. I improved all the rooms in the house, especially Charito's. The garden looked differently; it had more life and was full of colors.

Leandro began to slyly bring friends home to play cards. Then he began having parties, and finally he ended up having dates with prostitutes. His friends would stay at the house until very late and wouldn't let me sleep. It didn't matter which day of the week it was; for them, life was all games, alcohol, and women. Leandro's brother-in-law, who usually went along on those ventures, came to my room one day and tried to touch me. "I like you, Lilia," he told me. Everything I had worked to establish was falling to pieces because of Leandro's activities.

Working was hard, because I couldn't sleep until everybody left in the early hours of the morning; the only work I could manage was to distribute mail at my office job. I was forced to abandon my other ventures; the clothing sales, the cundina, the empanadas, and everything else became less convenient. I didn't have the same energy. The routine of parties started to be repeated twice during the week, then, three, until groups of people arrived daily to play and have sex in all corners of the house.

When I was home in the evenings, I stayed upstairs on the second floor with Charito while Leandro carried out his activities on the first floor. Heroin had arrived at our house, and Leandro sold the syringes. Every day, all day, people came to buy from him. He continued having his mysterious boxes full of medications he stole from the hospital. The doorbell would ring during the day, at midnight, or early in the morning.

One night, I approached the stairway to go downstairs in the middle of the night, but when I peered down into the living room, I saw Leandro having sex with a woman on the armchair. I went downstairs and confronted them. The woman, petrified, grabbed her things and ran out of the house. Leandro was outraged and began to push furniture and break the windows around the room. Then he left the house, yelling that he was going out to find prostitutes.

Problems began again, my nerves were aggravated, and the desperation settled in until I confronted him and everything turned into hell. He pushed, and I pushed back harder.

"Do you think you own this house? Do you think that because you bought furniture, you can tell me what I can and cannot do?" he asked one time as he jumped on top of our furniture.

"They are our things," I cried, "and I worked hard to buy them."

"I don't want you working again! You don't attend to me like you did before. You are out of the house all day, Charito stays with the servant, and you, all you do is work. Money is not lacking, so I want you here, taking care of me."

We had taken some steps forward, but that day we lost much of our progress.

Soon my sister Mili came to visit. Damián, who at that time was studying biology at the University of Morelia, had already come to visit, as had Esmeralda (my youngest sister) and my mother, who feared for what Leandro could do to me or my daughter. They didn't know the truth about the accident on the stairway, but they had seen my face. Esmeralda, who had always been brave, stayed for a week. She said that if Leandro tried to hit me, she would run out to get the police.

Mili stayed for two months, helped Consuelo, and took care of Charito. I still remember the smell of the tortillas that she would prepare, her attention to detail when cutting cilantro and tomatoes; it was like her therapy. Mili's concern and patience were the most beautiful signs of her love. She had to tolerate Leandro and his drunken friends, who on more than one occasion asked her for oral sex. One of those nights, Leandro told us to leave the house.

"Get out of here and take this mental retard!" he yelled, looking at Mili. "I am going to sink this hammer into your head."

"Someday you are going to find yourself without a wife," Mili yelled at him, "without a daughter, with nothing!"

That was the first time I had heard her yell. Leandro lowered the hammer but continued to look at her with fury. We left and went to the house of María Jesús, or Chuy, as we called her affectionately. Chuy had a business selling vegetables near her house; she lived on the side of the store with her son and sister. I had gone there to shop so many times that we ended up becoming friends. The truth was that she had become my guardian angel and hidden me several times. She would have been a very special godmother to Charito, but when I told Leandro about my wish, he said, "That woman from the store? Are you going crazy?"

So that night I escaped once more to her store and said, "It's just for tonight, Chuy. I promise I won't bother you anymore." I was embarrassed.

"It's okay, Lilia. Let the effects from the drug pass, and tomorrow you can go back more peacefully," she said with a soft voice, and gave a small plastic butterfly to Charito. "Sleep well, and don't worry about a thing."

That night Mili slept on a cushion on the floor. My daughter and I slept on the armchair. Charito closed her eyes three hours before I could. When I fell asleep, I had one of those dreams in which there are no real forms or places. I dreamed I was a butterfly, but had my own real legs. I dreamed that I had wings, but I still carried Charito in my arms. We went flying away from Leandro's house and arrived in a rainy desert with a large door and a sign that said TIJUANA. In the distance, I could see a city darkened by an almost black cloud. I tried to fly, but the raindrops wouldn't let me. So I took Charito by the hand and we began to walk toward the city, which seemed farther away with each step we took. As soon as we entered the city, a ton of women started running toward us. They were naked, and covered with bruises on their arms and legs. I tried to cover Charito's eyes, but my fingers fell off, and then my arms, without losing a drop of blood. Because of all the water, the women slipped in the mud until they were kneeling and asked me for help. I tried to fly but couldn't; Charito cried, and the women clung to my knees, saying, "Take us away from here." While pleading with me and getting closer and closer to my body, they began to crowd out Charito, who drowned between the rain and the crying. One of the women covered my face with her hand and I woke up. I had had many dreams during those years, nightmares in which I died, but never that sensation that felt so real on my skin. I lay still.

The next day, we returned to the house as though nothing had happened. Mili decided to leave because her presence altered Leandro's behavior more than normal; it would be best for her and for everyone. Leandro didn't throw me out or hit me again until the day he put a pistol to my head.

Tijuana
The Miracle of Saint Joseph

Liliana Kavianian

Charito was almost two. We left the house at six in the morning one Friday in 1987. I didn't sleep the night before, preparing for our escape. Like many times before, Leandro wasn't there, surely having fallen asleep on the floor of some bar or in some girl's house. He had told me that he was sick of me and that I was useless to him because he had lots of women from which to choose; the one he liked most was Marilú, his ex-wife with whom he still slept. I didn't move a muscle from hearing that, but this terrified me: "If you aren't out of here tomorrow, I'll kill you," he had said with his pistol to my head. "Now you've got me sick of you."

I was so sure of it that I thought I was going to leave as early as possible without doubting him or he would kill us. His face was like a demon's, full of veins on the verge of exploding. I had heard his threats, but that night was different. In his face I saw death. After he put away his pistol, he angrily left the house. Consuelo, upon hearing Charito's cries, went up to the bedroom to see if I was still alive. "Leandro is crazy, and he's going to kill us, which is why I have to go. Stay here—I'll be back in the early morning," I told Consuelo.

I took Charito and left for Chuy's house. As always, she took me in without asking for specifics. Consuelo stayed to put the clothes together. I told Chuy that I had decided to leave Leandro and that I needed a taxi for six o'clock that morning. I didn't sleep at all that night, thinking about what to do and hoping that Leandro wouldn't be home when I went to get the luggage. Chuy helped me organize everything. I also talked to my mom on the phone. When the sun came up, the taxi was already waiting for me. Chuy came with me all the way to the house, but she stayed in the taxi.

We slowly entered the living room and then the kitchen, and I told Charito to wait there for me. As I started up the stairway, Consuelo appeared, dressed in a robe.

"Leandro hasn't arrived, ma'am," she said nervously. "I've already put together your clothes. Where are you going to go?"

"Up north, but first I have to go to Salamanca."

"I'll get dressed then," she said hurriedly.

"You can't go with me," I replied.

"Please don't leave me here," she said with her hands clasped. "If you go north, I want to come with you guys."

"It'd be better for you to return to Ario," I warned. "I don't know where I'm going to live, and I can't promise you anything."

She wanted to get in the taxi anyway; she said she was doing it for Charito. Those few minutes were full of panic. I imagined that Leandro would take the girl, kill the cabbie, and then kill Consuelo and me. I almost couldn't coordinate the movement of my hands because I was so nervous. None of that happened.

I hugged Chuy and thanked her a thousand times. I didn't take all the bags that Consuelo had packed. I purposefully left one of Charito's bicycles in the entrance so that Leandro would see it and be reminded of his daughter. It was like a type of punishment so that he would think about what he had caused.

I left that house thinking about how he had forever lost us and that we would never return to that place. I was determined. As in everything in my life, the times I had the gumption to abandon something forever, I would leave and there was no turning back.

The taxi took us to the bus station, where we hopped on a bus to Salamanca, Guanajuato, where my mother had been living for some months to escape the marijuana smokers of Irapuato. I thought this would be the best way to calm down and plan for the trip to the north. Since my mom moved quite frequently, I don't know how Leandro ended up finding us. I don't know whom he must have threatened. In any case, Charito was at a neighbor's house because my mom had said, "I have a feeling that that man will come here at any moment."

I kept imagining bloody scenes: Leandro would open the door, kill my mom and then me, and take the baby. I couldn't sleep or eat during those days. Any noise could conjure the image of his demonic face and that pistol to my head.

The following week, my mom's prediction came to pass. It was nighttime. My mother looked out the window and saw Leandro's car approaching. Leandro broke the glass of a small window and tried to come in. I hid under a bed and heard the conversation. My mother confronted him through that same window.

"If you don't go, I'll call the police. Also, I'm not alone," she lied to protect us. "Some of my cousins are here."

"Where are Lilia and the plump little girl?" Leandro asked. He called Charito in that way because she had gained some weight; Consuelo had been ordered to feed her well.

"I know nothing about them, and I don't want any scandal in my house," my mom kept repeating. "I told you I'm not alone."

"I know they're here. I know it, so don't tell me otherwise," he insisted as he hit the wall.

Leandro started yelling until the neighbor who had already been warned by my mother and had heard the breaking glass went to help. Days before, my mom had confessed to the neighbor that I had escaped a nightmare. She had also described Leandro to him in case he saw him around the house.

"If you don't get out of here, I'll take my pistol and kill you," said the neighbor with his hand in his pocket. Leandro left without saying anything. In that instant, my mom's support was a courageous spark; rarely had she defended me, and hearing her made me feel safe again and reenergized me to keep on with my plan. At the end of the day, she was a survivor. She wanted to take care of us, but we both were aware of the inherent danger of such a decision.

"The earlier you go, the better. That man is crazy and has poison in his eyes," she told me.

In the next few days, I moved over to the neighbor's house. Besides being crazy, Leandro was sick; drugs had started to warp his brain from a very young age. He had grown up without his mom because she was a woman dedicated to high society, and Teodora, his grandmother, wasn't aware of his dangerous path until the insanity caught up to him.

After a week closed up in the neighbor's house, Lidia, another of the ladies I had met in Morelia, offered me her sister's house in the north. Lidia knew Leandro perfectly well; she had even helped me out one time when he broke a bottle over my head in front of the baby. We had become good friends because on Tuesdays, close to her house, there was a little market where we would meet and shop for fruit and fish. Another early-morning taxi. Consuelo insisted on following us, and I accepted her without much certainty about the future but with a destination in mind: Mexicali. Lidia had spoken with her sister, Rosa. Another option was to go to my sister Susana's house in Tijuana, but Leandro might know to look for me there.

"Go with my sister. In Mexicali you will be safe," Lidia told me. It meant being closer to the United States, which I was determined to enter someday.

Each time I had to run away, I felt like a criminal; not only did I suffer, but the moves also precluded the possibility of Charito having a peaceful childhood. I didn't understand Leandro's obsession. I wouldn't be able to know what would make him happy. Maybe it was to see me dead.

It was an exhausting trip. On the bus, all forty of us had to share the little air that came through the small window in the roof. The smell of humidity and heat suddenly made me feel like fainting, all of which mixed with uncertainty about the future: *What am I going to do?* I repeated to myself. Charito, red from the heat, slept for almost the whole trip, along with Consuelo.

After thirty hours, we arrived in Mexicali. Upon arriving at the bus station, I called Rosa, who appeared within minutes. She helped me with the bag while I carried Charito, and she took us to a house close to downtown where she rented a room.

The first few days, we settled in as much as we could because there was little room. The third day Rosa said, "The four of us don't all fit, but I know someone who can rent us an apartment." I gave her all the money I had, and we moved to a building six blocks from where we were. Consuelo stayed with Charito while I went out to look for work, but after two weeks, she left me because I couldn't pay her. Later I learned that her intention was to get closer to the border. She herself yelled one night, "I came here to better myself, not to help you. It'd be better for me to look for another job."

The little cat retracted her claws and backed off a bit. Rosa came and went without a regular schedule, which meant that I had to leave Charito closed up in a room while I scoured the streets in search of work.

One day, a woman saw Charito crying up against the window all afternoon. She offered to take care of her, and in return I gave her some jewels that I had saved for an emergency.

After much searching, I found a position as a secretary for a magazine, but first I had to make it through an interview with a man in his fifties, tall with white hair and a deep voice. He told me what my responsibilities would be and the kind of money I could come to earn if I did my job well. At the end of the conversation he invited me to dinner, saying that it was to explain some extra things that would help me get the job.

"Can we not talk about those things here in the interview?" I asked him, starting to feel funny.

"It would let us talk more in a more relaxing manner," he said seriously. "I need to give you more information and a few bits of advice.

"Okay, that's fine," I responded as I shakily rose from the seat. "I'll call tomorrow to confirm with you."

I left his office as fast as I could and never called him.

Later I found an opening at a hotel. With the money I earned cleaning rooms, I could pay the woman who watched after the baby, although Charito kept crying at the window and clung to my legs every morning.

The days with Rosa were darkening. Her character changed according to the climate, hour, and wind; it was impossible to guess what her mood would be. She had medicine bottles all over the place, and she would close herself in the bathroom to vomit. She ate a potato, a tomato, and a piece of lettuce, and sometimes rice; she said that being slender helped her keep her job, and she had no intention of becoming the overweight woman she had finally left behind. On an afternoon when Rosa was in a friendly mood, she told me about her change. She showed me old pictures of her parents and siblings and the picture she kept under lock and key: a fat woman with black hair. The change was remarkable; she had become a skinny blonde with green eyes.

She was convinced that the best way for me to forget about Leandro was to meet other men, which made her apartment Cupid's house. She would invite male friends over, introduce them to me, converse with them, and after an hour leave me alone with them. It was impossible for her to imagine that men made me nervous and afraid. I didn't know what she did for a living until one day when she told me she could offer me work.

"And what do I have to do?" I asked, interested because the money from the hotel wasn't enough.

"You have to go out with the men I tell you to and accompany them to their dinners, meetings, or wherever they take you," she said as if she were talking about selling tortillas. "It's easy!"

"So you're a …"

"No," she said as she furrowed her brow. "If you do what I tell you, you will have your daughter in the best school and be able to buy her all the clothes she wants."

"You're crazy! I can't do that."

She never said the name of her profession, but for me, an escort and a hooker were the same thing. During the day she sold samples of medications in pharmacies, and at night she went around with whoever's turn it was, mainly North Americans—whoever preferred blondes. Sometimes she would bring them back to the house, and other times she wouldn't arrive until the next day, with the thick scent of liquor.

Lidia had sent me to Rosa with all the generosity and care in the world, but she didn't have the slightest idea about what her sister had become. Rosa wanted to take advantage of everything. One of her friends was Tom, an American. I never found out whether he was a friend or client, but Rosa went out with him a few days each week. He even brought gifts for my daughter, and we spoke a couple of times. Rosa said that he wanted me and that if I didn't take the opportunity, he was going to drop it and go for her instead.

157

"Are you kidding?" I said. "The last thing I want is a man around." Even though she was jealous of the fact that Tom wanted something with me, she insisted on getting us together.

One weekend, the four of us went to the San Felipe beach. While Tom played with Charito in the sand, Rosa made my jaw drop.

"Would you be capable of marrying him so that he would be your daughter's stepfather?" she said to me as she watched the fresh scenery.

"I already told you that I don't want anything to do with men. You take him—he doesn't interest me."

"It's just that I don't interest him," she said sadly. "He wants you."

"And what do you want me to do?" I asked her, bored with the conversation.

"If you marry him, the three of us can cross over to the United States."

"You're really crazy …," I said compassionately.

On one occasion, Rosa proposed to the landlady's son to give us a discount if I slept with him.

Rosa noticed that I wasn't any use to her, and as a result the days became darker. She left her dirty clothes in the bathroom or thrown in the hallway; she dirtied up the bathroom with her vomits and left them for me to clean up. She almost didn't talk to me, and when she did, it was to insult me or ask me for money. I did my best to make sure that Charito didn't talk with her and did even more so that she didn't see the filth Rosa left behind.

After two months I ran into Amalia, a friend of Emma, who was one of Leandro's aunts. I had seen her at Charito's baptism and a few times when I went to visit Grandma Teodora. She told me that she had heard of our disappearance but knew the reasons very well. I told her the specifics of our story, and she offered to look after Charito: "It's better that she is in familiar hands," she said. Naively, I believed that Amalia would protect us because she was so sympathetic about my situation when I told her about Rosa. I innocently trusted her and didn't believe that she would betray us.

Amalia even found me a job at a car dealership. The owner was Mr. Tadeo, a nice little old man who designated me his secretary. He didn't ask for private interviews, nor did he appear interested in me, which made me think that things were getting better. Amalia promised not to tell anyone that I was in Mexicali.

Rosa went nuts.

"Are you thinking about going to Amalia's house?" she said, laughing. "To that pigpen of a house, you're thinking of leaving me for her?"

"You know her?" I asked her, surprised.

"Of course I know her. I saw her a few times in Morelia. She isn't going to help you, of that I'm certain."

"I've never thought about going with her, but if the future looks like this, there is no way, Rosa. I'll have to go," I responded, secretly hoping that God would, in fact, distance me from Rosa.

A few days later, Rosa left a letter on the table. She wrote that the best thing for everyone would be for me to leave the apartment, because I didn't deserve to live there. "Go with Amalia. I prefer to accept it before you tell me so," she concluded.

We went to Amalia's house, which included her five sisters, a brother-in-law, a nephew, and her stepfather. My aunt Barbara had warned me: "Don't tell anyone that you escaped from Leandro. You have to say that you are working in Mexicali and intend to cross into the United States." But I didn't learn; I went where the wind took me.

Amalia's stepfather had a store in the market, from which he took toys for Charito. He played and spoke with her as if he were her own grandfather. He gave her lots of attention—so much so that after a few weeks, Amalia got jealous because her stepfather was more worried about us than about them. She changed her attitude, and in a conversation with Leandro's aunt, told her that I was in Mexicali. The same stepfather discreetly informed me and recommended that I depart.

"Leandro heard about it, and he's coming to take your daughter," he said. Upon escaping from Morelia I had legal protection, declaring that I had abandoned my home because of death threats, but in reality, I feared that Leandro was capable of going outside the judicial system.

When I heard that he was going to take my daughter, I went crazy. He could hit me, kill me, but I was never going to let Charito grow up with that devil. When I heard the news, I ran to Mr. Tadeo's house, next to the car dealership, to ask for help. "Let me talk to my wife to see how we can help," he told me.

The next day, while I was organizing paperwork at the office, Mr. Tadeo and his wife came up to me: "There's no problem; get your things together and come," she said.

Just as bad people appeared, I had also found generous ones. I helped Mr. Tadeo in the office and his wife around the house. In exchange, I got a bed, food, and kindness. I was more comfortable, but I remained traumatized and with scenes of panic on my mind; Leandro would kill Don Tadeo and his wife, and then me, and he'd take Charito. It was like a horror movie that played out in my head at every moment.

Each day, as soon as I woke up, I asked myself, *Now what comes next?*

Mr. Tadeo also lived with Marcela and Daniel, his twentysomething kids. Marcela sometimes helped me watch Charito, mainly when the little girl wouldn't let me work.

The third Saturday, during a weekend lunch, two policemen came asking for me. Mr. Tadeo let them pass through. One of them showed me a document that I didn't read and said that Leandro was outside waiting to see his daughter.

I don't know how long I talked to the police. I didn't stop shaking, not even for a second while I told them the whole story. I showed them copies of the report and the marks he had left on me. Don Tadeo and his wife offered to be witnesses; their children watched motionless from the table. The police took their time as they went through each one of the documents, until they broke the silence to tell me, "Ma'am, you have to leave here. We can say that you weren't here, but he won't rest. He's determined to take your daughter from you, and we can't assure you that he'll leave this house."

Marcela suddenly got up from the table and proposed that she sneak me out in a car. The police supported the idea. "Leave, and we'll see to it that he doesn't suspect anything," one of the officers said.

I packed about half my clothes and some keepsakes in a suitcase. We all said our good-byes and they wished us the best of luck. They had loved Charito so much, it was as if she were part of their own family. Don Tadeo handed me some money for the bus trip to Guanajuato so that I could go to my aunt Milla's house.

We went out to the garage, and Marcela opened the trunk door: "You guys get in here; it'll only be for a few minutes." My body became like a block of ice as I adjusted to that dark corner. Charito asked what game we were playing. I kept still until Marcela opened the trunk and I could see that we were on the side of the road. She told me that she had pulled over there because it was better than going to the bus station and that surely I would find a bus that could take me to Guanajuato. As such, about a half hour later, Marcela stuck her arm out to stop a noisy bus. I thanked her again, and Charito gave her a kiss. Marcela told the driver, "I'm putting you in charge of her because she's leaving due to a life-threatening situation."

Hearing those words felt like a pail of cold water. I imagined myself in front of a mirror, and I looked sad, helpless, and once again running from that devil. Upon sitting and thinking about what I was doing, I noticed that despite everything that I saw in that image, I kept on trudging along, ready for the next battle. I looked at Charito and lifted her head up; she was the only thing that kept me going.

Days before, during a long phone conversation, Pillita had mentioned the possibility of Charito hiding out on a ranch. She was referring to the area full of fertile farmland inside Guanajuato but away from all the urban parts. Just as Pillita had suggested, we went for a few days to my aunt's house to come up with a plan. We headed back southward, another long trip. I was going over everything in my head again and again, trying to find the exact moment when I had lost myself, the day I had let that whole tragedy strangle me. Even if that trip had taken me around the world with time to meditate on my situation, I wouldn't have had the mental clarity to understand how I had let myself get stuck or how to solve my problems.

At the first stop almost everyone got off the bus to buy supplies or to use the bathroom. We stayed aboard the bus, watching everyone. Charito complained that she was hungry, but I didn't have a cent. At the second rest stop, and in those that followed, the driver offered me food and candies for the girl. Another little angel on the trail.

My aunt Milla took us in for a few days. She was concerned about the fact that someone might know that we were in her house and about the conversations between Pillita and the ranch family. I also spoke with my sister Susana so that she could receive us in Tijuana.

"Are you sure that family will take good care of her?" I asked Milla, terrified as I imagined the day that I would leave my daughter.

"Don't you worry—Charito will be taken care of there," she said assuredly. "They will treat her like a princess. There, she will be able to play freely. You'll see."

"And what if Leandro finds out where she is?" I asked fearfully.

"He won't find out, because no one will tell him."

I agonized about the decision to leave Charito, but I decided finally that she would be safer separated from me. If Leandro succeeded in finding me, at least Charito would be protected from a childhood with him. Besides, with someone taking care of her, I would be free to work as much as possible to save up for our next move, whatever that may be.

We prepared for another trip. We left early in the morning on a Friday. Another Friday escape. Although it was within the same state, the ranch was in a remote area where buses didn't go. I thought for hours and hours about what I would do in Tijuana and how I would live far away from Charito. The idea was to let a few months pass so that Leandro would desist from his search. Then I would find a job and cross over to the United States with Charito. The thought of abandoning her for a long time was not at all part of my plan.

I took a bus, a taxi, and then a wagon. Upon arrival, I forgot all about the anguish of the trip as the countryside reminded me of the feeling of existence, assigning a name to that feeling because I was far from knowing it. The wind caressed me with an air of tranquility, and the smell of earth reminded me of the coffee at my grandfather's country house. I wanted to sleep there forever. I'm referring to the estate owned by Fina, one of Pillita's cousins. Fina, who lived with her children Finita and Trino, was an adorable woman; she spoke gently and moved smoothly like leaves with a breeze beneath them. It was a beautiful place, surrounded by trees, animals, and cropland, where they grew papayas and strawberries to make jams that would later be sold to merchants in the city. There was also a chapel where the priest went every eight days to offer a Mass.

I convinced myself that Leandro was never going to give up with his daughter and that Charito would enjoy life more in that place than in any other. I hated him, and with that feeling I became cold and full of the courage to defend her like a hen protecting her chicks. I desired to keep Charito with me as my comfort and motivation to keep going, yet I realized that maybe it would be selfish to subject her to long trips, uncertain conditions in Tijuana, and being taken care of by unfamiliar neighbors or friends while I went out to find work.

I left Charito with Fina and with all the pain that a mother can feel leaving her little one. I knew that she would be happier in a stable environment with trustworthy relatives. Although the situation wasn't the same, I remembered the day when my mother left me with my grandparents; history repeats itself. I left the ranch, hidden from Charito in a wagon, a taxi, and later a bus on its way to Tijuana.

I didn't speak much with my grandmother or my aunt Barbara, but they were always on the ball; besides finding a home for Charito, they had even talked with Paco in Tijuana, a man whose work was taking people across the United States' border. From the first day in Tijuana, the only thing that I wanted to know was about a guy named Paco and how to cross over to *gringoland* so that I could make some money. I idealized that country as a distant land, and I dreamed of it as a paradise full of gold coins where, upon entering, all problems disappeared. In dreams, anything is possible.

My sister Susana lived in Tijuana with her husband, and so did Glafira, one of Pillita's distant relatives. Rumors were blowing from the south that Leandro was continuing his search; some had heard that he was reformed and wanted to persuade me to return to Morelia; others mentioned that he had gone crazy repeating the word *revenge*. Susana asked Glafira, the owner of the house, if she would take me in for a few days. The woman, without sparing words, responded, "I don't want problems here" as she turned her back to us.

"Don't worry," I replied, convinced of what I was saying. "I'll be here three days, nothing more."

"Just as well, but even so …," Glafira said as she raised her eyebrows.

"I promise you," I assured her, embarrassed to beg.

"Okay. I'll make something to eat," said Glafira.

After two hours, Glafira was touched by my story. She listened as she cut up vegetables for enchiladas. I didn't know if it was the onion or the sorrow, but her eyes were swollen and her arm was wet from wiping her nose; the story of Leandro reminded her of her own tormented youth. She cried for what she hadn't thought about in years, and between sobs she offered her support. That day and the second she was gentle and kind.

The next day, I met Panchita, Glafira's daughter-in-law, a warm and generous woman. They lived a few blocks away from each other. We spent almost the whole afternoon chatting, and she promised to help me find a job.

On the third day, Glafira ran me out of her house, not because my time was up, but rather because someone had told her a new story about me. Sometime after, I found out that Susana, although I don't know why, had said that I was running from the police for having killed a man down south. On top of that, Paco didn't show up. He had escaped with Pillita's money and that of another ten people. As such, I decided to cross without papers and return later to look for Charito. I went to Panchita's house to say good-bye.

"What do you mean you're leaving?" she said, frozen in the door and carrying her only son on her hip.

"I'm going to cross without papers. Paco didn't show up, and Glafira threw me out of the house."

"Then stay here," she said as she opened the door even more.

"Really?" I asked her, hoping it wouldn't turn out like the past offers.

"Sure! I just live with my husband and Gerardito," she said as she kissed the baby and backed up so that I could come in. "Stay here, and tomorrow we'll go look for a job so that you can get your papers together. You can't cross like that—it's dangerous."

I took Panchita's offer and calmed myself down. As always, I didn't cease from doing things around the house: I cleaned the rooms, helped with groceries, and played with little Gerardito.

One week later, I started working as a receptionist at a hotel. They didn't pay me much, but it was enough for Panchita to buy groceries. I bought shoes, clothes, and toys for Gerardito as a sign of my gratitude and nostalgia for Charito. I hid away a few pesos in a box for a trip to the ranch in Guanajuato where Charito was.

The rumors kept blowing like the wind that Leandro knew where Charito was, as did the lie that I had abandoned my daughter forever. I played out the movie in my head again: Leandro arrived at the ranch, shot the whole family, and made off with Charito. I tried not to call the ranch to ask if the rumors were true; it would better if I kept thinking about how to scrape enough money together for the trip.

Panchita talked to me about her friend Sandra, a young woman who served in a bar in downtown Tijuana. With what she earned, she was able to keep her kids in a big, comfortable house.

"You can go to the hotel during the day and work nights at the bar," said Panchita, enthusiastic about being able to help me. It sounded like an excellent idea. The next weekend, we went to look for Sandra, and her house was just as splendid as Panchita had described. Without much ado, Sandra responded that she would love to introduce me to the owner of the bar. If I wanted, she could do so that same night. She scrawled a map on a scrap of paper, and as she said her good-bye, she said, "We'll see each other tonight. Don't forget to wear heels."

We met up at eight o'clock in a northern neighborhood, *La Cohauila*. There were fast food restaurants, clothing stores, drugstores, and liquor stores with creative names in Spanglish. People came and went from innumerable bars with brightly lighted signs; music mixed in with the sound of cars and street conversations. Upon turning the corner, the lighted-up letters were lost in a little blue side street where we were walking, and for about a quarter of a block there were women in miniskirts and half-naked transvestites. The cars filled the street, hoping to see the spectacle; arms came out through their windows to immortalize the moment with cameras while the prostitutes and transvestites turned toward the wall.

"Here it is!" Sandra said, smiling to the guard at the bar. The bar was named *El Burro*. It was a small place with about ten tables and was dark, not for a lack of light. Upon entering, Sandra left me with the owner and disappeared down a hall. "Good luck!" she yelled. The man took me behind the bar counter to explain to me which tables were mine.

"Numbers four, six, and eight," I repeated seriously. He reminded me that the first day was always the hardest because the competition was fierce, but that if I did well, I would soon have generous clients. "But today I only came to …," I said without being able to finish, because he continued with the instructions. He also suggested that I wear a shorter skirt the next day I worked. As I chewed on that notion, table number four was the first to be inhabited by two characters.

"They're all yours," said the owner as he turned me toward the table and gave me a soft push. "Table four ordered tequila and three glasses."

When I returned with their order, they tugged my arm into sitting down at the empty seat. "I've got other tables to attend to," I told them. They asked me if I was a new employee as they filled my glass. After thirty minutes of senseless conversation, they both got up from the table: one went to the bathroom, and the other took my hand and moved closer to the bar counter to tell the owner, "I'll take this one."

That night, for a half hour of service, they paid me thirty dollars. Prostitution and everything that went with it made me into an even colder and more fearful woman. The third day, I hadn't gotten used to it, but I understood how the business model worked. I don't understand how I didn't die there. In reality, I was in the throes of death a number of times, but I stayed alive. All the while, I thought constantly about Charito, how much I missed her and how the money would eventually help us have a decent, stable life.

I had been in that bar for a week when one night a seemingly decent character, the kind who wore a jacket and tie, asked for my services in Rosarito, about twenty minutes from Tijuana, and said that he would pay me more than a hundred dollars. The owner gave the okay, and the man took me to an apartment in a building a few blocks from the beach. In one corner was a guy discussing something with two girls, who had been contracted in another place. One of them slapped the guy in the face and left. Through the hallway appeared two young boys, both with a glass in hand. They signaled for me to sit down and gave me a cup.

"What happened with those girls?" I asked, without realizing that it wasn't any of my business.

"Nothing," one of the guys said. "They just came, and now they went to look for some other girls."

"Cheers!" said the other, and he clinked his glass with mine.

The doorbell rang. Two middle-aged men joined the party. Each minute I found it more and more difficult to distinguish between the faces. I had drunk only one glass and my head was spinning. I got up to go to the bathroom, but someone pushed me into an armchair ...

When I opened my eyes, I was in a bed and couldn't move. I saw them taking turns with me. I counted ten of them. When they got bored with their feat, they put me in a car and abandoned me in a dark spot on the beach. Some guys from a *lunada*, a typical Mexican beach party, took me to the hospital. One of the men told me that I was purple, unconscious, barely clothed, and almost in the water when they found me.

The dream I had in Chuy's house had come true, only I was one of the beaten, naked women who appeared in it. At the hospital, they didn't exactly treat me like a princess, but they did stabilize me and let me call Panchita.

When I arrived at her house, she asked that I not return to the bar. Rather, she said, I should go talk to another friend who worked as a cashier in a restaurant. I was so shaken by the experience that I was numb, yet my drive to scrape together money for myself and my dear Charito pushed me to look for work.

The next night I returned to the bar, not to work but to talk to Alberto, a man who delivered plastic glasses. I told him what had happened to me and he suggested another bar. "Something more decent," he said. Alberto was referring to the Razas Club, a more prestigious bar.

The day that I went to check it out, I met a skinny man with a stooped back, who smoked while he peacefully used a broom to sweep, collecting the thousand pieces of broken glass. *At least they use glass here,* I thought. He was Benjamin, the owner of the bar. In the entryway, there was a security stand, and at the end of a hallway were small, round tables, but with enough room to serve clients their alcohol. On the left was the bar, and next to the bar was a dance floor and a small stage for the band. The bar was elegantly lighted with a faint light that illuminated the red velvet of the walls and armchairs.

"What's your name?" he asked me as he swept up the last few pieces of glass.

"Jessica," I invented as I opened him the trash bag.

"Do you have experience?" he asked as he clenched the cigar in his jaw, "because here, sometimes there are up to thirty women, and they all have experience."

"I was working in that bar … in a bar the next block over," I improvised.

He took the cigar out of his mouth and said, "Go tend to those men"—he pointed to some guys in the corner—"so that you can practice."

The best part about this place was that you could work anytime, day or night. Next door was a hotel with which Benjamin had a deal to take his clients. The women who didn't leave with men earned points; for each drink their clients ordered, the women got a point, which they later exchanged for money. This wasn't very profitable, because the management gave us a very low percentage of the price of every bottle served.

The first week was normal: I met a number of girls, some kinder than others, and I got some clients. There were all types of men: young and old, nice and ill humored, sober and drunk. Before going to the hotel, we talked about the terms of the service. Some asked for nude dancing, and some wanted orgies or had weird requests. I preferred normal services and hoped the clients were drunk so that the service was fast. Sometimes, when they stayed half asleep, I faked it. Sometimes little old men showed up. These were the most demanding, because they asked for a different girl every time.

One of my favorite outfits was black, tight to my body, with which I rocked black panty hose and heels. I didn't look like a hooker, but like an elegant woman. One night, the "Pantera," the leader of the house band I admired, told me that some of the clients thought I was working for the police.

"Get out of this world—you aren't built for this environment," he said that same night. "You don't seem like a hooker."

"I'm getting some money together for a trip," I responded. "I don't have much time left in this city."

"You want to go north?" he asked me, as if he had discovered my secret.

"Yes, but first, I have to go fetch my daughter, who's in Guanajuato," I told him mysteriously. Charito's absence hurt me more than the discomforts of that difficult work, but I continued to believe that it wouldn't be long before I was with her again.

I felt afraid and embarrassed for being in that line of work, but the money was good enough to get me off of Panchita's couch. Panchita knew what I was doing but did not make comments or get involved.

I rented a room on one of the side streets close to the bar, where I could cry for Charito without having to explain it to anyone. I also left my job as a receptionist, which was more effort than the money was worth. The street was a nest for drug dealers and hookers who worked around the clock; they argued about too few grams of drugs and too many hours worked.

Despite the environment, I did my best to live peacefully. At first I didn't have problems with alcohol. I would drink at work in order to better tolerate my job and so that I wouldn't feel guilty. I hadn't bought even one beer, nor did I smoke at home; that was all just part of the job. I minimized my drinking to keep my senses sharp and alert in case some guy became dangerous; the other girls warned me, because they knew that among our clientele were a lot of drug dealers. They met up in the bar to have fun, but also to start or finish a business deal.

I once again passed close to death when a white guy in his thirties, took me to a hotel and threatened me with a knife. No sooner had I opened the door to the room than he pushed me toward the bed; it was in that instant that I could see the drugs from the look in his eyes.

"Don't move!" he ordered as he pointed his left index finger at me with his right hand in his pocket. I was afraid, but I had asked for the money beforehand, as always.

"Don't fuck with the money!" he said as he pulled out his right hand from his pocket to show me the knife. "Stay on the bed!"

Then he started the water in the bathtub. "First you have to give me my money," I said bravely, "or I'm leaving here."

"I'll give you your fucking money!" he said impatiently, and leapt onto the bed. "Now shut up if you want to live," he said as he pressed the knife to my face.

He sat on top of me and started to kiss and hit me. Alternating one with the other, he furiously tore my clothes off with his hands.

"Now get your fucking body in the bathtub!" he yelled.

"That water is almost boiling! I'm not going to …"

"You will do what I tell you to!" he screamed. He grabbed my arm and threw me down in the doorway to the bathroom.

He opened my wallet and took out the six hundred dollars I had made that week. Before he kicked me, I had a chance to look into his demonic, red eyes.

I'm going to die right here, I thought. *God, help me, I don't want to leave my daughter all alone.* I don't know where my strength came from, but I stood up and pushed him, and we both fell to the floor. I tried to open the door, but my hands slipped on the handle. I kept trying while he started to get up off the floor. He picked up his knife, and just as he came at me again, I was able to open the door and sprint naked toward the reception desk of the hotel.

"What happened to you?" asked the receptionist as he covered his eyes with one hand.

"Call the police," I instructed him as I held myself up on the counter. "He wanted to kill me!"

A few minutes later, two patrolmen arrived. The man was still closed up in the room. I waited on a couch, covered in a pink gown given to me by the receptionist, until I saw him pass by, handcuffed. I had thought that my life would end right there, in that room, and that I wouldn't have a chance to find what I was searching for or see Charito again. I didn't even know what that was, but I kept calling it "a purpose for my life." I sometimes called it "a sense of peace," but I was undoubtedly looking for it in the wrong place. The more I wanted to leave my past behind, the more I returned to situations even darker and more painful.

Many years before, Tijuana had become a place of enormous growth in technology and health. However, it had also become famous for its nighttime bar scene and sex trade, on top of drugs, violence, and human trafficking. Being a border city, it had a very particular identity: it still brought in North Americans hungry for diversion and sex, as well as the thousands of Mexicans and Latinos who wanted to cross legally, or illegally, into the United States. Those deported from the United States lived together, many of them forced to work in places full of drug trafficking and prostitution.

La Coahuila, the same street where I worked, is still an area full of guns, drugs, strip clubs, coyotes (illegal-immigrant smugglers), and street-side prostitution, the most difficult and precarious of all because pimps make the prostitutes charge low prices and take all of their profits anyway. Luckily, I didn't have to work in those conditions. In a certain sense, my work was more discreet, but it was not free of corruption. At any time, the municipal police would show up at the bar asking for health department documents; they ended their visit with some combination of arrested prostitutes and cash in their pocket, or tangled with one of the girls in bed.

José Luis and his cronies planned to lock us up one night. On the way, Irma, one of the more experienced girls, made them a deal: she offered them fifty bucks for each one of us, and those who didn't have the money could pay with an hour of fun. We paid our debt and they let us go. In the visits that followed, the officers saved the negotiations and went straight to asking for a service.

After the episode at the hotel, and after spending a week depressed and in bed and crying for my daughter, I returned to the bar. That afternoon, before going in, I went down to the sidewalk to call the ranch to see how Charito was. I spoke with Fina to tell her that I was pretty sure that within a month, I'd be able to come and get her. She didn't stop telling me all that Charito did and how happy she was together with Finita and Trino, her honorary aunt and uncle. This is how Fina put it: "They adore her and care for her as if she were their own sister," she told me. I took a deep breath so that she wouldn't hear me crying.

After I hung up the telephone, I dropped all the coins I had in my hand onto the ground. I squatted down and saw the hands of a man who picked up all of the coins so quickly that I couldn't grab even one.

"Thanks," I told him as I dried my tears.

"Do you live close by?" he asked me with an accent I didn't recognize.

"More or less," I replied without taking my eyes off the floor.

He took my arm and helped me to my feet.

"I'm looking for some bar ... you know ... somewhere fun where I can hang out for a bit," he said while he moved his hands around as if what he said wasn't sufficient. "Do you know a place like that?"

"What country do you come from?" I asked him as I stepped away.

"Australia, but I'm Argentine," he said with his little accent.

"I work in that bar." I showed him with my finger. "If you want, I'll take you there."

"Perfect!" he blurted out.

He bought me a glass of wine, we chatted, and later I accompanied him to the hotel for the rest of the night. Roberto had brown hair and his eyes were almost green; he was a kind and cheerful man, which made me feel at rest and understood. He told me that he was in the middle of a divorce, and I remembered when Leandro had told me the same thing.

Roberto was in Tijuana figuring something out about medical treatment. The transplant that his thirteen-year-old stepdaughter required was prohibited in Australia. He assured me, without me asking for it, that his relationship with his wife was strictly friendship and that he loved the girl as if she were his own daughter. When he asked about my life, I didn't know where to begin. I started saying that my husband was crazy and that he wanted to take Charito from me.

The next three nights we met up at the same time. We kept the same routine, but each time we learned more about each other;

he told me that the girl had suffered an accident when she was five years old and that his wife blamed it all on him because he was driving drunk. I explained what had happened with Leandro and my torments from childhood. During those four days, he was my only client.

The fourth night he gave me a surprise.

"Come on, let's go!" he said before sitting down at the same table at the usual time. "I have a surprise for you."

"I don't like surprises," I said angrily and without looking at him.

"You're going to like it, I promise," he said as he put his hands together. "I swear to you that it's not anything bad; you have to trust me."

We left the bar and took a taxi, and he covered my eyes with a tie. Several minutes later, the taxi came to a stop. When Roberto removed the tie from my eyes, I saw that we were at the airport.

"What are we doing here?" I asked him as we got out of the taxi, afraid and ready to run. "The last time I strayed from the bar, I almost died," I told him as I fought back tears.

"I'll show you right now," he said with a mysterious twinkle of happiness in his voice. "Give me your hand."

"I'm not going anywhere!" I told him with my arms crossed. "You tell me what we are doing at the airport or I'm leaving."

"We're just traveling within Mexico—don't worry. We're going for Charito."

He showed me the tickets for Guadalajara and told me that from there we were going to rent a car to get to Guanajuato. I couldn't believe what was happening. It had been four months since I had seen Charito. I was happy but scared at the same time, because I knew very well that favors were to be repaid, and were expensive at that.

We took the flight, and then Roberto drove for eight hours to Guanajuato and three more to arrive at Fina's ranch. I cried during the whole trip, filled with excitement because I missed her so much, and with anxiety and fear that I would arrive and find that she wasn't there.

We arrived at six o'clock on a Sunday morning.

Fina answered the door, surprised by our unannounced visit from so far away. She led me upstairs to see Charito: there was my little girl, asleep in her princess room, hugging a teddy bear. A wave of relief and happiness came over me, and at the same time I felt sad for having left her. Finita, Fina's single daughter, had been in charge of looking after Charito along with her brother Trino, also single. The two of them had become Charito's honorary godparents for almost six months, but they weren't there that morning. Charito had stayed with Fina because the rest of the family had gone to the city for a wedding.

While we waited for Charito to wake up, Fina served us breakfast. She served us a jar of strawberry jam so delicious that I had to buy ten jars from her. Fina was friendly as always but did not hide her disappointment when I announced that Charito would be leaving with us that day. Charito was very loved by everyone in the family, and no one would want her to leave. Fina said that if her children, Finita and Trino, were there, they would make their greatest effort not to let me take Charito.

"I came for the girl," I told Fina as she looked at me with a face of horror and the bread halfway to her mouth. It was quiet.

"But here she is just fine," she said, setting the bread on her plate. "You don't have to take her. We have taken very good care of her, and she is happy."

"It's just that I'm afraid of Leandro. They say that he knows she is here."

"That's not certain, my dear. Everyone adores that girl, especially Finita and Trino. No one is going to let him take her."

"Understand me, Fina: she needs to be with her mother."

It was quiet again.

"What more can I say? She's your daughter," she said as she shrugged disappointedly.

When Charito woke up, she was surprised to see me and acted strangely. In the hurry to prepare for the return trip, we took Charito with one change of clothes and a pair of white shoes. She cried as we all left Fina's house and continued to cry on the flight to Tijuana. She lamented leaving and mentioned the goose at the lagoon and her honorary aunt and uncle, whom she called Mamá Finita and Papá Trino; both would cry inconsolably upon hearing that Charito had gone. She talked about her white shoes, which "Mamá Finita" had given her.

"Stop crying," Roberto told her as he stroked her face. "People are going to think that we're beating you." I couldn't believe that Charito was with me; it wasn't the best moment, but I couldn't make it even one more night without her.

Three days later, Roberto returned to Australia, but he said that we would see each other very soon. I went back to work part time at the bar and left Charito at home at night. Since there was no one to look after her at that time, she stayed alone in the apartment, which I would leave child-proofed. By removing all possible hazards and leaving the television and refrigerator accessible, I made the apartment safe for her.

A short time after Roberto had left, he sent me flowers at the bar, and in one of his calls he asked me if I would like to travel with Charito to Australia and get married. "That's impossible," I told him. "How can I ask for a divorce from Leandro without him killing me? I won't be able to get the girl out of the country that way."

Robert's plans for Charito and me sounded good, but I hardly knew him, and life had taught me not to trust anyone. That became even clearer when one of the girls told me, "Forget it, Jessica. In Australia he's going to want to trick you. Lots of them do it like that. They come to look for women, and there they turn into your bosses … Don't believe him … Keep him far away."

On the next call, I repeated everything that girl had told me as if they were my own thoughts, but that wasn't enough to get Roberto to quit insisting. Afterward, one of Roberto's female friends called me. She said that she also lived in Australia, and with the same little Argentine accent told me, "Roberto is sad; he barely eats or sleeps and can't stop thinking about you. You have to believe him—he is a good man."

I asked the bar owner to either not give me his calls or to tell him that I had left Tijuana. Roberto gave me happiness, care, motivation, and of course the trip to Guanajuato. He paid for the trip to the ranch and motivated me to bring back Charito, something that I hadn't dared to do because of the conditions in which I lived. Roberto was an angel from heaven, but who knew if the angel would turn into a demon? Leandro had saved my life, and it had all gone to hell afterward.

With Charito back, the room had a different feel to it. I forgot about the drug dealers, the hookers outside the house, and the scandals of the transvestites on the corner. I could understand that world, but how was I supposed to explain it to a three-year-old girl? I tried my best to make sure that Charito didn't see any of that and hardly took her out of the room. There was no way I could stop working, so I went back to the bar, but only at night. In the meanwhile, I continued to search for someone to take care of Charito so that I could also go back to working during the day.

In the first week I had to leave her alone. I didn't know all the details of her time in the country, but she had learned something that made her more mature than most children her age. We talked about a lot of things. She didn't ask for her dad, which helped me to not lie about Leandro.

"Where are you going?" she asked me one night.

"To work, baby," I sighed.

"And what do you do at work?" she asked as she grabbed at my skirt.

"I'm like a nurse," I said after setting her down on my lap. "I give massages to people when they feel tired or sad or if they're in pain," I explained.

"I don't want you to give massages," she said as she hugged me tight. "Don't go. I don't want to be alone."

The memory of those words and her angelic little face make me cry. Many times I left her closed up in that room, and despite her young age, she understood that it was important for me to work. She never went hungry, and I made sure that everything was safe and in place; I left a glass, the milk in the refrigerator, and the television where she could get to them, and paper, fire, and plugs out of her reach. In the mornings, while I recovered from the night before, she opened the little refrigerator, took out a glass of milk that I had left ready for her from the night before, turned on the TV to a quiet volume because she knew all the buttons and their functions, and lay down next to me without making any noise.

It was a relief when Norma, a Colombian colleague, told me that she left her daughter with Gina, a woman who lived close by and took care of a number of kids. For a month, I left Charito with Gina at night, but each day she claimed something different: that Gina had pushed her, that she had scratched her, that she had yelled at her. "I prefer to stay by myself," she said.

I didn't pay attention to her allegations until one day, when I was bathing her, I found a purple mark on her back. With all the fierceness that a mother has to defend her kids, I went to Gina's house. When I confronted her about the marks on Charito, she was obviously startled but tried to hide her surprise and told me quite calmly, "That's not true. I haven't laid a hand on these children. Kids are like that. Sometimes they hurt themselves lightly and tell fibs about people doing them harm." I saw that the other three children Gina was paid to take care of were also scratched, and knew that I wouldn't let Charito stay at her house anymore. Gina had suffered many losses, including a daughter who died of cancer. I realized that Gina's suffering had made her bitter, lazy, and even destructive. But although I pitied her, I would not risk Charito's safety.

I started to leave Charito alone again, although just for a few days, because I didn't have the energy to go to the bar. I felt more helpless than ever and like I wasn't going anywhere with my life. I missed two weeks at the bar, days I took advantage of to be with Charito and to think about what was next for us. We walked all around the city and visited the circus in the Plaza Río. Those were simple times and became the most beautiful of times for Charito and me. Her smile rejuvenated and motivated me.

Upon returning to my job, I decided to get Charito away from that street. Alicia, a coworker from the bar, came with me to look for an apartment in the same part of town where she lived. We found a small studio with enough space for a bed, a small kitchen, and a few pieces of furniture. Alicia took care of filling the house with all the furniture we needed. Switching houses filled me with energy. I organized it with Charito; we made a spot for her games and filled it with color.

The rent was twice as much as at the last place, which meant that I had to work to compensate. There we met Jesús, the man who fixed everything that was broken. The owner had contracted him a year ago and in exchange, let him live there in one of the apartments. The first day he introduced himself and offered to help. He told me that he was from Guadalajara and that he had come to Tijuana looking to rehabilitate from a past drug problem; he had become a true Christian. He was a fervent churchgoer and evangelized as many people as he could. Many times we got together to eat and talk, and sometimes he watched Charito; he said that she was a very intelligent girl. He was a very fun man. I remember that the first time we went shopping. "Wait, Indian, you aren't in your town anymore—you have to wait for the light," he yelled at me as I ran a red light. From that time on he called me "Indian." His company was important for me.

Although I didn't know where I was headed in life, I decided to keep with the routine. Yet again, Charito had to stay alone, although Jesús would keep an eye on her. I felt like going to the bar even less than before and was drinking more than the usual amount necessary to put up with the men and their craziness.

One night a Japanese guy came in named Suzuki, just like the car. The first night, after bowing to me a few times, he told me that he had arrived three months earlier to assess an electronics company and would be returning soon to Tokyo, where he lived with his parents on the fortieth floor of a building. He had learned Spanish because his grandfather had grown up in Spain and had always wanted his children and grandchildren to speak the language.

For the next few days, as soon as he came in, he asked for me. We would sit there, chatting for hours, but I understood only half of what he said until one day he said, "I have to return to Japan, but if I come back to Tijuana, I'd like to marry you. What do you think?"

I laughed as if it was the best joke in the world. Suzuki looked at me and understood my laugh as a "yes." He was happy. They were vague promises from lunatics who landed in the bar.

I didn't make myself wishful for anything with the John Does, or with anyone who dreamed of rescuing a lost woman and turning her into a princess, but I did realize that I could remake my life in that place or another. The offers from the Argentine and the Japanese, if that's what you could call them, awoke a yearning inside of me form a family. The North American paradise and the gold coins became part of what they always had been: an immature dream. I set out to meet a good man even though the fear of falling into the hands of a psycho, drug addict, wife beater, or who knows what killed me.

With each John Doe I talked to, I tried to see what was underneath it all, what his life was like, and what plans he had for the future. While they talked, I made my evaluation and asked myself if I was looking at the right man, if he could offer me peace, a family, and a different life from the hell that I was living at the bar.

But each night was worse than the one before. The anxiety of not knowing who I was going to meet, which man I was supposed to please, and the things that I would have to put up with took me to a state of extreme anxiety. I started to shake and didn't sleep for days. To face every encounter I upped the alcohol dosage, but I began to feel more lethargic, depressed, and sick. I came home without being able to attend to Charito, so I began to pay Sofia, a very kind woman, to take care of her while I worked. I called my mother and cried about my anguish. "You should offer candles to San José," she said to me.

A friend from the bar who dealt prescription drugs brought me prescriptions for Valium by the tens. With these fraudulent prescriptions, I went to pharmacies all over Tijuana, buying that drug. It became a vice for calming my feelings of anguish, but between the liquor and drugs, I started to get sick. I wanted to quit at the bar, but it was the only way I was able to keep Charito.

I even thought about saving money to buy a little cart to sell tacos on the street. I was saving well until my fever and stomachache took everything I had saved. I went to three or four doctors, and all said the same thing: I had an infection that could be fixed with antibiotics. The doctors injected me with pain medication so that I would pay and leave their office without really knowing what my problem was. Despite the meds, my fever didn't go down and my stomach made me twist in pain constantly, so much that I often had the sensation that I was suffocating. In the bar on some nights, the men slept peacefully—not because they were tired, but because I slipped a pill into their glasses to help them sleep. I didn't have it in me.

Anyway, the John Does started to switch me out for other girls. Angélica, a fat, scary-looking woman, started to tell them that I was really a man who'd had an operation, that I had AIDS and that she had seen me in the bathroom vomiting blood. She was a woman who envied those of us who didn't have a pimp who managed our cash. Her pimp, lover, and owner collected her cash each night, and if she didn't reach quota, he would beat her in front of everyone. The same went for Antonio, the type of guy who wore sunglasses all the time. He had ten women, and besides taking their money, he made them sell cocaine.

One day they let me know that I had a job at the hotel and that the man was waiting for me in room number 20. When I got to the room, I saw Antonio seated on the bed holding two cups in one hand. He sat me down next to him and told me he had noticed that I had been very nervous the past few days. He handed me one of the cups and took a little box out of his bag. I told him I had been exhausted and sick. He said, "I have the cure for all misfortunes." He opened the box and took out a line of cocaine.

After that night, I fell as far as you can in this world, and I couldn't help myself up until the miracle from San José came to pass. All the while I kept taking drugs and drinking, but the fever wouldn't let up, and one day it broke me. That night, I was at the bar seated at a table with two men when I lost my balance and fell onto Teresa's feet. Teresa, one of the older women there, took me home, prepared some water with I don't know what, and warned me that I needed to rest. I slept all night with Charito in my arms.

A few days later, we went to a new clinic. There, in the gynecological department, the X-ray technician hadn't been told to X-ray my abdomen, but on a hunch, he performed the X-rays and didn't charge me. After the doctor took a look at the images, he said, "Your fever was a result of a tumor in your uterus." It had been six months since my pain had begun, and the tumor was the size of a small watermelon and even had veins of its own. The doctor told me that he would have to operate immediately to remove the tumor along with half of my uterus and one of my fallopian tubes.

Charito asked, "What's a uterus?"

The taco cart idea faded quickly.

In order to scrape together enough cash for the operation, I persuaded a couple of the girls at the bar to offer themselves as masseuses. I promised them that I'd set them up with the best clients. It was a nice gig because I visited the swankiest bars and dropped off some cards, and later I'd set it all up over the phone with those who would pay what I asked for. The tumor bothered me every day, but the fever would calm with a few red pills that my doctor had given me. I followed my gut and installed a phone in the apartment. I became a pimp, but a good pimp, because I didn't rob the girls of their money. I offered three services with different prices: I contracted a room in a hotel, set up the client and girl face to face, and collected the cash. After paying the ladies, there was not much cash left over, but what I earned, I had to use for the cost of the surgery. Some clients asked for me to be included, but I told them I wasn't a masseuse; rather I worked as an agent for the company the girls belonged to. Business got better even when I raised the prices. I kept working at the bar, but only a few times a week, and it was on one of those visits that the miracle of San José came to pass.

Earlier, I had talked with my mother and listened to her advice. She said that San José helped women find good husbands, and she was sure that if I asked him faithfully, he would grant my wish. I went to the basilica of Guadalupe on Revolución Street, bought ten candles, and prayed all afternoon to San José. "Give me a good man who can help me leave this sin," I asked.

About two weeks later, the miracle came to pass. It had been a strange day because I had slept almost all day. Charito was watching television when I woke up with the urge to leave. The fever wouldn't let up, but for some reason I wanted to go to the bar, even though I knew that Sundays were bad for business. I told Charito that I was going to leave her alone for a few hours, but she started to cry inconsolably. "I want to stay with Jechu!" she said in between sobs. To satisfy Charito's request, we went to Jesus's apartment.

"It's just for the night, Jesús."

"And who are you going to scare with that face?" he replied with a chuckle as he greeted Charito with a kiss on her forehead.

"I'm headed to the bar," I said so that Charito wouldn't notice.

"Are you sure?" he said as he touched my forehead. "You have some scary-looking bags under your eyes."

"I know, but I've got a feeling about it," I said as I handed him a few bucks. "I have to go today."

"Okay, we're headed to your apartment in ten."

"Yeah, that'd be better because it's a pigpen in here," I said with a finger pointed at some toolboxes and papers he had shoved into a corner.

I put on a blue denim skirt that I had bought in Rosarito and a gold sequined shirt and attempted to cover up the bags under my eyes. Never had I dared to wear those clothes, but I thought it would help compensate for my sickly face. When I got to the bar, all the tables were empty, but the house band was playing.

I sat in a corner table; Angélica and the rest of the girls sat at the other tables waiting their turn. Their pimps came in and out, pissed off because of the lack of clientele. I ordered a drink and waited. A bit later a big, tall man came in looking serious. He looked around and chose a table. When I saw him, I got goose bumps and started sweating. He sat close to the women's bathroom and waited to be attended to.

Marta, the oldest waitress, approached him and took his order. Angélica ran to mark her territory. Her pimp watched her from the other corner. The music kept playing as I tried to decode why I had shivered when I first saw him come in. I paid attention to the conversation, but I could see that Angélica was the only one talking and he didn't reply more than nodding. Knowing her gestures, I could see what she was scheming. She was going to order him some drinks, she would offer him a service at the hotel, she would sell him some blow, and later she would hand the cash over to her pimp.

Almost half an hour passed and the gentleman was still there, sitting and drinking his drink. I went to the bathroom to try to get my fever down with a splash of water on my face. Upon returning to my table, I noticed that Angélica wasn't there anymore; she had left. He didn't look at me until Marta came over to tell me, "The gentleman says that he wants to invite you over to his table."

"What about Angélica?" I asked. "She's not with him? I don't want to have problemsm so tell him I can't."

"Nom darling, Angélica left. Her pimp took her with him."

"Well, she'll surely come back. I have neither the energy nor the time for problems," I said as I looked at the ground.

I stayed right there waiting for another client. Marta came back with another message, "Darling, the gentleman says that he's not a client of Angélica and that he wants to talk to you, not her." Marta had a drink in her hand. "He ordered you this drink."

Before sitting at his table, I went to the bathroom again. Upon returning, the client started to talk to me without pause. He had grown up in Iran but had arrived in the United States at age twenty-one and was visiting Mexico for business. He understood Spanish, but it was harder for him to speak it. He had mastered English, but I couldn't understand that. Still, though, the tone of his words demonstrated that he was a respectful man. In our first conversation we created an interlanguage; we moved our hands to describe this thing or that and used monosyllables to fill in the blanks. He talked to me about eggplants and pumpkins, which grew in the United States and Mexico. He told me that he had a daughter who lived in San Diego and that his first wife, with whom he had been for more than twenty years, had left him for an old boyfriend. He asked a couple of things about me, but I replied without the main details. We kept moving our hands until he said, "I'm in the hotel next door. Do you want to come?"

"Do you not want to go with the other girl?" I replied as I opened my arms up to signal Angélica's fatness. "I don't want problems," I insisted.

"I don't want her," he said in broken Spanish as he gestured. "I want you."

We were able to enter the hotel despite the fact that the manager, worried about the bar's bad reputation, had given instructions not to let in any women with short skirts. The receptionist took the order: vodka, orange juice, mineral water, and a margarita.

A half hour later, one of the hotel employees came to the room and said, "The manager says that he doesn't want prostitutes here. I'm sorry, but you'll have to leave the hotel." My companion said a few things that I didn't understand, and he kept talking until we hopped in a taxi. Embarrassed, I followed him to another hotel, which was much better than the previous one. At the reception desk we placed the same order and headed to the room. We talked for hours about his life, mine, and the rest of the world. I felt a trust that I had never felt with a man before.

The next morning, I thought I would say good-bye just like I did with any other client, but he invited me to breakfast. I replied that I couldn't because I had to run and get my daughter. To my surprise he wanted to take me to the house and meet Charito.

When we arrived, Charito hung from my neck. Jesús went to his apartment.

"Who is this mister who came with you?" was the first thing Charito said.

"He's a friend," I replied.

"A friend? … And where'd you meet him, Mama?" Charito asked.

"Don't ask so many questions," I quickly said. "I'll explain later, but right now my friend is going to come in and eat breakfast at our house."

"That's fine," she said as if she was giving us permission.

That morning I made toast, fresh orange juice, granola, and fresh fruit. Charito drank her milk and took it upon herself to tell him all about her games and her friends, real and imaginary. We spent almost the whole morning at the breakfast table. I also told him why we had come to Tijuana and how I had started working at the bar; he listened attentively to each detail until he looked at his watch and said that he had to run to a business meeting. He wrote down my phone number and promised to call later. I said good-bye to him as a friend but didn't think I'd see him again.

That night, the phone rang. It was the man. He asked about Charito, he told me what he had done that day, and he got off the phone with *"Mañana, yo llamarte,"* meaning, "Tomorrow, I'll call you." He kept his promise.

A few days later at the same time, I answered the phone. He asked about Charito again and left me with *"No bar, no más bar, yo dinero, yo pago,"* meaning, "No bar, no more bar. I money, I pay." The next day he showed up at the house with his big briefcase and some gifts for Charito. I remembered the prayers to San José and got nervous thinking about my prayer being granted; the man for whom I had asked was in my doorway. His name was Radesh, and he was twenty-one years older than me.

That day, I made pozole and we talked all afternoon about the details of my story; he was more interested than anyone had ever been. Years later, he would confess to me that after listening to me that day, he contemplated my behavior, my beauty, my attentiveness and caring, and who I was overall. He thought, *This woman is from another world.* Before leaving he gave me some money so that I could buy a bed for Charito. I bought not only a bed, but some furniture that made the apartment truly beautiful. It looked like a dollhouse.

∽

Radesh visited us every day for a week, but because life is no fairy tale, he told me that he wasn't alone. He had a nineteen-year-old girlfriend in Rosarito, in an apartment he had rented. I worried at first but later thought that everything would change, that Radesh would realize that I was a good woman and I could give him everything he needed. A few weeks went by like that. They were peaceful days, far from the smoke, liquor, and drugs.

The girl that Radesh had told me about was named Pilar, and she was a dancer at a bar in La Paz in Baja California, where Radesh owned land. The existence of that woman and the pain of my tumor would not let me alone, but my heart was healing. Radesh stayed with us every day, and the shadow that was Pilar appeared to be just that—nothing more than a shadow.

Radesh thought it would be a good idea to move to a different apartment. I told him that wasn't necessary, that I liked how the house was and that I felt comfortable. He replied that he was going to travel to Tijuana more often and that we deserved to be comfortable.

"Look for a bigger place," he told me. I asked him about the girl, and he told me that it was a thing of the past, that he had bought a car for her and her fake brother, who was actually her pimp, and that he had sent them to La Paz so that they could manage some of his land. I started to distrust, to feel that furious heat that something was going wrong. Yet I didn't say anything.

I asked Ricky, a nice old man I had met at the bar, to help me look for a bigger, more comfortable apartment in the Las Palmas area, where he lived; he knew Tijuana like the back of his hand. I also told my sister Susana about the move. Ricky never asked for my services; better yet, we had forged a friendship that lasted a long time. In reality, Ricky visited the bar to kill time. He was interested in neither the women nor the liquor; he could spend all night chatting with whoever would give him the time of day. He had been born in the United States but had immigrated to Mexico in search of "something different," he said. He had been married five times to American women. The first was an alcoholic and adored casinos. The four who followed robbed him of his money and then left with other men. I'll never forget his support, especially the last time at the bar when he sat and talked with me for hours.

When we moved closer to his house, our friendship became even stronger, so much so that we named our pet parrot after him. It seemed entertaining to name him as such, and it didn't bother Ricky. The worst happened one day when the parrot got sick and Susana stayed with him while we were traveling. Upon returning she told me, "Yesterday, Ricky died."

I almost died from the news and said, "I'm going to his house."

Susana grinned and replied, "Ricky the parrot, not your friend."

In every moment of urgency we counted on my friend Ricky's help. Radesh said that this place was temporary because he wanted to arrange my papers so that we could live in the United States; he was going to help me with my divorce and write a letter to hire me in his company. He visited us a few days each week in between his travels. Radesh grew crops in La Paz that you couldn't in California because of the change of seasons, like pumpkins, eggplant, and melons. It was a successful business, but it required much time, money, and sacrifice.

The apartment that we found was on the third floor, and it was spacious and comfortable. Charito was happy with her new bedroom; she started to attend preschool and live a normal life. Radesh bought a car and told me that we would marry soon. *Then it was certainly the miracle* was the first thing I thought. The routine of the bar was exchanged for that of complete dedication to my daughter and the house. I received the help of Paula, the same woman Ricky paid to clean his apartment.

Then suspicious things began to happen. One night, when Radesh was out of town on business, I called his hotel and the receptionist said there was no one there by that name. "Search well—I'm sure he's there," I insisted. I called more than three times, at different times throughout the day, and each time they gave me the same answer. No one was there by that name. The strangest was when Radesh talked to me the next day. I told him that I had called, and he kept saying that he was in that hotel. A few hours later, a receptionist called me to apologize. "It was a mistake, ma'am. Our employees got confused with the system, and the gentleman was indeed at the hotel. We ask you to forgive us for the error."

Radesh had convinced me that Pilar wasn't part of his life, but one call changed everything. I picked up the phone at the same time as him and listened in on the conversation in which the supposed brother of that girl told Radesh that Pilar was in the hospital, gravely ill, because of hemorrhaging. "You're her partner—you have to help her and send us money," he said. I didn't want to hear any more and hung up the phone discreetly. I didn't say anything, but I felt like leaving him and running with Charito to the place we had just left. "How is this possible?" I demanded as soon as he was off the phone. "You have two women; you go to La Paz and sleep with Pilar, and later come here and sleep with me. I want to know what your relationship is with me. What do you think of me? What do you want from me?"

"Do you think I didn't realize that you were listening on the other line?" he said angrily. "If Pilar knew that you listened to other people's conversations ... imagine what she would think of you."

"What's she going to think?" I responded sadly. "I see that what she thinks is more important."

"You're stupid," he replied without looking at me. "You don't know anything, and you'd better shut up or else."

"Or else!" I screamed. "What, you're going to hit me? I'm used to men like you."

"I already told you that I go to La Paz to work, I stay at a hotel, and I don't sleep with her," he said serenely and closed the topic.

After the discussion ended, I left Charito with an elderly woman who lived across the hall—and I disappeared for a month. I went straight to the bar that night, not to work but to run into people I knew and to drink for hours. I ended up sleeping at one of my girlfriends' houses. During the next month, each of those "friends" took turns taking me in and stealing from me. Since I was drunk or high on cocaine most of that time, I didn't notice that someone took my bank card and must have seen me enter the password when I withdrew money. I later found out that someone had withdrawn all the money I had saved up. I didn't understand why my life couldn't be normal; I asked myself what had changed. *Could it be the miracle?*

Radesh spoke with Susana and her husband so that they could put ads in the newspapers. They looked for me with the police all over the place, except in the bar. After being gone for a month, I decided to go back. Upon my entering the apartment, Charito ran to hug me. Radesh cried, "I thought they had killed you."

I never checked to see if Radesh had misled me about Pilar, but I was sure she was a gold digger. Even Ricky had accompanied him to the countryside a few times to keep Radesh company and see the towns where he worked, and had seen that woman. Ricky told me that it wasn't too hard to realize that she was destroying the business.

I tried to tell Radesh what was happening and that he should keep an eye on his money, but he believed that all of my warnings sprang from jealousy. A few months passed, and it was Ricky who warned him. Then Radesh paid attention.

That woman's presence bothered me, and it occurred to me to ask John, my sister Susana's husband, if he would like to work in Radesh's fields in La Paz. John and Radesh accepted the proposition. We had a meeting, and the responsibilities were made clear. John would be in charge of paying the employees and supervising the planting, irrigation, and harvesting. He would send the harvested products to the United States by either truck or airplane, take care of customs procedures, and ensure delivery to Los Angeles. John agreed with the arrangements and left for La Paz without Pilar knowing about it. When he arrived, he introduced himself as a new employee.

"I think you're confused," the girl told him. "There aren't any other employees here except for me. I'm responsible for this field, and more so, I'm Radesh's lover. No one is more important than me," she insisted, her hands on her hips.

"I don't care who you are," John told her with the same soft tone as always. "He sent me here to work. He'll call you later to explain."

"Who do you think you are?" Pilar said as she straightened up her pants.

She leapt on top of John and started to hit him. She was so out of control that my poor brother-in-law couldn't fight her off. I never met her, but he told me that she was a tall woman, muscular, and that judging by her clothes and the ways she moved, she was a lesbian. Radesh had met her at a bar in La Paz, the type he was accustomed to visiting. I couldn't change his past; that was the same way he had met me. But I wanted us to leave that life behind and build a new one.

With time, he realized the type of woman he had been with. Pilar asked him for money to contract with one hundred workers, but she got fifty and didn't even buy the pesticides for the crops. When John was put in charge, he recovered the sales, but the situation was a delicate one; there were debts, and payment to workers was in disorder.

In the midst of the chaos, Radesh decided to contract a lawyer to initiate the divorce documents between Leandro and me. The lawyer went to Leandro's house in Morelia, but he wasn't there. After all, it had been almost five years since we had last spoken. A neighbor told the lawyer that the man he was looking for had sold the house and that the whole neighborhood was pleased as a result. He told him that the neighbors got sick of Leandro's parties and early-morning fiascos. The lawyer then headed to Leandro's mother's house and found him there, explained the situation, and asked for his signature. Leandro refused. The lawyer presented us other ways to secure a divorce, and that's when we asked Ricky and Paula to be witnesses against Leandro's abuse and sickness. They didn't know firsthand, but were familiar with the whole story.

One day, I decided to call Leandro instead of having the lawyer return to Morelia. I was no longer scared of Leandro. I had realized that he was a coward and would provoke only someone who was weaker than him. Since I had Radesh to protect me, I knew that I could be strong and that Leandro wouldn't bother to come after me anyway. I asked him to sign off on the divorce and told him that if he refused, we were going to take other measures. After asking me who I lived with, he demanded recent photos of Charito and an address where he could visit her.

"I can't give you that because we are going to move," I replied. Finally, with the witnesses plus the police report I had made before escaping from Morelia, Leandro had no choice but to sign the papers, and the divorce was finalized.

In the Las Palmas house, we started to see friends and family; I showed off my typical dishes that were Radesh's favorites. On one of these visits, Pillita and my aunt Lancha showed up. It was so exciting to see them after so many years away. We took to the beach and chatted about everything that had happened since the last time we had spoken. Despite the difficulties, I wanted to show everyone the good things in my life and how I had survived the rest. Radesh fit in well, sharing with us, and that was a real treat for me.

Later my mother traveled with Ernestina, Damián, and Esmeralda, who was now a teenager. My older sister, Nataly, still lived in Querétaro. No one knew anything about my father. On the second visit, Esmeralda decided to stay because she was on a school break. She was sixteen years old and in that typical period of teen angst when you don't care about anything and feel like the whole world is weighing on your back. She seemed sad, and hardly ate or talked. While we were all having a good old time, she was lost in her thoughts.

When my mother and my siblings returned to Salamanca and we were alone, I was able to ask her why she was upset. She told me that Ernestina was the favorite and that she barely talked with my mother. She didn't feel like staying in school or thinking about the future.

"Nothing is worth it," she told me. That afternoon it was just the two of us in the apartment. Radesh had crossed over to the United States and Charito was playing with a neighbor's daughter, the same girl with whom she attended piano class. Esmeralda vented her stories and the few memories she had of our dad, which weren't actually memories but what Damián and Susana had told her. I grabbed a liter bottle of whiskey. Esmeralda watched me intently. I went to the kitchen, and when I returned, Esmeralda asked for her own glass.

"Are you nuts? I can't let you drink alcohol."

"Mom lets me drink, but just a little bit," she replied.

"We'll call and ask her then," I proposed.

"Uh, that's okay, don't give me any," she said resignedly as she crossed her arms and leaned back on the couch.

I had gotten used to drinking in the house. I didn't get drunk, but alcohol produced a state of relaxation for which I was grateful. We kept talking for a few minutes. She kept saying she didn't care about anything, nor did she want to remember her father, and she didn't want to be with anyone. She looked lost. I finished my third glass and went to the bathroom. When I got back, the bottle was about two glasses less full, and Esmeralda had a glass. When I tried to take it away, she got irritated. From that moment on I didn't control the conversation or the whiskey.

I told her about Pilar and the supposed relationship she had with Radesh, and I confessed my fear about starting to mess up again. When I went for more ice in the kitchen, I heard a shout. The window was open. I ran to look and saw her lying on the ground. I went downstairs and saw that she was pale white, with blood coming from her nose. A man came over and I asked him to take her to the hospital because I couldn't. I could hardly believe what was happening. I gave him the keys to my car and begged him to take her to the best hospital. Now hysterical, I went back to the apartment. I saw that she had torn the window screen out of the window on the third floor where we had been drinking and talking. I was terrified;

everyone was going to think that I had pushed her. My family saw me as a problematic person because of everything that had happened with Leandro. I couldn't get the image of my sister on the concrete out of my head. I called Ricky on the phone and asked him for help. He went to the hospital and took care of informing my mother.

They never said it, but I felt everyone's rejection and their suspicions that I had pushed her. She was in the hospital for three weeks, recovering from back injuries. It was a miracle that she came out alive from a three-story fall. I didn't want to show up at the hospital. I felt guilty because she had been my responsibility at that moment and I had allowed her to drink alcohol; I even thought that the authorities at the hospital would want to charge me for allowing her to access the whiskey.

In the days after that tragic experience, Damián told me not to feel guilty; Esmeralda had been working through problems and had already attempted to kill herself twice. He had saved her on the first occasion, when she combined an overdose of her prescription sleeping pills with alcohol. On the second occasion, she was with Ernestina and yelled, "I am going to kill myself" before sinking a kitchen knife into her abdomen. It was not a deep wound and, thanks to quick work by Ernestina, Esmeralda was taken to the hospital and recovered.

More than ten years later, on an occasion when all of the sisters were together, Esmeralda told them the truth. She confessed that she had been drinking and had jumped out the window. She even sent a long letter to my aunt Barbara, who had supposedly faulted me for what had happened.

One year after the accident, my mother had the idea of looking for my father. After Esmeralda tried for the third time to commit suicide, and the difficulties that I had gone through, she wanted support as a parent and as a woman and felt that she needed to know if my father was alive. After all, he was still the only man she had been with, and wanted his companionship. She had heard from one of her cousins that my father was in Los Angeles, so I asked for

Radesh's help, and we started to work with a private investigator. The first thing we found out was that my father had lived with the Madrigal family right in the middle of LA. The investigator handed us the address and telephone number.

Radesh wrote a letter that certified that I was an employee at his company and secured papers that would allow me to cross over to California without fear of deportation. It was September 1992, and we were still living in the apartment in the Las Palmas area of Tijuana, but we were checking out some houses in a place called Escondido, a county about half an hour from San Diego. Radesh wanted to get out of Tijuana as soon as possible, saying that in the United States everything was going to be better, that everything was more orderly. He told me so many marvelous things that I imagined entering a city of cotton on top of a cloud. Never had I been outside of Mexico, and the idea of leaving the country terrified me.

On September 5, we left early in the morning for Las Vegas to get married. Charito stayed with Panchita. At first I wanted to get married in a church, as I had always imagined, but that wasn't possible. Those weren't the times to go around planning a wedding. Radesh was busy with work, and things with my family went from bad to worse. After knowing that I wouldn't have the wedding in a church, I didn't care about having a party or guests—I wanted to do it as quickly as possible before either of us changed our minds.

We left from Tijuana by land, which took about five long hours. We headed north, and while I watched the countryside change from yellow to green, I imagined Radesh stopping the car and telling me, "I changed my mind." My stomach turned just thinking about it. We brought some supplies in the truck so we didn't need to stop to eat or use the bathroom. I had told many people that I was going to get married, and I wasn't ready be embarrassed by a change. Life with Radesh had been so much better than everything before that I was scared that this fragile dream could fall apart at any second. Especially now that we were so close to marriage, something that would make the dream concrete, I was anxious for our wedding. I had to arrive in paradise; the United States would be the heaven for which I had waited so long.

The trip was direct, without stops or difficult conversations. When we arrived, I was showered with lights, colors, and shows. Everything—the freeways, the streets—was enormous and organized, orderly. I was ecstatic and impressed by all of the bright lights. Summer was over, but the city was still partying, everyone in the street looking for the best casino, the best shows, and like us, the right place to get married. In Las Vegas, there was everything: open-air chapels or chapels inside hotels, from the simplest to ones with huge ballrooms straight from a storybook. There were limos, colorful pools, and stairways where you could sit like a princess waiting for your prince. If anyone wanted to marry without dedicating even a year to the marriage, this was the place. If you had money, of course. Thousands of American couples and foreigners came every month to look for sacred matrimony; at times they chose a themed wedding or for Elvis himself to preside over the ceremony.

When we arrived at the hotel and entered the room, I couldn't stop registering every decoration detail in my memory. Like a typical tourist, I leaned out the window to see the city lights. We left our bags and went down to ask for a chapel that was close by. A few minutes later we arrived at a little white building with a sign that read CHAPMAN. We liked it because it was small, discreet, and simple. The manager told us that we could return in three hours to celebrate our matrimony but that first we had to buy our license for fifty dollars in an office that was open every day of the year, from morning to midnight. We went to walk around a block of luxurious shop windows. The wardrobe was nothing special. Some mannequins waved to me, but I didn't want to pay them any attention. It wasn't worth it to spend so much money for a couple of minutes. Nor did I want to change clothes, so we had gone to get married and we did it. The official was at the ceremony and so was a paid witness; the official read us the speech and in fifteen minutes we were a married couple.

Afterward, we went to one of the many casinos, playing all night until we won four thousand dollars. Radesh was simply lucky with those things. During the weekend we got to know other hotels and typical places in Las Vegas. I was happy. I had gone toward a destination, and I was doing the right thing and in the right order. On the way back, I was free of the anxiety of the trip to Las Vegas, and the countryside looked even more beautiful.

When we returned to Tijuana, we got some details from the investigator and left to meet the Madrigal family. Charito was eager to meet her grandfather. On the trip, I imagined my father as a new man. I was hoping to see him happy and that he would be happy to see me. I would tell him how much I had missed him and we would be able to get along like a real family. I could never forget his temper, his fury against my mother, the nights that he came home drunk, and his coldness and craziness. But I tried to make my mind create a new story. Maybe Esmeralda could accept him too. I wanted him back.

When we arrived at the address given to us by the private investigator, Mr. Madrigal and his wife received us with kindness. They told us that my father (their cousin) had been with them for a few years but that it had been years ago. They said that he was a good man, but alcohol had been his downfall. While he was living with the Madrigals, he got into lots of trouble. The police were looking for him, and he had even been in prison. He was a fugitive of the law and he owed people money. They told us that his life consisted of shooting pool, going to bars, and dealing drugs. That was him, without a doubt. They also told us that he was living near Sunset Boulevard. "On that street there's a restaurant where he goes to eat," Mr. Madrigal told me. We left for that place immediately and found a local Mexican restaurant, poor and ugly. I went in to ask, and the woman cook told me she knew him.

"Sometimes he comes in for a whole week; later he'll disappear. It's like that all the time," she said. "But the gentleman frequents a bar over there," she said, pointing toward the other end of the street.

"And you don't know where he lives?" I asked.

"I have no idea, but if you want, you should ask at that bar; maybe they can tell you."

We went to the bar. Upon entering, I remembered the day when Damián followed our father to the whorehouse. This place didn't have any hookers, but the smell was similar. The man at the bar was cleaning glasses with a yellowish dishcloth that looked like a rag from the floor. The tables were plastic and whitish and still had cigarette ashes and empty bottles from the night before. The man told us that my father came there every night but lately he hadn't seen him.

"They told me that Don Vincent was sick," he said, scratching his head. "But I'm not sure if that's true or not."

"You don't know where he lives?" I repeated again. That question was like a broken record.

"No."

No one wanted to give us clues about his address; nevertheless we gave a nice tip to the man. On the way out he said to me, "Hey ... Omar knows Don Vincent very well and he comes in at ten. Come at that time and you might get lucky." We decided to wait, as Radesh knew the streets of LA quite well and had some Arab clients close to Sunset Boulevard. They were businessmen who bought products from his fields, some had stores, and others sold to restaurants. During the afternoon, Radesh took advantage and visited them. Later we went to eat and Charito played a little bit in the park. Afterward, we waited two hours inside the truck, until 10:00 p.m.

At night, the bar got even shadier. The loud noise of drunken voices and clashing glasses, the dim light, and the smoke hardly let you see the heads of men. Charito clutched my hand. We approached the bar and asked for Omar, who showed up a few minutes later. He was a dark fellow, with frizzy, messy hair. I explained to him why I was there, and we went out to the street to chat.

"I really need to speak with my father," I said.

"You're really his daughter?" he said as he moved a bit closer. "Yes, you look like the other daughters I know."

"Can you take us to his house?" I asked him impatiently.

"Yes, I can, but it's pretty ugly where Vincent lives," he said as he looked toward Charito. "He's very sick, and he spends the whole day closed up in his room."

"And he lives alone? I thought he lived with family," I confessed.

"I came here from close to Guadalajara," Omar said. "I met your pop here in a bar, and I live with him to help him with the rent. Honestly, it's better if you go and speak to him. I'm shaken up, because sometimes he vomits blood.

Without noticing it, I imagined the place, smell, and humidity where my father was. Omar entered the bar and came out with his jacket in hand. We got in the truck and stopped a few blocks away at a horrible apartment building. Radesh, Charito, and I got out and followed Omar. On the walk, the smell let us know that the puddles contained more than water. The doors to some tiny rooms were open. In one of them I saw a woman seated on an old couch while her purple arm touched a small boy; in another, a naked woman with disheveled hair danced drunkenly for a pair of fat men. I couldn't believe where I was, but I wasn't afraid. Maybe it was my fleeting past in that faraway world, where many times I was close to death. Omar gestured to us with his hands that he should go in first. We lost him in the darkness of the hallway, but he soon returned: "Vincent says that you can come in," he said as he moved to the side. My father was seated on a filthy bed with a spittoon to his side. We looked at each other and didn't move for a moment.

As if he were focusing on an image, he lifted his eyebrows and wrinkled his forehead. "I thought that you were the one who had jumped out the window," he said painfully.

"That was Esmeralda, but she's okay. What happened to you?" I asked him as I fought off tears.

"Alcohol, darling ...," he said as he looked at Charito. "Who's this little lady?"

"This is Charito, your granddaughter. She's six," I said as I dried a tear.

He got up from the bed and went toward the dresser to put on some music by Pedro Infante. Someone knocked at the door, and a tall man came in who spoke to him secretly in a corner. Meanwhile, I went to the bathroom but came right back out because I had interrupted a cockroach party.

"I'm old, baby," he said, picking up where he had left off when the tall man left and closed the door.

"Don't worry. I'm going to come see you again, but promise me that you'll take care of yourself," I said as I grabbed his hand. "Why don't you change things up? It's never too late," I continued as I dried another tear. "This is Radesh, my husband, and he can offer you work. Maybe God brought me here to help you."

"No, daughter. It's my destiny," he replied. "If you want, you can come back to see me, but I won't move from this spot. I'm tired now."

Despite it all, it killed me to see him sick. While he talked nonsense words, I promised myself that I was going to take care of him, that I wasn't going to let him live like that. When we said good-bye, I slipped him some money. Charito watched me, and then looked at her grandfather and told him, "Granddaddy, I want to give you these dollars so that you can buy some food." She hugged him as she gave him four hundred dollars that I had given to her to give to him.

Without any results, we returned to Tijuana. In the car, I couldn't believe the conditions in which the same man who had beaten my mother and been the reason I had to grow up with my grandparents was living. I cried and asked Radesh to go back another day. It was no lie that Radesh could give him work, but my offer was useless for someone who didn't know the meaning of that word. He had been an alcoholic and was violent, but never sick and dirty like in that room. I remembered many things ..., but there was mainly one thing I could never forget. There was one day when I was visiting my mother's house; Damián was small, sitting on a rock at the entrance to the house. That day my father arrived, staggering all over the place, as if he were avoiding holes on the ground while he lowered his zipper. My father moved toward Damián and started to urinate on him. When Damián cried, my father's drunken breath hissed, "Sorry, kiddo, I thought you were a dog."

One month later, on the second visit, he was a little better. Omar had persuaded him to go to the doctor, and he was following through with his treatment. The apartment looked abandoned, but my father was well dressed and sober. We even went to eat. Radesh told him about business, and Charito entertained him with her stories.

"Can I meet your daughters?" I asked him in the middle of lunch.

"Yes, you may, but I can't go in," he said naturally and kept eating.

He had fought a long time ago with María, the mother of his other daughters: Ana, Valeria, Victoria, and Constanza. Later I found out that he had beaten María and that he couldn't put a foot in the house, so he waited for me in the truck with Charito and Radesh.

The place where María lived was just as poor as the building where my father spent his days: overflowing trash cans and gangs on the corners. When I met María, she took me in without any problems, like a family member on a normal visit. She told me about her daughters and her story, which, tearfully, was the same as my mother's. María seemed like a woman three times as closed off as my father. She was of short stature, with straight, long hair with streaks of gray. Her face, pale like the winter, showed a scar that crossed her lips. I felt that this woman desperately wanted to share her story with someone, and who better to listen than me, who knew my father's character well. With clear signs of being tired, she got up and walked down the hallway until she stopped and got on her tippy toes to take a picture off the wall.

"This is around the time when I met your father," she said with a slight smile. The woman in the photo didn't look much like her: without any gray, with bright eyes, and with her little twins.

I left that house with more memories than my own. I had incorporated her story into mine, and had guarded her grief next to that of my mother. With a broken heart, I returned to the car not knowing whether to smack my father or hug him for being so miserable. He never knew how to respect women or be grateful for the effort that my mother and María had put forth for him. Both had fallen in love with the wrong man. Both would cry after his brutal death.

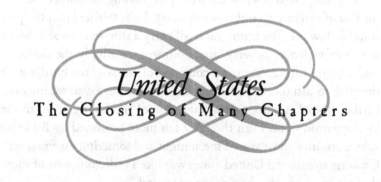

United States
The Closing of Many Chapters

Two months had passed since the wedding and seeing my father. With all of those images and conversations, the day to move to another house arrived. In Tijuana, the route to the United States is called San Isidro. From there, doors were opened to a better future, far from my land and far from what I knew. Tijuana is one of the most-frequented frontier routes in the world; it is a city that has grown rapidly because of emigration by Mexicans, Guatemalans, Ecuadorians, and people from many other countries whose emigrants want the same thing: to triumph. Many of those who don't succeed in crossing the border end up living in Tijuana dedicated to smaller and sometimes degrading jobs; some triumph, others die. It is also the obligatory route for thousands of Mexicans and Americans who pass daily between one city and the next for business.

It is difficult to describe the feeling of crossing the border. Besides the fear of entering an unknown country, I was terrified that the past could follow me. We immigrants all carry a story on our shoulders: stories of violence, poverty, abandonment, or simply the desire to find a better future. My story consisted of crossing the border with the wish to distance myself from the bad memories, to escape even further from Leandro, and to take care of the family given to me by the patron saint. Even though I felt more protected by Radesh's side, Leandro's ghost visited me at night and sometimes seemed real. Crossing over to the United States was like a milestone, one of those that we use to mark a beginning or an end.

That day, we said good-bye to Susana, John, Panchita, and Ricky and began the short trip to Escondido, California, which would last less than an hour. The truck carrying our things had left at dawn. At the border with the United States, I felt like the protagonist in a movie. I review my story. And more than the abandonment, the lies, the life with Leandro, and the beating from the men at the bar, I questioned my ability to feel at ease. I had lost something as a child, and I think that it was the trust and security that my aunt Barbara worked so many times to take away from me. I grew up doubting whether there was anything truthful in her insults of "stupid and ugly." The power of those words remained stored with a lock in my head, and a very few years ago I found out what had caused that nonsense in her mind.

My aunt Barbara adored Hitler and practiced every doctrine of that man. She had arrived at those ideas after one of the trips to DF, where she helped my uncle Fermín and aunt Mary in their pharmacy. There, she had met a Jewish man who was going against his own town and justified each of Hitler's actions. I never assigned very much importance to the photos that she saved in the junk storeroom. There, she kept pictures of that man with the mustache, to which she silently paid her respects every time she entered that storeroom. My aunt collected many books about his life and took it upon herself to brainwash me with racist ideas and speeches; in fact, she is the most racist person I have ever met. She even sent me to high school with the mission of speaking about Hitler's work. Since I never had the courage to tell her no, I had to take the books in my bag to share them with the teacher, but I never showed them, nor did I read them; much less was I interested enough to ask her who that character was.

My aunt was a strange woman. She kept many secrets from her parents, snuck out at night to be with her friends and required me to stay up late to help her sneak in and out without my grandparents knowing. She was accustomed to being alone, and said that everyone else was a miserable person, good for nothing. However, she lost sleep over what everyone said about her or any of our family members. She wanted a perfect man, and although she had a few suitors, she never had a serious relationship. She wanted the best, cleanest and most wealthy man. Any detail that deviated from that ideal man caused her to throw a man out. One of her boyfriends was discarded because he slurped his soup during their first dinner. He was a man with a considerable inheritance. In a photo he sent, I saw everything, including a luxurious bathroom that was meant to convince my aunt of the good life that awaited her. But she remained alone with her cats, kissing them on the nose because she said that they got very cold. She treated them like children; she combed them, at noontime she gave them prime meat in a porcelain dish, and later she laid them down in their bed. I had to take care of the errands and clean up their feces.

But one day, I couldn't stand anymore and killed one of the cats. It was a summer morning, a long time after the night of the fritters, and I was already fourteen years old. It was very hot, and Barbara sent me to buy prime fillet for her yellow cat. I took one hour for the errand, but that was not the problem.

When she unwrapped the package in the kitchen, she saw that there were small pieces of fat that the butcher had failed to cut off.

"Look at this meat! Stupid! I told you I didn't want fat!" As she put the cuts of meat on the floor for the cat, her voice seemed to amplify. "My cat doesn't like fat!" As she complained, she was suddenly screaming.

She reached down on the floor, grabbed the raw meat from the floor, and stuck it in my face, stuffing part of it into my mouth. She stormed out of the kitchen, and I took the raw, filthy meat out of my mouth and threw it in the trash. A minute later, Barbara returned to the kitchen and asked sharply, "Why did you take that meat out of your mouth and throw it in the trash!? You will go back to the butcher and buy a new fillet with your own money! Go!"

I performed the errand, crying the whole way. When I returned home with the superior fillet, Barbara gave her cat the treat and set me to work cleaning the house, which she made me continue until well after midnight.

Two weeks later the cat would cause me problems again. When we bought fresh cow's milk in those days, we had to boil it four times to eliminate the bacteria before we could drink it. That morning, after boiling the milk, I let it cool as I did other chores. When I returned to serve the cooled milk, I saw the cat licking from the pot. The filthy cat that killed and ate rats from the street all the time was licking from the pot of clean, white, pure milk! I grabbed the broom and waved it near the cat to shoo it off the counter. In my rage, I remembered the episode of the fillet and the countless other times that I had caught the mischievous cat contaminating freshly purified cow's milk. I hit the cat a few times and felt more rage, so I continued. All of a sudden, I realized that the cat was dead.

The yellow cat was my aunt's favorite; she said that he brought her luck with money. I left the body in the courtyard of the deserted house where Buki used to live, and I think the vultures eventually picked its bones, because no one ever found the body. In the afternoon, my aunt began to look for the cat in all the rooms and held the hope that he had escaped; she even offered a reward for his retrieval. I barely slept that night, dreaming that I had killed her instead of her cat. I was very agitated by my deed, but had alleviated some of my fury toward Barbara.

As I remembered the cat and other episodes of my life, we crossed the border. I presented my documents, which the official stamped, and we continued on our way. I was fortunate to enter the country with all of my papers in order and not to have the same bad luck as a ton of women who try to enter with false papers, are raped en route, and appear dead in the desert.

We passed through San Isidro, Chula Vista, National City, and San Diego ... all of the places that belonged to Mexico before the Hidalgo Treaty, when Mexico granted several states to the United States in exchange for a price of several million dollars. We preferred Escondido because Radesh had a ranch in Valley Center, thirty minutes from the house, where he grew Mexican squash and various types of herbs used by Arabs, Persians, and Jews to season their dishes.

Paula also came with us to help us for three days; she had children and grandchildren in Tijuana whom she couldn't abandon.

The new house we were renting had three large rooms, two bathrooms, an enormous living room with a chimney, a large garden, and a water fountain in which there were many things except for water. Paula and I cleaned it and put in a few colorful fish. There was also a Jacuzzi in the garden that I think I used only one timem because it was always full of twigs, seeds, and bark pulled off by the wind. It was November 1992, and even though California is not cold, sometimes the winter comes without an invitation.

On the third day at the house, Paula packed her bags as planned. We were commenting about the repairs and decoration when Radesh appeared to take her to Tijuana.

"Do you like this house?" Radesh asked me.

"It's …," I managed to say.

"If you like it, we can buy it," he dared to say. "Charito will be happy about that enormous backyard."

"Let's wait a while to see if we all like it," I replied.

Paula left. Radesh continued with the trips to La Paz, and I dedicated my time to the house.

The first weeks were full of activities and frustrations because of the cultural adjustments. I had to get used to going to the supermarket, finding the correct ingredients, and using the machines that did everything for me. What can I say about the language: the little I had learned in school didn't seem anything like what they spoke in the stores. Shopping … that was my hobby. I wanted to have the house impeccable, which was why I spent the whole day inside as therapy to think about what would become of my life. I convinced myself that learning English was a good task so that I could later find work, but despite all the stimuli, I felt strange, alone, and frightened by the noises and by Leandro's ghost. I couldn't stop remembering the episodes in the bar, and Radesh's supposed lover continued to occupy my mind.

I began to feel like I was in a bubble. Escondido (meaning "hidden" in Spanish) is a place that does justice to its name, and the street where the house was located was even more hidden; it didn't even have traffic. Later on, I would realize that Escondido was a place where many Mexicans, predominantly immigrants, lived. For years, the residents had proposed regulations to reduce the immigrants' rights. There were all kinds of people—hard workers and humble people in search of a chance, but also people with bad habits, without any motivation to advance.

In that place especially, racism was very high; I was not a victim because I left the house very little or never, but I saw uncomfortable situations that affected other people. Besides, it was enough to see how the gringos interacted with Mexicans; even simpler, you could see in the newspaper the denouncements of liberty and security by U.S. citizens.

One day, as I waited in line at the supermarket, the woman a few people in front of me couldn't understand a simple question that the cashier asked her. The cashier became impatient, and kept repeating the question in English with a harsh intonation. The woman was so embarrassed that she decided to abandon her large grocery load and left the supermarket without paying. The cashier turned to her coworker and complained loudly, "I don't know why these people are allowed to live here when they don't even speak English."

On one occasion, a petition was started to deport illegal immigrants. I frequently had to go to the supermarket and clothing stores, and I didn't feel comfortable. In the beginning, I felt like I was being watched and was fearful of everything. I was not prepared, but I was confident that everything would get better and that at some point I would get used to things.

I would sit on the bed, open the window, and spend hours looking at the garden. I already had a routine, even though I was frightened when Radesh was gone. In the neighbor's house, some men had jumped the fence and taken several valuables. That made me more nervous. During those nights of fear, I would cling to Charito so that I wouldn't feel alone. The first winter the rain was violent, and the sounds in the backyard intensified with the presence of small armadillos looking for seeds.

One night, it rained so much that the driveway flooded, and when the water receded, cadavers of cobras and other strange animals remained. The owner of the house was named Patricia, an American woman who always walked around with a flask of alcohol in her purse. She lived nearby and came by the house whenever she felt like it. Whenever she wanted, she would arrive with scissors to pick roses and inspect the state of the garden. After that heavy rain, I told her that we had lost important things. The rain that drained in the garage on the first floor destroyed Radesh's biology books, boxes with important legal documents, and expensive shoes. Patricia remained quiet and said, "Those things happen."

For the third time that year, I went to visit my father in October. He was drunk with a swollen eye; he had gotten into a fistfight with some men at the bar. I wanted to take him to my house, but my mother had said in one of her visits to Tijuana, "Under no circumstances."

"You were the one interested in finding him," I reminded her that day as we drank tea.

"Yes, but I asked you to find out about him, not for you to give him money and rescue him," she replied.

"So … why did you want to know if he was still alive?" I asked her, irony in my voice.

"Because his sisters said that I had ruined his life, and I wanted to show them that he was the same old drunk."

"But Mother …," I said, crossing my arms. "I want to help him."

"Back away," she warned, raising her voice. "If you want, help him, but don't take him to your house."

"My father is old now. What damage can he do?"

"Vincent will never change," my mother said sadly, as though she were remembering some episode of her life. Do you want someone to kill Radesh or kidnap your little girl?" she threatened. "Is that what you want?"

"Don't say those things," I said as I held my face in my hands.

"Then distance yourself, because he is very dangerous."

In any case, my father didn't even want to leave his pigsty.

María, and sometimes her daughter Ana, called the La Paz ranch. Since the beginning of my marriage had been turbulent and I had been mildly disturbed by seeing my father's difficult situation, I did not want any visitors or contacts that would distract me from my goals as a mother, wife, and new immigrant. For that reason, Radesh and I decided not to give María and Ana an indication of our whereabouts, but we did offer to help them. They had corresponded with us a couple of times to charge us the rent for my father's apartment. María was just like my mother; she worried about my father until the end.

But in the early morning of November 7, 1992, Ana's call was for a different reason. Radesh was traveling. I was bothered by the ghosts and noises and was hugging Charito. At two in the morning, I felt like someone had lay down in my bed. It was so real that I can still feel the sensation in my legs. Later, I fell asleep. The next day, Radesh arrived with the news. Ana had informed him of the death of my father. Radesh sat me down in a chair and took my hands. Before he began speaking, I snuggled up to his legs and told him what I had felt that night.

"It's so good that you arrived," I told him. "I was very scared."

"Why?" he asked as he caressed my hair.

"I don't know, but yesterday someone else was here and sat on the bed," I told him, crying. "I am going crazy in this house …"

"That's not it. What happened was …"

Radesh told me the news and gave me details. I had known that at any moment my father's time would come; he had already confessed to me that he didn't want to live, was tired of life and of carrying things on his conscience. His death was a settling of scores, as were many in the bar. A drug dealer from the north of Mexico had gone to recover a thousand dollars my father owed him since a month before, when the dealer had given him a thousand dollars' worth of drugs. They began to argue at a table until both stood up to demonstrate who could yell louder. "Pay me, or I'll kill you," said the dealer.

"Kill me, you bastard—I'm not scared," responded my father, who then went to sit at the bar. The dealer disappeared, but a few minutes later, he gave the order to turn out the lights. He took out his pistol and fired ten times. My father bled out and was dragged to the pavement outside while others cleaned the bar. That tragedy fulfilled my mother's words: *"One day you will die in the street like a dog."*

Radesh, Charito, and I traveled to Los Angeles to take care of the funeral. No one from my family attended, but Maria and several of her relatives were there, as were many of my father's relatives, including the Madrigals. Among the things that María gave me was my father's watch, still with streaks of blood on it. My mother refused to accept it, so it was Damián who eventually kept it.

There were many people who stood over the coffin at the funeral; the majority of them were drunks and prostitutes, including a young woman with a two-year-old boy. The woman was almost twenty years old, and the boy was my father's son. In the midst of the sadness, a man brought out a bottle of wine, distributed glasses to everyone, and said, "We will avenge your death, Vincent ... Cheers!"

Charito was frightened by the war cry and clung to my dress. Later, she timidly approached the coffin and extended her hand to touch her grandfather. My father didn't look old, but rather swollen; yet his handsome face had been preserved. Seeing Charito next to my father's body reminded me of how he looked when he was young and made me see myself as a child for a moment. I wondered how different my life would have been if I had established a relationship with my father when I was Charito's age. That possibility was lost forever.

We left the funeral in the direction for the Mass and the wake in a chapel of the Virgin of Guadalupe; the drunkards and women followed in other cars. It was a long trip during which I thought about the last moments I had talked with him, and I thanked God for having let me find him before his death. In the church, after going up a long stairway, we put his coffin next to some pews near the entrance. There, María was waiting with her twin teenagers and three of my father's four daughters. One of the twins looked sad and had tears on his face. The other didn't show any emotions. He stood still like a statue.

Two weeks after the Mass, my father's body was transported to Ario de Rosales to be buried with his parents, Trina and Vincent. I sent money to my aunt Estela so that they could have a funeral in the town. Some Arienses felt compassion, others lamented having lent my father money, and others simply said, "He deserved it."

My sisters didn't want to accompany my mother, so Damián had to travel with her. He was the one who told us that my mother cried during the whole funeral and didn't stop looking at the man who had hit her so many times. Damián also told us about the scandal that ensued when my aunt Estela yelled at my mother. "You always made my brother suffer!" she said from the other side of the coffin. "You never gave him the attention he needed."

"This is not the time to be yelling," my mother replied, composed, with her handkerchief at her eyes. "Let your brother go in peace."

"Ask him for forgiveness instead of crying," my aunt continued yelling, and almost grabbed my mother's hair. "It was your fault that he became a drunk."

"You know that Vincent made us suffer a great deal—me and my children," my mother said, her eyes drenched in tears. "How do you not see that?"

Finding my father and having to say good-bye soon afterward was a very hard blow. I felt stifled, depressed, and with no one who could understand what I was going through. Despite the mistreatments of my mother, the drunkenness, and the insults, I wanted to rescue him, but I had arrived too late to prevent his death.

The first year in the United States was not what I had imagined. I continued receiving blows that, although they were not physical, were equally painful. Radesh brought my mother to Los Angeles so that she could meet María. My mother had always been inquisitive, and wanted to compare her life with Maria's. They would find out that their lives were eerily similar.

I had informed her that Ana was Maria's oldest daughter, that Valeria had a special personality—she almost killed a teacher at school—that Victoria was very quiet, and that Constanza, the youngest, had died from a stomach illness. I had already commented that they lived off food stamps that María received from a government office. Their house was a small room on the third floor of a building in East Los Angeles. They had only a small kitchen that used an oil stove, and they washed dishes in the bathroom. It was a poor life, full of suffering.

When dropping my mother off at Maria's, Radesh asked what time he could return.

María replied enthusiastically, "At night ... like at ten—that's fine."

They got comfortable at the table and spoke a little about everything, including how they had met my father. María told my mother that she had seen him driving around through the apartments in a red car in which he also slept. One of the times that María went out to shop, my father offered to carry up her grocery bags. That's how they began talking.

"What are you doing around here?" María asked him.

"My wife died," he said desperately. "And I had to come to look for work around here."

"Do you have children?" María asked, concerned.

"Yes, but they remained with my wife's family," he replied with an innocent expression.

Since my father was very attractive, María fell into his game of conquest, especially because her husband had died some years before at the hands of the mafia in Mexico, and she had remained alone with her twins. A few days later María accepted my father into her home, and weeks later she realized that it had been a mistake.

María also told my mother about the year in which Vincent returned to Mexico for a couple of months. That day, he disappeared without saying anything and left a hundred dollars on the table. Later, she found out that my father had escaped from the police and that he had left with his wife. My mother remembered that day perfectly, when my father appeared in Salamanca to persuade her to sell the house and give him a portion of the money. Next to the hundred dollars my father left for María, he had written a fictitious note: "I am going to San Francisco with a friend."

During his absence, María found out the truth about his trip and his wife. When he returned, she confronted him. "You were not a widower!" she cried. "Why did you lie to me?"

"That woman is dead to me!" my father replied. "She was trash!"

Later, he brutally beat María. And he might have killed her if the neighbors had not called the police. Vincent spent seven months in jail because of the battery charge and could no longer get near María or their daughters.

Seeing that both my mother's and Maria's suffering had been caused by my father was good for my mother in some way. Many of my father's relatives had believed that my mother had been the problem in the marriage; on the contrary, my father was the problematic one in the relationships with both of these women.

When I offered to get my father out of that life and he answered, "This is my destiny," I thought that it was a cowardly attitude, but after his death I continued to think about that phrase. I imagined myself in a trip to the past and saw, as in a film, why all of the things in my life happened the way they had. I began to think about why I had put up with everything that had happened. I didn't want that life for myself or for my family, but the things I went through had been unforeseen ... and time passed. It was like a scale loaded on only one side with sadness and violence. If I had made a life with my first man, and he had respected me, maybe I would have changed my destiny. If I had not met Leandro or if I hadn't allowed him to humiliate me, maybe I would have changed my destiny. If my mother hadn't left me with my grandparents, would that have changed my destiny? It was a succession of episodes, each one worse than the last, and gave me no rest. Damián, in his attempt to become a priest, once said, "This is a chain that we must break." The question I never answered was "How do we break it?"

So a brief chapter was closed: the reunion with my father for a couple of months. I believed that I would quickly get over his death, but I felt more and more lonely and lost in my emotions. Without having clarity about what to call them, I continued my life as though everything was the same, but with other ghosts.

The house in Escondido was in good shape and I liked it, but I didn't see any growth in myself and felt like a prisoner. I was willing to change everything just so that someone could tell me what it was that I was feeling. I went to the gym to feel stronger, but neither the machines nor the entertaining dance classes helped me. I fell into a sad silence. Radesh asked me to find someone who could help me clean the house. Since Charito was already seven years old, she started going to school, and while she was at school I took English classes. I hired a woman from Tijuana who traveled on Mondays and left on Fridays. Just like Paula, she had relatives on the other side of the border.

Having more children was not in my plans. I didn't take contraceptive pills, nor did I use any method to take care of myself because I had lost my ovary and other things on my left side when I had the tumor. The possibility of becoming pregnant was remote, as the doctor advised me before operating. I liked the idea of having more children, and thought that maybe that was what was missing. I also thought about Charito, and about giving her a brother to play with and protect, but I didn't fool myself. Even though I had always dreamed about having a family, with everyone gathered around the table, I had accepted the fact that I couldn't have any more children and didn't ask any saint; I just resigned myself to my fate.

But destiny had another surprise in store.

In March 1993 I began to feel strange, with dizziness and nausea. I attributed everything to my state of sadness. But the maladies lasted so long that Radesh took me to a clinic, against my will. I didn't like doctors, and I liked them even less after the last doctor, who had taken out half my uterus. I was scared that the doctor would say something that I didn't want to hear, but the news hit like a thunderbolt on water.

"You are pregnant and I can hear two heartbeats," said the doctor joyfully. Upon hearing the news, I remembered the twins who lived in Ario de Rosales and the Gypsy who had read my hands and predicted that I would have twins. I felt sadness, joy, and fear—a confusion of feelings. I was excited to have more children and glad that I was healthy and free of illicit substances, but I was scared about them being born with some defect because of the drugs or alcohol that I had used in the past. I was also insecure about my capacity to protect them as a mother. Once again, the fear was circular; it had happened with Charito and was happening again seven years later.

Radesh took it as a normal occurrence. He called his family to tell them about having twins, especially his younger sister, who had already had a multiple pregnancy.

The next day, our landlady Patricia appeared on the porch. When I told her that I was expecting twins, she was so happy that she went to look in her car for a bottle to celebrate. I didn't like her visits because she always arrived smelling of wine. She would settle into the house for hours, talking about the world, and would later sleep, drunk, on the armchair. That day, she did the same thing. During the following months, she was more enthused than I was; she visited me every day and brought me clothes and cuddle toys for my babies before they were even born.

We found out from the gardener that Patricia was ill and traumatized because she had never been able to have children. Insisting on her desire to be a mother, she adopted—or rather, she bought a girl from Italian parents.

As the weeks passed, my anxiety about the pregnancy grew. I tried to relax but I was trapped in a mountain of torments. Radesh invited me to eat and we would go to the zoo, but I continued to sit in front of the bedroom window for hours, still, with my eyes fixed on the trees. I wanted to move but couldn't. Nostalgia, the passage of time, and the bitterness at not feeling happy would all trap me.

One of the neighbors—who lived almost right in front of our house—was from Ecuador; she had emigrated many years before from her country, and had three daughters who played with Charito. She was a good person; she offered to take Charito to school and often invited me to her house, but I didn't feel up to having a social life. I was living in a world I didn't know how to share. Only once I invited her to my house, and she told me the story of her father's hard work; they had been poor until her father began to work in the fields. Later, he bought land and transformed it during large farming seasons with which he was able to carry his family ahead. She told me that everything started like that—slowly and hard, but with time everything got better.

My problem was not the money; Radesh still had a few problems with paying the laborers, but was working out the crisis that Pilar had left for him. We were fortunate to have rid ourselves of any involvement with Pilar, yet we were still dealing with the problems she had created. My problem was larger than those of our business; it was something like recognizing that the years had passed and that I had chosen nothing that had happened to me. I was in a safe place, but with a totally different culture from my own and looking for something that not even I knew what to call.

Carrying two boys inside me was not easy. I was thin and barely succeeded in carrying the weight on my two feet. In the fifth month, my feet swelled like balloons, so my only pastime was being in bed. I didn't know that my sickness had a name; I just locked myself in my bedroom for hours, not thinking about anything.

To empty my head, Radesh got an English teacher for me. Marlyn came two times a week, and with a great deal of patience, she taught me how to speak and write in English. She was a woman with deliberate movements, a soft voice, and large, blue eyes. She dressed very elegantly. I still have the photos that we took one day on the porch of the house. We became friends, and hers was the only visit I liked to take. She and her husband had dinners with us; I took the English classes, but she also gave me strength to face the world from my profound sadness and a different culture. We built a great friendship, so much that when I went to the hospital to give birth, she took care of Charito.

Mathew and Kent were born on December 21, 1993. All our lives changed, especially Charito's, who was only eight years old and, without a choice, became my helper. She had to leave aside her dolls and replace them with bags and jars of milk. She was an excellent sister; she was concerned with the babies and didn't complain when she had to travel on long trips, during which her help was fundamental.

Marlyn could not continue teaching me classes; she had a problem in her knee and the doctors wanted to operate. She needed to rest for five months, and besides, she would travel to the other end of the United States to recover close to her family. I was saddened by her trip and missed her angelic smile. After her departure, I dedicated myself completely to taking care of my children and Radesh.

When the boys turned three years old, I received a visit from my friend Teresa, which brought back many memories. She had gotten married after eight years of engagement to Oscar, son of the 1980s president of Ario de Rosales: Gonzalo Escobar. That visit was magical; I conversed with Tere about everything that had happened in my life—almost everything. It was an encounter filled with melancholy brought back by reminiscing about our stories. Tere had also participated in the incredible story of the Ouija board, and had been with me at Grandfather Rafael's funeral. We remembered our adolescence and how our lives separated at one point and took different paths. We spent hours in the garden, enjoying Mexican and Persian dishes. I was filled with joy, except for Oscar's comment, which left a bitter taste in my mouth.

"What are you doing living in such an ugly, abandoned ranch?" he asked, looking around every nook and cranny in the yard.

"It's not ugly," I said nervously, fearing that Radesh had heard the comment. "The thing is that it's different from Mexico. Here it's more deserted … There are no people walking around in the streets, but it's calm."

"Lilia," he said, coming near my face, "there is nothing near here, nothing for a few miles around. You don't seem so happy to me."

"Don't be a spoilsport," Tere said to him. "This place is different, that's all."

"I am happy," I said to Oscar. "The thing is that I am tired … You know how it is … three kids …"

There was some truth in Oscar's words, which I was not prepared to accept. The trees, the earth, the house … everything left a bitter taste. The nature and peacefulness of the place had become saturated with my sadness. It was Tere's and Oscar's only visit.

I ran into Teresa a few years later, but only in a photo. It was in the pages of a book about Ario de Rosales. She was about five years old, wearing a white dress, and looking serious with her big black eyes. She carried a large bouquet of flowers in offering to the Virgin Mary.

I decided to continue with English classes, but at a "college" where thousands of immigrants study English for free. It was a place where I found a piece of Mexico and the world. I went every day for three hours in the morning. I experienced the diversity as I never had before, not just because of the accents but because of the smells, clothing, and customs. But they all were there for the same purpose: to learn this language. In the beginning it was an uphill struggle, but after two weeks, I dedicated myself completely to reviewing my class material, going through my books, and repeating the pronunciations.

Mrs. Watson, the teacher, chose me as her favorite student because I always arrived with the assignments completed and the verbs memorized, and I followed her instructions. When I was able to express some ideas in English, a lightbulb went on in my head. For a moment I understood that everything was mine for the taking; all I had to do was stand up and not let myself be defeated by anguish or sadness.

One morning, I woke up with that conviction and saw things in a different light. With that in mind, I met Eam Chung in my English class. She was an elderly lady from Cambodia who told me about the Vietnam War and how she had survived those times with her family, eating only roots. She liked to sew, so one day she made a pajama set for each of my children.

Another friend was Sagad Ammar, a young woman from Jordan. She brought her children to play with mine while we did exercises in English. She liked to give Charito chocolates. She was younger than me, but we forged a friendship worthy of envy. Together with Lucia, an Ecuadorian with two children, we would go shopping and cook. We would sit and talk until the tiredness took over. Lucia always succumbed to sleep before us; she was a nurse and took shifts at a nearby hospital. It was a time in which I had many activities to entertain me, and I learned things that I would never have had the opportunity to learn had I not crossed over to the United States.

A couple of months before, a woman named Luz from Tijuana had arrived to help me with the house and the children. Luz was very shy but dedicated to her work. In Tijuana she prepared food in a small restaurant, so the able and quick way in which she worked was enviable. She was able to play with the kids, prepare lunch, and clean the kitchen all at the same time, although that wasn't why I had hired her. I wanted her just for my children, and always told her that.

One day, after English class, I came home to a surprise. Luz was sitting in a chair with a frightened face, her hands trembling. She stood up. Before she could say a word, I thought immediately about Leandro, but it was impossible that he could have found me. I touched her arms and asked her to speak.

"Stay calm," she told me. "There was an accident."

"Speak, Luz … What happened?"

"It's that Mathew was playing on the floor"—she turned around to show me where—"and I was watching from the armchair," she continued nervously. "All of a sudden, he lost his balance and fell, hitting his head on the door."

I didn't say anything. I ran to look for Mathew and Luz followed me to the room. I looked at my little one's face and saw that there was a cut on his forehead.

"Don't worry," I said, holding Luz's hands so that she would calm down. "These things happen. You will see that in a few weeks there won't be even a trace of the cut."

"Forgive me, ma'am," she clasped her hands and begged me. "It wasn't my fault; the little boy was …"

"It's okay …," I interrupted. "I already told you that I believe you, and I understand what happened."

"I am going to have to dismiss myself, ma'am," she said, afflicted. "It is a lot of responsibility to take care of children."

I couldn't believe it the next day when I saw that she had packed her bags. I realized that she probably hadn't been paying enough attention to the children and knew that what distracted her was the cleaning and cooking. All I really wanted was for her to take care of the children.

"Don't go, Luz," I said, almost begging. "I don't blame you. All I ask is that you be a bit more careful."

"No, ma'am," she said without looking at me. "I have to go." And she left the house as though she were running from the police.

I think that her husband advised her to leave before I decided to take judicial actions. She must have become frightened, because that kind of case in the United States is serious and is punished; many years later I would prove it myself. Luz's job was to take care of the children, not to work in the house; I had worn myself out telling her that, but she had insisted on tidying up and washing the dishes. Surely because she took care of everything, she hadn't been careful with the kids.

As a consequence of her departure, I was obligated to leave my English classes and return to the bubble.

John, my brother-in-law—after Pilar's lies and stealing—improved the planting, harvest, and entire business. To increase our profits, Radesh began working with Mike, an Arab man who had dedicated his whole life to agriculture. Mike was about sixty years old and a total gentleman. He would come and go from La Paz in his pickup truck, trying to regulate the situation with the field workers. He lasted a short time in that position because one day he stopped to help a young man on the road. The man said he needed a ride up to the entrance to La Paz. He got up on the truck bed, where Mike was carrying boxes with some eggplants. On the passenger's seat Mike had a portfolio with the workers' payments. Mike looked back through the rearview mirror from time to time. The man went along calmly until he suddenly turned around, clenched his fist, and punched through the glass. He took out a knife and began to stab Mike in the back. Mike continued driving, accelerating and fighting to steer the pickup truck. I don't know how much time must have passed, but the young man succeeded in wounding Mike until he lost control of the pickup. The young man was frightened and jumped from the truck bed, but Mike bled out in the front seat and crashed into a tree.

The next day, the event appeared in the newspaper with photos of the truck and details about the young man, who was arrested a few hours later. All of the scenes traumatized me for a long time. I was scared by the thought that the same thing could happen to Radesh. In my dreams, I saw more and more deaths.

Work in the fields was so difficult that Peter, a friend of Radesh—and also his childhood neighbor in the town of Machade in Iran—advised him not to plant in that locale, and also not to wear himself out by being in charge of everything related to the business. Peter bought fruits and vegetables in Mexico and sold them in the United States. He advised Radesh to devote himself to distributing produce in different cities because he would not have to worry about the harvest, the workers, or the weather. But Radesh has always wanted to do everything in his own way, so he ignored the advice.

Before the accident, Mike's brother had also been involved with the business, but as soon as the tragedy occurred, he withdrew from that alliance. Radesh continued planting in Valley Center and La Paz, and also added to his capital by acquiring crops on a farm in San José del Cabo, near Cabo San Lucas, also in Baja California. The trips repeated themselves every week, and sometimes I went along so that I wouldn't have to remain alone with the kids in the bubble of Escondido.

On one of the trips, we went along the whole coast until we reached San José del Cabo. It was a beautiful route. I remember an occasion when we stopped in Santa Rosalía, a small city that looks upon the Gulf of California, which had its period of glory with copper deposits in the middle of the nineteenth century. It is said that Porfirio Diaz—the president at that time—told the French businesses to take all the minerals that they wanted, but in exchange, asked them to build a town of highest quality. The French filled the town with houses, churches, schools, and businesses and brought in all of the development associated with a site rich in mineral deposits. They exploited the land for decades until the mineral ran out. When the businesses left, the place turned into a ghost town with half-

223

European, half-American children. When we passed through that town, I felt as though I were in a different place. It was neither the United States nor Mexico, and the houses had conserved a European style. The most beautiful was the Hotel Francés, where we stopped to eat. I don't remember what I ate, but I do remember that when I stopped by the restroom and returned to the table, the boys had lost their shoes; they were neither on the floor nor in the car. It was a mystery. Nevertheless, the passage through that town was unforgettable.

On that same trip we stayed for a couple of weeks in La Paz. Radesh had made a reservation for a rustic wooden house inside a subdivision. It was enormous with three bathrooms, three bedrooms, and a large pool. The first thing I did was buy knives, pans, and all other things for the house. The second thing I did was clean it, especially the bathroom and kitchen, and make food before attending to my children and the guests. They were mostly Radesh's friends who enjoyed the Mexican dishes I knew how to cook from memory and the Persian dishes which Radesh was teaching me to prepare.

Among the visitors, we hosted a very special couple. The woman was Mexican and a housewife, and her husband was Italian, owner of various farms that he later commercialized in California. They were our neighbors, so we shared many times with them. The Italian was one of those machismo men; he didn't allow his wife to handle money, not even to buy food. He prohibited it, not because they were poor (of course not)—he was the owner of the condominium—but to have control over her and all the things in the marriage. That's what she told me at one of the parties that they organized for the children. I will never forget the strawberry sauce that she herself had prepared. She complained, saying that it was the only thing that she could contribute.

"My husband wants us to use the things we have in the house," she said. On another afternoon, in order to celebrate some of the women's pregnancies, we went to buy gifts. She bought a rattle toy, but when she got to the checkout, she counted out all the money that she had in a small money purse and realized that she had only eight dollars. She looked at me with embarrassment and asked to borrow the two dollars that she needed. We became such good friends that on the day I moved away, I was packing the suitcases and she came in to say good-bye. She stood in front of me and said so naturally, "Can you leave me your knives and the cutting board for meat?"

I couldn't understand how it was possible that her husband wouldn't give her money to buy those things. At that very time I remembered that, at the children's party, she had asked another woman to take care of her daughter's clothes. We exchanged phone numbers and addresses and wrote to each other a couple of times, but the friendship melted away little by little throughout letters.

After Luz left, scared because Mathew had fallen and hit his head, my mother found a young woman from Salamanca to replace her. She knew the woman because she frequently cut her hair. Juana had lost her mother recently and was interested in working in the United States. I sent her money so that she could fly to Tijuana and asked Ricky to help me with the documentation. He got me in contact with a man who gave Juana a false passport. After putting makeup on her so that she would resemble the woman in the passport photo, he succeeded in helping her cross the border. Radesh waited for her in San Isidro and brought her to the house.

Juana was dressed as though she were in a graduation party. I couldn't imagine her walking around in her high heels or getting down on her knees to take care of the children. As soon as I saw her, I offered to let her take a shower while I went to buy some things. I bought comfortable sandals for her, a bathrobe, and other clothes. Both she and I were content with my purchases. I was going to be able to return to my English classes and go to the gym.

After one month, everything was going normally. The young woman wasn't excellent, but I was content with the fact that she took good care of the children.

One afternoon, however, when I returned from the gym, I entered the house and nobody responded to my greeting. Charito was watching television in her room. There weren't any dirty dishes, which was strange because Juana would accumulate them during the whole day. I waited nervously for her, starting at seven in the evening. At ten o'clock she entered with the boys, each of them without T-shirts. She smelled like beer. She had gone to the house of one of her friends, who also took care of children, and they had put on a party in the yard. Mathew and Kent came running to hug me. They looked happy, but their faces were dirty, and they had scratches from twigs on their backs. I looked angrily at the girl. I took the boys, bathed them, gave them soup to stabilize them because they had surely been eating junk all afternoon, and laid them down to sleep. I didn't say anything.

The next day, I woke up as though nothing had happened and asked the girl to go with me to the doctor. I talked with her during the whole trip, and even put on Tigres del Norte music so that she wouldn't forget about her dear neighbor, who frequently put on that music at full volume when the bosses weren't home. I had seen and heard the young woman playing that music because she lived in the house kitty-corner to ours and would go out on her balcony when the music was playing.

After some time we arrived at the border.

"Why are we crossing the border?" she asked when she finished singing.

"It's a surprise … You'll see," I said, smiling.

"But how am I going to get back in later?" she asked as she turned down the volume of the music.

"You won't have to get back in," I said with a serious face. "I'll take you to the bus terminal so that you can get back home."

"Why are you doing this?" she asked, practically jumping out of her seat. "I have money saved at your house."

"Don't worry, I'll have my mother take the money to you," I said as I left her at the bus terminal. "You came looking for a party, not to work. I don't want to see you anymore."

I regret having acted like that, but I felt that I needed to protect my children. I would have done anything for them, and because of my personality, I wasn't going to confront her. Therefore, returning her to her land was the best way I could find to defend myself and, even more important, my family. After taking the irresponsible young woman back to Mexico, I felt proud and justified because I was protecting my family. After all the times in my life that I had allowed injustices to be incurred against me, I had finally taken a stand to remove someone who did not have my family's best interest in mind.

One month after leaving that girl, my sister Mili arrived. What better than to pay someone from my family to take care of my children? She had accepted the offer because she was going through a difficult time in her life. She had something of a vocational crisis because she wanted to be a nun, but I would later find out about her real problem. The old man whom she had married had stayed in Salamanca, in a house that they had succeeded in buying. To bring Mili to the United States, we paid an American man who knew smugglers in Tijuana who could help her cross into the United States through a place on the border without police security. It was a moment full of anxiety when I found out that Mili hadn't arrived on the date they had promised. It was a risky undertaking, but Mili was determined to face it. The man had told me that it would take Mili three days to arrive. When that time passed, I called him on the telephone to ask what had happened. He told me that the border area where they had planned to cross was guarded by police, and they had to travel almost double the distance to find another place to cross. On the third day after that call, I was more insistent. The man repeated the same story to me about the police control on the border, and assured me, "The young woman has already crossed the border ... She will definitely arrive tomorrow afternoon."

It was true. The next day, the man called me to inform me that Mili had arrived, was hungry, and in a few minutes he would leave her at my house. When I saw her, it wasn't hard to imagine where she had been. She was covered in dried mud, with her hair so messy that it seemed like a clown's wig. It was impossible to see what color her clothing was.

"Please go take a shower and leave your clothes in this bag."

"Are you going to throw them away?" said the saintly Samaritan who saved and took care of everything with love.

"Yes, but don't worry. I bought you some clothes," I told her, showing her some bags. Stay for a while under the water so that you can wash off that swamp you are carrying."

We sat down to eat, and she told me she had had to hide herself for several hours under a tree, and later waded through an enormous mud puddle, fought mosquitoes, and walked for miles through weeds. Charito didn't understand what we were discussing, yet she didn't ask questions.

Mili was a beautiful young woman. Her hair shone like a princess's curls, and her skin was perfect, almost like that of a doll. My aunt Barbara never loved her, calling her a "mental retard with a cut ear."

When she was born, the doctor who attended the birth was missing an ear, which is why everyone said that she had been born the same way. Those were nonsenses of the town. Mili always had reasons to suffer, because of my aunt Barbara, my father, or any other person who didn't understand her sensitivity. I still feel chills when I remember one of the first times she suffered. She was five years old, and that day was playing in the plaza in Ario de Rosales. Mili wanted to pass through the grille that protected the hero Victor Rosales's monument; it was a small grille, but the danger was at the tips. Mili followed her impulse but didn't succeed in passing over; she ended up burying one of the iron spikes in her crotch. I ran to get my mother, who was visiting Pillita, and they took Mili to the doctor.

Unfortunately, she never had a normal life. She faced the responsibility of taking care of my siblings while my mother lived in her world of tears. While my mother stayed locked in her room, waiting for the days on which my father wanted her, Mili calmed the younger Esmeralda's and Ernestina's crying, and mediated the fights between the older Damián and Susana. In the midst of the chaos of a house lacking both a mother and a father, Mili would go out to find milk from the neighbors. My mother prayed. That was a time in which my grandfather no longer wanted to help my mother; he was tired of asking her to leave Vincent. Money was never a problem for my grandparents, and it would not have been for my mother either if she had not continued to be bent on rehabilitating my father. For that reason and many others, Mili grew up timid.

Among all of the sisters, she was the most quiet and discreet. She could spend hours staring into the distance; you never knew what she was really thinking. Just like me, she lived far from love, and when she had the chance to find it, she also went wrong. In Salamanca, she studied social work to help the poor; her heart was always as great as her patience. In that very place, she approached the church and began helping the priests in the preparation of Mass and in collaborating on social projects.

Before I left Tijuana, Mili had come to help me there for a few months. During that time, she fell in love with the first man who entered the house. He was the young man who cleaned the carpets; he was very humble, and it seemed that he loved her a great deal. On occasion they would go out, not to eat or dance but to walk around and around the city, and the young man always gave Mili a bag of pistachios. She felt content with that, but the relationship ended one day without notice and we knew no other details. Later Mili returned to Salamanca and met an old man. My mother pressured her to marry him because he was wealthy. Yet after the wedding we all learned that he was addicted to alcohol and drugs and made Mili work in a restaurant in the city; she had to prepare salsa for tacos and distribute it to all the restaurants in the district. Besides sustaining her husband's restaurant, Mili had to slave to take care of her husband, their house, and her mother-in-law. Mili got bored and didn't want to help him anymore. She disappeared for some time and later returned to my mother's house. My mother offered to have her help me for a time in Escondido, to distance herself from the old man and to rest.

Mili was good at cooking and her mothering abilities were unquestionable. I was at peace because my children were in good hands. I paid her to take care of the children, and the poor thing had to send all of her earnings back to her cranky old husband in Mexico.

Radesh didn't like her very much, and looked for any mistake to justify his distrust. He also said that Mili was not normal, and that she was hiding something behind that obedient look. I asked some of my friends from English school to take her out of the house, shake her up a bit, and introduce her to a young man. On three occasions, Mili accepted. The only problems were the three times that Radesh arrived home before her and left the door locked. I don't remember the exact day when Radesh began to sleep on the armchair. He didn't do so because we were fighting, but rather because he preferred to watch television until late and not to wake me. The three times that Mili went out, she had to knock on the door when she got home around 4:30 a.m. The third time, Radesh said to her, "Instead of going out at night, you should be taking care of your husband!" His intention was not to offend her but to say something that would motivate her to stay home and therefore avoid the dangers to which women are prone when they go out unprotected late at night.

It is true that Mili had a few strange behaviors, but given the story of which I was aware, I never wanted to pressure her or blame her for her character. She took pills all day, but I never asked her what they were for. She was sometimes unstable, timid, and compulsive, and we would later find out that she had nonchronic schizophrenia. Radesh insisted that I not trust her too much, and he was right. It wasn't because she was a bad person, but because she was sick. One day, after I arrived home from English class, I proved it.

"I'm leaving," said Mili, desperate as she held her head with her hands and compulsively tugged at her hair.

"What's wrong?" I said, taking her face in my hands and examining her.

"Are they in there?" she said, signaling to the kitchen. "I saw them there."

"Calm down." I grabbed her hands so that she wouldn't squeeze her head so strongly. "Who's in there?" I asked, and began to get scared.

She looked at me for a couple of seconds. "I have to go," she said, and started to cry. "I feel like I am going to kill the children if I stay here ... I need to get help." She ran to the bedroom.

Her words fell like ice down my back. I followed her to the bedroom, and she told me that she saw demons and angels, and that the chairs were floating.

"I need to look for help!" she yelled, and grabbed the bag where she put her clothes. "You need to take me to Susana's house."

Scared, I prepared the kids and we left for Tijuana. There, Mili locked herself in a room and slept for hours. Susana told me that she had seen Mili that way and that it would be better for Mili to return to our mother in Salamanca.

After some time, we found out that the reasons for her hallucinations were not the demons who visited her to punish her for sinning—as she said—but were rather the effects from the schizophrenia that she had hidden since childhood. She returned to Salamanca but after a couple of months, she disappeared. She left a note, which my mother read for me through the telephone.

Don't worry—I am going to be fine. I am going to a better life with God.

During that same telephone call, I told my mother that I was going to have plastic surgery to flatten my stomach because I had been left in bad shape after having the boys.

"I would like to take care of the kids," she offered happily. Radesh agreed.

My mother traveled to Tijuana without a visa. I didn't want to contact the smugglers again, or buy false papers to have her cross; that had been a traumatic experience. She waited for me one day at Susana's house until Radesh arrived from his trip. We got her into the car and told her not to worry; Radesh would speak with the frontier official. When we arrived at the control booth at the border, Radesh explained some things to the official.

"Come aside for an inspection," I heard.

We drove forward and parked. Radesh and my mother got out, and I stayed in the car with the children. A very tall, thin American attended to my mother and Radesh, who made up the story that I was sick and that my mother was going to take care of my children. The official listened while he slowly looked over the documents. I continued waiting in the car and saw how the man flipped through the pages once and again, and looked at my mother.

"Are you Elia?" he asked her. The official came to the car, and looked at the children and at me. I was very nervous and sad, and imagined returning my mother to Tijuana without being able to take her to my house. The official folded the papers and let us pass. It was a miracle.

The next week, Radesh and I returned to Tijuana. To my surprise, the doctor in charge of the plastic surgery had been born in Ario de Rosales. With his stories and childhood anecdotes, he helped calm my nerves. The operation lasted seven hours. When I woke up, I was in a bed next to a white woman who had had an operation on her face … The poor woman was all purple. The next day, Radesh and I stayed in a hotel because we would have to return for a postoperative checkup. Everything was in order, the doctor said.

My mother was waiting eagerly to see my new figure. When I arrived at home, I went to the bedroom and put on a bathrobe, walked to the hall where she was, and opened the bathrobe.

"Surprise!" I yelled. She ran to the kitchen. She wasn't frightened because of my yell, but because of all the bruises I had. She covered her mouth with her hands and said something that continued to ring in my head.

"How can you stand so much pain?"

She stayed with us for a month, until my sisters started asking for her from Salamanca. But the main reason was that she began to have trouble breathing. We would be talking, eating, or doing any other activity, and she would begin to feel suffocated. On the last days, she asked me for tranquilizers. As soon as she returned to Salamanca, she called to tell me that Mili had sent a letter from the convent.

I have changed a great deal and I am at peace. I found what I wanted from life and it makes me happy …

My mother explained to me that Mili was working with some priests who had helped her to manage the schizophrenia and had persuaded her to start treatment. I was happy for her; she had risked her life many times for others, even for me at times when my life with Leandro grew dangerous, and now she deserved to focus on herself.

My mother also confessed to me that she hadn't liked her days at Escondido. She had been happy to be close to her grandchildren, but the place made her feel uncomfortable.

In December 1997 we finally moved to another place. I chose Chula Vista, a city near San Diego, because Radesh traveled twice each week to La Paz, and each time I had to leave him in Tijuana. The properties of Valley Center didn't interest him too much, so he agreed that we should get away from Escondido and move farther south. Since I didn't have anybody to take care of the children and didn't trust anybody to do so, I preferred to travel with them to Tijuana, where Radesh took the airplane to La Paz. Each time he returned, we would be there waiting for him. John was doing a good job, and the business was picking up after the disaster left by Pilar.

There were many reasons for us to move to a new house. It turned out to be stressful to drive on the roads that I still wasn't used to, given the wide lanes where rapid streams of cars entered and left the highway from every direction. Chula Vista was almost half an hour from Tijuana, which made the trip to leave Radesh much shorter. Besides, the house in Escondido was so large that I could never finish cleaning it. But the main reason was that I felt that if I left that house, I could find a change, get out of the bubble and out of my depression. We moved to an apartment on the third floor. The moving truck had to make two trips to bring all of the furniture, and there wasn't enough room to put everything. My sister Susana came the next week to take some furniture to her house.

Mathew and Kent had turned five years old, and Charito was twelve. The three entered a new school and began making friends. I continued with my English classes at a different community college. Everything was going well, and Radesh even got up the courage to ask me to look for a place to set up a Mexican restaurant. I said, "Now I *will* be at peace."

The idea of the restaurant was an old project from my childhood. Grandfather had brought down my business, but he couldn't take away the ability and love I had for cooking. After he destroyed The

Bonfire, I helped Aurora prepare some dishes. Since I spent hours in the kitchen, I could see which spices she put into the pot and how she cut her ingredients. From seeing food so much, I had less of a desire to eat it. On some occasions on which Pillita went to Guanajuato for her medical exams and Aunt Barbara was in DF, I had to serve Grandfather food when he arrived early in the morning. Pillita asked me not to leave him alone. I served Grandfather the food which Aurora had prepared, but I felt just like a cook. The few signs of care from Grandfather were shown through a "thank you"; I felt fortunate with just that.

When I was ten years old, I had to prepare my first breakfast for fifteen people. It was a morning when there was no one else in the house. Grandfather awoke me to tell me that some coffee buyers would be arriving in an hour. I got dressed rapidly and went down to the kitchen excitedly. I made sure the table and chairs were clean, and began to cook. I broke three eggs, spilled a carton of milk, and burned some bread, but the breakfast was ready and impeccable when the men entered the house. I served coffee and attended to them for two hours while they talked of business. They ate everything I put on the table. Grandfather told me that they would want the same breakfast on their next visit.

The idea of setting up a restaurant was on the verge of becoming a reality but was capsized by the dishonesty by Arthur, the owner of the land on which Radesh farmed. Arthur didn't just steal money; he also destroyed the business. After John stopped taking care of the ranch, for reasons I no longer remember, my brother Damián took his place and moved in there. But after some time, he had to return to Guanajuato to dedicate himself to a career in biology. That was when Arthur appeared. Radesh commented to him that the ranch had been left without a manager and the man said, "I know how to manage these lands. Don't worry; I will take care of things." In spite of the fact that Radesh didn't know very much about him—he was just the owner of these lands—he trusted in what he said. After all, the man knew how to plant and was perfectly familiar with how the business worked. Radesh did not need to know more, but he should have found out earlier that Arthur was an alcoholic whose life consisted of bottles and women, on the ranch itself or in some pub. Arthur stole money set aside to purchase pesticides and from the workers' wages. Everything seemed normal during the first months, but later Radesh began to suspect something because the workers were not content with their wages. Radesh asked a friend to spy on Arthur, which is how he found out that the guy put on enormous parties in the house and paid prostitutes and dancers to heat up the spectacle.

The business began to decline and the fall became severe when the United States' whole market suffered in the aftermath of the attack on the Twin Towers. The trip that we had made before, enjoying the landscape and virgin beaches, became headaches and constant arguments. The last trip was the least pleasant of all; besides the affront by Arthur, the price of eggplants, which had always given good business, began to go down. Radesh was desperate; the land was full of produce but there were no workers to harvest it. That day he stayed to think about a solution. I returned with the children to Chula Vista. It was a sad trip; I felt trapped without any way to help my husband. I understood little about numbers, but I felt that any kind of effort would help to support him with the expenses at the house. The problems of debt to the workers and suppliers continued to grow. From one minute to the next, the money invested in the La Paz land had been lost.

To save the land, some of Radesh's relatives put down money. They created a society that permitted us to recover part of what had been lost and to plant again. Radesh took care of managing the sowing season and to put back together that which Arthur had spoiled, but a few months later, the society began to have problems. I don't remember how things happened, but something broke the commercial relationship and Radesh remained alone once again. Peter continued insisting on the business of buying and distributing products within California, but Radesh continued to say that he was going to lift up his business, however possible, just like his father. A few months later, Peter would meet my sister Ernestina and our relationship would become more familiar than financial.

Ernestina had been married a few years before to a man who seemed good at first sight. Later, he turned out to be a sick man who mistreated her, even when she was pregnant. That is why my mother had taken her to Salamanca—so that her son, Rafaelito, could be born in peace. But just like Leandro had pursued me, the sick man continued to pursue Ernestina.

I spoke with Radesh about the situation that Ernestina was going through and asked him to think about another boyfriend, somebody who would treat her better. Radesh remained silent, but when he spoke of Peter, I didn't think twice. He sounded like an ideal candidate. His only vice had been opium, very common in Arabic countries. But Peter became addicted to opium in the United States. His addiction put him into debt and caused his wife to abandon him and take away his two daughters. He also had problems with one of his first businesses. At that time, it was one of Peter's uncles who helped him get out of the crisis, but in exchange he made Peter promise that he would leave opium and put his family back together. His wife never came back, but he again took up his business in Los Angeles.

He stopped smoking opium but became depressed and fell into a problem with alcohol. He began to frequent bars and brothels in Tijuana until he fell in love with Araceli, a dancer who had seven daughters. He took Araceli to his apartment and made her into a princess. He gave her flowers daily and pleased her in every way possible; he even paid for paperwork that enabled her daughters to come to the United States. For those daughters, he rented a house, perhaps in an effort to compensate for what he hadn't done for his own daughters. He made Araceli happy until he found out that, on her trips to Los Angeles, she would sleep with another boyfriend.

The same day that Peter confessed his story to my husband, Radesh told him that he had decided to enter into a deal to buy and sell merchandise. Peter invited Radesh to work for him, but Radesh replied that he would try alone at first, and that he couldn't risk losing it all because he had a family to maintain.

"This is my wife," he said, and showed Peter a picture from his wallet. "And these are our children," he showed another photo.

"Is she Mexican?" Peter asked.

"Yes," responded Radesh and closed his wallet.

"What a beautiful wife you have!" Peter exaggerated. "Does she have sisters?"

"Of course," responded Radesh, remembering the conversation we had had a few days before. "She had a sister who might interest you; her name is Ernestina."

He was so excited about the proposal that he blurted out, "Tell her to introduce me to her sister, and I will take care of you all. I promise you that I will help you with your businesses."

"I will tell Lili to ask her sister, but I can't guarantee anything," he responded to Peter.

Radesh had placed all of his attention on the lands of La Paz, ignoring the sowing season at Valley Center. He abandoned the land at Valley Center and ended the contract with the owner of those properties. He bought a truck and began the business of distributing fruits, vegetables and herbs throughout the south of California. He arrived late, slept in an armchair, and went out again early. Sometimes he would not arrive home for two or three days.

One day we argued because I asked him about a casino receipt I found in his pants pocket. He responded that he had the hope of recovering what he had lost, which was why he went sometimes to the casino to try his luck. From the top, we had fallen to the floor and I got irritated about not being able to work. I could manage with English well enough to find a job but I didn't have the courage to face the world, and Radesh didn't want me to leave the house.

I called Ernestina several times to see if she would accept the invitation to meet Radesh's friend. My mother also agreed on giving it a chance. No one knew Peter but everyone wanted to help lift my sister's spirits. Yet she refused to meet him, saying, "I have suffered too much with my husband to want to get involved with another man."

I don't know how they convinced her, but one morning Ernestina called me to give me the news. Peter was happy to have an chance, and as soon as he could, he took a plane from Guanajuato to Salamanca. In the airport arrival hall Ernestina, along with Damián and Esmeralda acting as body guards, waited for Peter. Ernestina had no trouble recognizing him; at the arranged time a man appeared with a large sign that read, "Soy Peter."

The four went around the city and ended up at a refined restaurant. Esmeralda looked at Peter with distrust, but that was not at all abnormal. She was the youngest but the most rebellious. She said that no one could brainwash her, and that she would never allow a man to mistreat her. She had enough bad examples.

The next rendezvous between Ernestina and Peter was in Tijuana. Ernestina, Jasmín and my mother flew from Salamanca and Peter from Los Angeles. Radesh, the children and I also added to the encounter, as did Susana and her husband. We met in a very popular restaurant in Tijuana named Los Arcos. It was pretty but I was bothered by seeing a pond with vipers at the restaurant entrance. Everyone there looked happy, drinking their margaritas with one hand and smoking cigarettes with the other. I didn't do either. Despite the fact that it was an entertaining meal because we were with our family, I couldn't enjoy it. The music, the noisy conversations, and the laughter started to stifle me. All of a sudden, I had the urge to be back in my house. As for the vipers in the water, I went to the restaurant sometime later with a Colombian friend. On that occasion, we asked the waiter about the cobras in the pond. He said that Mexicans and foreigners bought bottles of that water daily to be taken as an aphrodisiac.

Peter immediately cared for Ernestina, and wanted to please her in every way. One day fifteen of us went to Rosarito. Peter took care of making reservations at the hotel and bringing us gifts; he was happy. Each encounter had to take place in Tijuana because Ernestina didn't have the paperwork to cross over into the United States. Peter was eager to have her see his house and begin to make a life together. As I had many times, I opened my mouth to make a suggestion, which I would later regret. Without thinking, I said, "In Coahuila there are many smugglers that could take her over the border illegally." Peter opened his eyes as though I had solved all of the worries in his life. Since I had worked in that sector, I knew that many smugglers got together in certain bars and on certain corners. I didn't have any contacts but I could take Peter to the place to ask.

Peter didn't doubt one minute, and that same afternoon I went to La Coahuila, a red-light district in Tijuana. After asking around in bars and speaking with various smugglers, Peter made a deal with the one who looked most decent. The man told Peter that the whole process, including papers, would cost him three thousand dollars.

"Done deal," said Peter.

The smuggler asked Ernestina a few things and then said, "Tomorrow at seven on the dot," and gave her a paper with an address.

I returned to Chula Vista uncertain about what would happen the next day. As always, Peter stayed with Ernestina in a hotel. Early in the morning, he took her to the address on the paper. The same man came out to greet Ernestina and asked Peter to return to the United States and wait for his fiancée in San Isidro. Ernestina told us that there were other women in the house waiting for the same outcome. They were given papers and instructions about the proceedings. It was nothing complicated; she didn't have to swim, climb fences, or walk through the desert. She just had to cross the border on foot with the false papers in hand. Next to her, a woman with enormous eyeglasses fixed her hair and put on makeup, trying to imitate the woman who appeared in the photo.

Ernestina left the Coahuila district nervous and took a taxi to the border. Upon crossing, the official looked at the document, looked at Ernestina and looked back at the document. They didn't let Ernestina cross, and put her in an office to make a police statement. When we found out, we all felt guilty; Ernestina had been arrested. Peter stayed in our apartment, smoked about five packs of cigarettes, and cried the entire night. The next day, the police returned Ernestina to Tijuana. She was free, but was punished with not being allowed to return to the United States for the next ninety years.

"If she tries to cross again and we catch her, she will pay in jail," an official interpreted from English to Spanish. Peter, who had not yet obtained U.S. citizenship, decided to wait for a time and complete a more complicated, but effective plan. I didn't open my mouth with any more of my ideas; I already had enough problems in my own house.

Radesh continued his work with the truck. The land of La Paz was a mystery; we had argued so much that I didn't want to ask him again about what had happened. Radesh continued the same; he arrived late, slept in the armchair, and left early. I continued with English classes, trying to make a normal life, taking care of Mathew and Kent and the problems I was beginning to have with Charito. The effects of her adolescence became more and more acute; she didn't like to go to school, share with her family, and especially take care of her brothers. Her friendships became the most important thing, and she was capable of making whatever sacrifice necessary to maintain them. The kind of people who waited for her outside the apartment concerned me. One night, Radesh and I sat down to ask her who her friends were.

"They are good people," she responded.

Radesh was the least calm with Charito's behavior; he insisted that she was hiding something from us. He said that Charito arrived at home with her eyes bloodshot from smoking marijuana, and blamed a girl whom Charito had brought to our house a few times.

I remained silent as I listened to his comments. I rejected the idea that my own daughter could be following in Leandro's footsteps. The girl to whom Radesh was referring was a beautiful and kind young woman. We spoke on more than occasion, and she seemed quite normal.

The problem exploded when Charito turned fifteen. Someone called me from the school to inform me that she was in the hospital in bad condition but was stable. The principal requested that, before going to the hospital, I stop by the school to talk about the incident. When I entered the school office, there were still mounds of sand on the floor. Charito had vomited in the classroom, on the schoolyard and in the principal's very office. The man calmly explained to me that it had to do with a serious situation. According to the first inquiries, Charito had stolen a bottle of alcohol from the supermarket and had drunk it with a male classmate in one of the men's bathrooms. Upon returning to the classroom, she felt ill and collapsed on the floor. As the ambulance was arriving, they tried to revive her but with no success. She had life signs but did not breathe normally until the paramedics connected her to an oxygen tube. I apologized to the principal and went to the hospital.

When I entered the hospital room, I saw Charito pale, connected to various tubes that made her seem in an even more serious state. I cried. I don't know if it was because I saw her defenseless in the bed or because of what the principal told me. I felt to blame, I didn't even think about her punishment, but about my own for allowing this to happen. *Where was I? When did all of this happen?* I asked myself. I dried my tears to listen to the police who were approaching me discretely.

"Are you this girl's mother?" he asked me as he wrote in his notebook.

"She's a good girl," I told him.

"Maybe," said the official. "Just like my daughters. But she almost died. The friend who accompanied her to the bathroom said that your daughter drank almost the entire bottle."

I was embarrassed. I could do nothing other than lower my head and listen to the policeman. That episode made me more anxious, but it would be just the beginning of a long path down the ravine.

For a while Radesh had been confronting Charito about missing work, disappearing from the house for two days at a time, and arriving at home with slurred speech and bloodshot eyes. He wasn't at all surprised by the alcohol episode at school.

The next day, Charito was released from the hospital in the evening. I was so worried about Charito not having recovered that I couldn't bring myself to pick her up from the hospital. My sister Susana and her husband, John, came from Tijuana to pick her up. The next day, I spoke with Charito to find out who had given her the alcohol. She lied, saying that a visitor at the school had arrived with alcohol and shared it with her in the bathroom. Her story somehow didn't match up with the facts.

A tan-skinned female officer showed up at the house to question Charito about the incident. After two hours alone with Charito, the policewoman had been able to get to the bottom of the matter. It turned out that Charito had actually stolen the alcohol from a nearby store and shared it with a classmate in the school bathroom.

Radesh talked with Charito, not to lecture or accuse her but to gently advise her not to put her life in danger with these destructive behaviors. Charito would have to change her ways in order to grow up.

Peter insisted on getting Ernestina across the border, and he succeeded. He sent her up in a small airplane and took her with little Rafaelito to his apartment in Los Angeles, the same place where he had lived with Araceli and Octavia, the woman who cleaned the apartment and cooked the food.

Peter and Ernestina got married in a civil ceremony in Las Vegas, and later in a church in Salamanca. Just like with the dancer, Peter treated Ernestina like a princess; he brought her flowers every day, took her out to eat in different places, said sweet words and covered her in gifts. One day Octavia said to Ernestina, "That gentleman treats you just like he treated Araceli, like a true queen." Ernestina didn't know what to say to her. I identified with her situation because, just like me, she acted like a marionette that everyone wanted to move. She spent the whole day within the apartment watching Rafaelito but not paying attention to him. Sometimes she had to host Peter's daughters, who wouldn't stop talking about the dancer. Octavia bothered Ernestina daily with her comments. "The gentleman always bought those chocolates for Araceli," or "Those flowers were Araceli's favorites," or "Those perfumes are the same ones that …"

Many times, I suggested that she fire that woman, but Ernestina said that she couldn't because Peter loved her like a mother. Besides, after each poisonous sentence, Octavia would ask Ernestina, "But don't say anything to the gentleman ..."

Ernestina became depressed in the darkness of her room; she filled with doubts and, without realizing the effects of Octavia's words, stopped loving Peter, especially when the woman said, "Araceli will never stop being the gentleman's favorite."

Ernestina decided to leave and go to Susana's house, but first she stayed at my house for a week. The two of us cried about our problems and about feeling strange and lost. Ernestina didn't know where she should go, and neither did I. We had husbands, families, and everything we desired, but we didn't feel happy. Ernestina didn't find comfort at Susana's house either. Peter arrived there to persuade her to return to the apartment. Ernestina told him that she was pregnant but asked him not to pressure her; if he wanted, they could continue to meet in Tijuana, but she didn't want to return to the United States.

"I want to go back to my mother's house, at least for some time," she told him. But Ernestina didn't return to Salamanca until a little while before the birth of her daughter. It was a day on which she argued with Susana, took the car, and drove for more than a day until she arrived at my mother's house. Upon arriving, she left Rafaelito with Esmeralda and lay down to rest. At midnight the labor pains began and they had to take her to the emergency room. The little girl was born at seven months and had to be kept in an incubator, where she survived only one month.

Susana felt guilty, and the rest of the family made her feel that way. I spoke with her but was unable to lift her spirits because I was even worse. I didn't understand why so many bad things happened. Why was I unable to leave this permanent state of sadness and help other people? If I resembled Susana in some way, it was in the sensibility with which we confronted problems. Any difficulty we had would turn into a two-headed giant. The same thing happened to Pillita, but the difference was that she faced those things in silence, without bothering anybody. She locked herself in her room and cried. As long as the room was locked and she had the key, no one could bother her. Several times I got close and heard her crying like a little girl. Hours later she would come out with her hair fixed nicely, her face washed and patted with a cream that smelled like vanilla. The only time she let herself go and didn't even make it into the room to lock the door was when Uncle Rodrigo died. After the funeral, no one could remove her from the room until she came out one morning dressed in black, with her hair down and without any perfume.

One dawn in 2001, Radesh woke up from the armchair and left in his truck, heading north. I prepared breakfast for him and packed some fruit for the trip. As part of the daily routine, I woke up Mathew and Kent to take them to school. Charito, without an alternative, also went to school. After dropping off the boys, I went along to the college. I was getting better at English and felt more secure about being able to get a job. At the end of English class, I went to the gym and then picked up the boys. When I entered the apartment, I received a call from Radesh. He was in the hospital because he had felt a sharp pain in his arm, which he didn't take seriously until his head began to shake, too.

"Don't worry, Lili," he said to calm me down. "I am okay."

"You always say that," I said, about to cry. "How can you be okay if you are in the emergency room?"

"I thought it was something less serious, but they say they are going to keep me hospitalized," he said, as though he was there because of a twisted ankle.

"What do you need," I asked him while I grabbed my pocketbook to leave again and signaled with my hands to Mathew and Kent to go out of the apartment.

"Nothing—don't you worry."

"I am coming to you," I said, walking down the stairs. "Tell the doctors that your wife is on the way."

That was the first of a series of medical complications that would change our lives, many of which would bring Radesh close to dying. I felt like the Chinese jugglers with their spinning plates, trying to keep them all from falling. Charito continued having her mysterious friendships, the money was more and more scarce, and the boys didn't understand what was happening. I said, "My head is going to explode," and I kept repeating that same phrase for quite some time.

Radesh stayed in the hospital for a month, so I did the same thing every day: I would wake up early, leave the boys at school, go to English classes, and then go to the gym; that was the only thing that helped me feel better. Then I would pick up the boys at school and we would all go to the hospital. Charito never wanted to go, not one day. No one helped us except for a Pakistani friend who organized a collection to help. The few people we knew became distant.

The debts were still waiting, and the taxes from the La Paz property increased fiftyfold. We became poor and had to seek help through the government. Feeling more shame than when my aunt Barbara used to say that I was ugly in front of my cousins, I had to go to the social security office. I didn't know what I was getting myself into, what I was going to do, or how I would explain my situation in English. When my turn came, I went to the window, looked at the woman across the counter, and remained silent. They called an interpreter who could give me a long list of documents that I had to get together. Luckily, many of the forms in California have translations in Spanish. The next week, I returned with a folder full of receipts, certificates, and stories about our poverty. Many times, I desired to leave and abandon everything. Many papers and interviews later, they granted money and food stamps to last one month. In the next interview, the social worker sat looking at me and began to laugh.

"Is there some paper missing?" I asked, looking again through the folder that I had handed over.

She entered the numbers in the computer again.

"Which paper is missing?" I asked her, sure that she was laughing because I had forgotten something.

"Wait a moment," she said, serious. She stood up from her chair, took some folders, and disappeared through a door.

She returned, sat down, and sighed. "How is it possible that you need money if you received a deposit of six thousand dollars?" she said, showing me the receipt.

"That deposit came from a collection that a family friend did to take care of the hospital costs from when my husband was there for a month."

"Do you have proof of the hospital bill?" she asked with a mocking smile.

At that moment my humiliation, anger, and nerves spilled over. When I had arrived at the office, I wasn't inclined to challenge anyone or even ask for help. But when I realized that the woman was trying to mock me instead of helping me secure benefits for my family, I decided to stop being submissive. I needed to be strong to protect and provide for my family. I left my embarrassment right then and there and said, "I am going to get a lawyer and we will see each other in court. You have no right to treat me this way."

"I will see you in court," she said as she closed my folder. "Next!"

I found a practicing lawyer and the law ruled in our favor. They paid us for the four months that they owed us in money and food stamps. I began to look for work. At least I had succeeded in studying tourism management, even though I was sure that the degree would do me no good. I didn't want a big job, but rather anything to help me meet the household costs.

I went around the neighborhood many times, until one day when I had lost all hope, I found something. It was the last store for which I thought I could get a job; it was one of those commercial stores that sell clothes, furniture, toys, beds, household goods, and so on. That morning I entered the store unexcitedly to ask a cashier how I could apply for a job. "Go to the computer in the corner," she said, pointing. "And leave your information."

I sat down and began to read each of the hundred questions. I was doing that when a tall, blond woman with red lipstick walked up behind me.

"For which department are you applying?" she asked, smiling. Because of her lip color, it was hard not to look at her mouth.

"To any department, even if it's the one that sweeps the floor," I responded.

She laughed at my joke.

"When you finish here at the computer, go down that stairway," she said, pointing to behind the cashiers, "and ask for Cristina."

I finished the hundredth question and went down the stairs. I found Cristina in a small office with large windows. She offered me water, looked for a pencil under a mountain of papers, and wrote my name on a blue piece of paper. She asked me a couple of questions to which I had already responded on the questionnaire in the computer and said, "You are hired. Come next week to sign your contract."

I became pale; I don't know if it was because I had gotten a job where I wanted it least or because the idea of changing my routine gave me vertigo.

Two weeks later, I was settled in as a cashier for four hours a day from Monday to Friday. The training was so brief that I barely learned how to press the buttons on the machine. I have lost count of the number of times I made mistakes. If my number of hours at the store depended on my performance, I owed the management. Managing cash and credit cards turned out to be a mess; I barely looked at the cashier monitor so that I wouldn't see the mistakes. Even then, I made an effort and made it to two months of employment by the time Cristina called me into her office.

"We are going to transfer you to the merchandise assistance department.

"Why? ... I know that it has been hard for me to be a cashier, but I am getting used to it."

"The manager gave me instructions to transfer you," Cristina said, "but don't worry. It will be a good thing for you.

My weekly hour load increased, so I was also able to raise my income. The money from the government ran out, but we continued to receive a number of food stamps.

Radesh got out of the hospital with a serious heart condition and also with a diagnosis of diabetes. We found out that some stores donated their products when the expiration dates were about to pass. When Radesh got better, he went with me to the supermarket and we succeeded in receiving food from there a few times.

We also met a man who offered Radesh a job selling key chains in the street. To my surprise, Radesh was enthusiastic about the idea because it was an independent job; he wouldn't have to explain things to anybody, and he would manage his own work hours.

"You aren't going to earn anything doing that," I told him. "It would be better for you to stay home and take care of yourself." Yet I quickly understood that Radesh felt useless and wanted to help.

During those days my routine was to take the kids to school, go to work, clean the house, and pick up Radesh from the bus stop after his passage through certain neighborhoods. He would go from store to store; some closed the door on him, and others helped him. Stubborn as always, he insisted on walking despite his illnesses.

"You'll have to cut off your foot if you don't go in for a checkup," I warned. But he didn't slow down until he had to go to the hospital again. One of his toes had become infected, and he had to have it amputated. He was frustrated by all of the problems, but he didn't plan to give up. He showed strength and courage facing life's challenges.

The change from a cashier to a merchandise assistant was exhausting, but better, even though I had to stop my English classes. I also changed my name to something shorter and more simple and direct, without losing part of the previous name; that is why I came to call myself Liliana officially. The increase in hours was a gift that the other women at work looked upon with jealousy. Some of them had been working there for years and had never been granted even half the hours that the store assigned to me. I felt lucky but also knew that my privileges were consequences of my own merit. I had proved myself to be more responsible, more available, and more trustworthy than my coworkers. I also had charisma.

I stayed in that position for several months, going from one side of the store to the other getting clothes, taking them to their corresponding places and replacing merchandise on the shelves. Sometimes I didn't have time to eat lunch and was the last employee to leave the store, but I was glad that at the end of the day I could buy food and anything else that was needed at the house.

Elena, a friend from Russia whom I had met at the English school, came to work with me, which made things easier; we would chat at lunchtime and leave the store to catch our breath. She worked to entertain herself, so instead of picking up clothes from the floor, she went to the dressing rooms to nap. She accompanied me at the store for only a brief time because she soon left work to dedicate herself to studying. She acquired a diploma in echo tomography, but we continued as friends for a long time.

When Elena left the store, I asked to be transferred from my department because at the end of the day my feet were swollen, and I had headaches and allergies because of the cotton in the towels. Selling shoes would be my next challenge. But my coworkers surprised me, saying that the shoe department would be impossible for me. Besides, I wouldn't earn money, because the women who sold shoes didn't earn a wage; they earned only commissions. It was true. Anyway, I asked for the transfer and they granted my request. The next week, I began another three days of training. I still couldn't learn how to manage the buttons on the cash register computer, but I had an incomparable gift for sales.

"Be careful of Samantha," said Jerry, a gay man with whom I enjoyed talking. He was humble, friendly, and honest. He said that Samantha robbed the other salespeople's commissions.

"At the first gap in the salesperson's attention, Samantha puts her code in the machine," he said.

I remembered my grandfather and put into practice all of his tricks for attending to clients. I made sure to suggest a product that the customers would be interested in buying and rarely let a client get away without purchasing something. I invested all of my effort and enthusiasm and was successful enough that after a few weeks I had enough commissions to share with Jerry, but he later became ill with hemorrhoids and had to go to the hospital. When Jerry left, Samantha succeeded in taking three days of my commissions, but I filed a complaint about her.

Coming home from work one afternoon, I found Charito outside the apartment with a group of teenagers who didn't leave a good impression on me. Besides their clothes, what caught my attention were their attitudes. They were leaning on the wall and got quiet when they saw me.

We thought that Charito was working in a café but then found out that she had been fired because she didn't show up on time and sometimes didn't show up at all, deciding instead to roam around in the streets with her friends. Our suspicions were confirmed when Mathew and Kent, playing in the room that they shared with Charito, found a bag of marijuana. It was hard to make the next decision, but I realized that at any moment everything could get worse. That very day, I confronted Charito.

"Where have you been?" I asked her angrily as soon as she walked in the door that afternoon.

"Working," she answered, and I could see that her eyes were red.

"That's a lie!" I said, grabbing her arm. "I already know that you were fired for going around with those friends of yours."

"Why won't you leave me alone?" she yelled and jerked her arm to free herself from my grasp.

"Because you are doing whatever you want with your life," I said sadly. "You don't study, you don't work. You don't do anything for yourself. What kind of example are you giving your little brothers?" My brain seemed on the verge of exploding. The giants were defeating me.

"Surely that man is putting ideas in your head," she said, signaling to Radesh.

She went to the bathroom. Radesh didn't say a single word.

I started crying when I realized that everything that I had done for her hadn't mattered. Neither fleeing from Leandro, nor working in the bar had been enough to better her world. I had not been able to change my daughter's destiny, and that hurt me. I was disappointed and angry about what was happening with Charito. But I felt that if all of the things I had done to try to give her a good life had not been good enough, then nothing would work to make her behave like she should. Because of the presence of drugs, my house was acquiring an atmosphere that I didn't like. I had to do what I had to do. I had to take the bad influence out of the house. I put all of Charito's clothes in a trash bag and said, "Go with your friends, far away from here."

She went to her room to look for a few things, grabbed the trash bag with rage, and insulted Radesh before leaving. Charito didn't find anything better than getting into new problems with a friend who had also been kicked out of her house.

Mathew and Kent knew Humberto, the man in charge of maintenance in the condominium; they watched him pass by every day in his golf cart, and they always chatted. He was the very one who showed them the apartment where Charito was living, not because she and her friend had rented the apartment, but because they had forced their way in to stay there every night. Humberto had promised Charito not to tell anybody, especially not the landlord, but he wanted to tell Mathew and Kent because they were worried about their sister. Between the three of them, they made a pact of silence to protect her; they thought that she would be better off there than anywhere else.

She and her friend put together a room in the unoccupied apartment, where they stayed for two weeks. But they were discovered by one of the landlords. We found out when a policeman showed up at our house. I imagined that it had something to do with Charito. The policeman interrogated us for half an hour and ended by saying, "I understand, you two; I also have a girl in the middle of her teenage years … and it isn't easy." We didn't see Charito for several days.

Humberto, the man with the golf cart, had traveled at the age of four with his mother and siblings in a train from Guadalajara to Tijuana. In Tijuana he lived with an aunt and four cousins in a tiny room in a building plagued with drug addicts. In that building, at the age of fifteen, he would receive a scar on his neck while defending one of his sisters from a beating by her boyfriend. Later, when Blanca married a Chicano who took her to the United States, Humberto crossed illegally to live with them. Humberto lived for nearly a year with Blanca until he became a burden when he lost his job. The biggest problem came from the parties to which he invited Blanca's husband, sometimes for the whole weekend. Humberto ended up on the street, living underneath cardboard boxes. He later worked as a salesman in an Argentinian café, a job he had to leave because of back pains.

Humberto had been living at the Chula Vista condominium since 2002. His work consisted of plumbing, painting, and security. He also rented an apartment there. He became good friends with Mathew and Kent, more than I would have liked. I first became worried because Humberto started to come up in the conversations at the dinner table. For instance, one afternoon Kent accused Mathew of having received twenty dollars from Humberto. When I realized that they were constantly talking of Humberto, I got worried and began to find out more about that man. Sometimes I returned early from work to find out what they were doing.

"Is he married? Where does he live?" I asked the boys. They told me that Humberto gathered several children from the condominium and took them to a place where the workers ate lunch. There, he shared food and candy with the children, and they played and spent the afternoon. Humberto this ... Humberto that, they would say. But there was nothing strange going on.

One morning, while I was getting ready for work, the bath got clogged. I called Jorge, one of the other workers in the building, so that he could fix the clog. Jorge arrived with his tools, solved the problem, and left. In the afternoon, the bathroom got clogged again. I asked Mathew to get Jorge again, but he had left earlier. He *did* succeed, however, in finding Humberto, who was riding around in the golf cart, as always. Humberto and Mathew entered the apartment together. I had been resting in the armchair with my legs elevated, after having worked on my feet for more than eight hours straight in the store.

"It's there in the bathroom," I said, pointing to the bathroom door without looking at Humberto.

When he finished the job, he told Mathew, "When something breaks down on your mom, don't tell Jorge. Tell me instead."

A few days later, I called the condominium management to say that the curtain of one of the rooms wouldn't close. When I came home from work, I saw Humberto fixing the curtain while the boys talked with him. As I did every afternoon, I went to the kitchen and prepared something to eat. Every day, I also bought beer, which I hid in my room and drank in the privacy of the bathroom. I liked to sit on the floor, rest my feet, and not think about anything. Radesh never knew it because he continued to sleep in the armchair. That afternoon, while I was preparing tacos, Humberto appeared in the kitchen.

"I have finished, ma'am," he said respectfully.

"Thank you very much," I said to him, in a more friendly way than the previous time. "Do you want a soda?" I asked, and before he could answer, I handed him a glass. "Sit down; I am going to serve you a taco."

The boys sat down with Humberto at the big table in the kitchen. Humberto began talking about his life in such detail that I followed only the first few sentences. A few minutes later, I was already tired of listening to him. *How annoying. Why doesn't he just leave so that I can have a drink?* I thought. He finished his taco and stood up. Before he left the apartment, I asked him why he wore his hair so long, but what I really wanted to ask him was, "Why don't you cut that ugly hair of yours?"

He responded that he wore his hair long to hide a scar on his neck, a consequence of childhood mumps. He later told me that it had been a cut from a blade in the apartment in Tijuana.

From that afternoon on, he hid, waiting for me between the bushes at the time I parked the car. He appeared everywhere, and when he left, he always uttered some stupid question. I told Radesh about Humberto's harassment, but he responded, "Leave him alone. He's just bored."

Charito had taken refuge in the house of one of her friends. Later, she met a young man named Sam, who invited her to live with him in a nearby county. Our relationship improved noticeably, and she began to come over to visit more often, but her destiny would be marked for the rest of her life, just like that of her future child. I didn't pay much attention to her relationship with Sam because, just at that time, I received the news about Pillita.

The doctor had recommended that she live in a warm climate, and much to her dismay, she had to obey those orders when the pain in her bones became intolerable. She had moved to my mother's house in Salamanca. There, they had hired a nurse who ended up taking care of Pillita only for a month and a half. Neither the spiders in her throat nor the bone pain killed her; it was a severe flu that suddenly caused her death.

I couldn't travel to the funeral because my aunt Barbara gave orders for no one to tell me. When I found out, I said good-bye to Pillita in my own way, alone, in a corner crying in silence and reliving the memories of my childhood and adolescence, and the eagerness with which she had said to me the last time, "You have to fight for your happiness." I didn't know how.

Ever since then, my aunt Barbara has lived alone in the house in Ario with her fifteen cats, without a husband and without children. She had a servant who worked there only because she needed to, and who hid away every time my aunt got angry. My mother, who always had hope for her sister, convinced herself one day of my aunt's arrogance, and dedicated a space for her among letters and verses in a notebook.

> *Once was, always will be …*
>
> *How difficult it is for a person to change. It's easier for an eagle to walk. You can change your appearance with surgery, but not your character or your stature. As children, they are a charm and sweetness, faces of angels full of tenderness. One has to have patience during the years of adolescence, which change one's temperament, character, and constitution. The happy, playful child is left behind, caused by a hormonal imbalance that placed his chastity at stake. There is vanity and nerve, changes in one's voice and language. Teenagers are intolerable and don't want anyone to even speak to them. They feel alone and misunderstood; it's because of the*

hereditary genes they carry with them. Through the difficult path of youthfulness, there are bouts of rebellion and restlessness. There is neither calm nor harmony; the profile of one's personality begins to come out clearly. So, someone who is frail will always be frail. Someone who is weak will always be weak. Someone who is mute will always remain silent. Don't you doubt it; a leopard will never lose its spots. Vices may be corrected, but difficult people will afflict you, are stubborn, foolish and obstinate, and make life heavy and hard. It is better to flee from their foolishness.

I remember perfectly the day on which Humberto and I began a relationship. It was January 31, 2004. I left work angry because I had lost a few commissions and my hours had been reduced. Many of my coworkers had been dismissed in the last few years because of the "economic crisis," as the managers explained. I was barely earning enough for food and rent. Radesh continued with weekly relapses, and I thought that I would be left without a husband at any moment.

After work, I went home to see Mathew and Kent, but before that I went to buy my beers, which I drank like water in the bathroom beyond the bedroom. I was in a bad mood; I didn't know whether to cry or yell. My head was spinning and seemed on the verge of exploding. This worried me, because I had begun to have brain convulsions a few years before.

When I came out of the bedroom, I saw Radesh watching television. I came into the doorway and saw the boys playing with a couple of neighbor friends. I returned to the room, walked around a few times, and left again but went directly to the car because I wanted to buy more beer.

Before I got into the car, Humberto appeared in his golf cart; surely he had been spying on me.

"Are you busy?" I asked as though I had been angry with him.

"No. Do you need something?"

"Take me to buy some medication," I told him as if he were my employee.

"Are you feeling all right?" he asked, concerned.

"No. I am sick, which is why I need to go to the pharmacy."

"Do you want to go in my golf cart?" he said with a smile.

"Of course not. Here are my keys; drive my car," I responded with authority.

I gave him directions until we arrived at a place that seemed very little like a pharmacy. I got out and bought a pack of beers, three or four of which we drank on the way back.

"So you weren't sick?" asked Humberto before he took the first sip.

"Yes, I am sick. Perhaps you haven't noticed? This is my medicine," I said, showing him the pack of beers. "Can we continue drinking these in your apartment? I can't in mine ... My husband and children are home."

When I entered his apartment, which was at the other end of the condominium, I was surprised by the dedication with which he had decorated the space. Everything was in harmony; it made me want to stay there for a long while. Since Humberto had a way with words (he spoke with everybody), he made friends with the neighbors, and they all liked him because he solved their problems. Humberto had decorated his house with gifts he received from the tenants when they moved out. We sat down to talk in an armchair that he had received a few days before.

With each successive beer, the conversation seemed more like a fight without an enemy. There are few things that I remember; Humberto told me the other details the next day. The whole night I said that he seemed gay and told him to be very careful. "No one touches my children." I swore to him that I was watching him and was capable of doing whatever was necessary to protect Mathew and Kent. I continued arguing alone for hours until I finished the last can of beer. That was when the fatigue and the drunkenness (I'm not sure which came first) took over.

"May I lie down for a moment?" I said, lifting my chin toward the door of the bedroom that he had shown me hours before.

"Of course—that's not a problem, ma'am. You can sleep there and I will stay here in the armchair."

I slept for a couple of hours, and then I came back to the living room. He was still lying in the armchair.

"Come with me," I think I said, holding out my hand. I took him to the room.

"Take off your clothes! And lie here," I requested.

Early in the morning, I couldn't believe it. I was in his room and didn't remember what had happened. I dressed in silence and walked on tiptoe into the living room. I peeked out of the window, made sure that no one could see me, and walked to my apartment. Those nights repeated themselves many times, but I always returned before the boys awoke. Radesh didn't say anything.

A few months later, the family next door to us moved out, and Humberto decided to move to the newly vacated apartment. At midnight, when everyone was sleeping, we would get together to drink beer, watch movies, and talk. Radesh was a very jealous man, but he didn't oppose the relationship. His health was more and more fragile, and for many years my life had consisted of serving him food, taking him to the hospital, and talking about household matters. He had been sleeping in the armchair in the living room for six years. So permitting my relationship with Humberto was the most honest way that he could find to keep me at his side. He had given up on our sexual life, not because he wanted to but because it was not possible because of his illness. He said, "I understand that you are young, and I cannot prevent you from having someone who loves you as a woman. So you have the right to go out with Humberto."

My mother's opinion was, "Radesh doesn't love you, because no man who loves his wife would allow that."

But that's how I ended up living: with a husband twenty-one years older than me and a lover younger than myself. Humberto became part of our family little by little, and my routine continued the same as before. I went to the store, and in the afternoon I took care of the boys, attended to my husband, talked with Humberto, and drank beer.

Everything was almost the same, with the same difficulties and no changes other than the ones we had already undergone. Charito even visited us with Sam to tell us that she was pregnant. Even though they were not in the best of conditions, I was happy to await my first grandchild. I really liked having Sam around and taking care of him by serving good food, because I knew he was taking good care of Charito.

Everything was better until we received a call from Leandro for the first time since the divorce proceedings fifteen years before. Berta, one of his sisters, had gone to the house in Ario de Rosales to find out our address but was only able to contact Susana. Leandro was dying from an illness of the stomach, just like his father, and his last wish was to meet Charito.

Susana was the one who called that afternoon to give us the news that would darken our happiness. However, the news that Leandro was sick changed my attitude, even though I doubted the situation briefly, remembering that Leandro was an expert in blackmailing. I asked Susana to give my phone number to Berta, who called immediately. It was a brief conversation to tell her, "I am going to speak with my daughter, but she is the one who has to decide if she wants to see her father. She will tell you her decision."

Charito, without any influence other than her memories, called Berta one day to tell her that she didn't want to see her father, but did want to hear him on the telephone. Charito didn't understand the words her father said to her; Leandro was already dying. He was living the last hours of his sad, miserable life. The next time Charito called, Berta answered, "Your father already died of sadness because you didn't want to see him."

I never asked my daughter why she really hadn't wanted to see him. I respected her decision and remained in silence. In that way, one part of our history with that man remained buried, although the memories would never disappear.

A few months later, on a day in March 2005, I arrived at home and saw Radesh sitting in the armchair, asleep. I sat by his side and rested with him. The routine at the store was exhausting; if I didn't sell, I didn't make commissions. I spent the whole day on my feet, attending clients who often spent hours choosing a product that they later decided not to buy. My feet would swell just like they had when I was pregnant with the boys. I lay there resting until Radesh opened his eyes and I proposed a bath in the bathtub.

"I can't, Lili. I can't move," he said, startled.

"Yes, you can—make an effort."

Radesh stood up slowly, leaned on my shoulder, and began to walk slowly. When we arrived in the bathroom, he was able to get into the tub. Everything was normal until he began to convulse. I called an ambulance and ran to get Humberto. A few minutes later, they took him to the hospital, where he would stay for another month. His heart was so weak that he couldn't take even the slightest exertion. He blamed Humberto for having poisoned him with a few tacos the night before.

"Why would you think that?" I asked him. I began to laugh because Radesh seemed like a child for proposing such a ridiculous idea. He was so agitated that he would get irritated with Humberto, and they would both behave like children.

Radesh was really in bad shape. His heart could stop beating at any moment, according to the doctors. I requested a leave from the store to take care of Radesh for a few days, but I never went back to work. I dedicated my time to visiting him, attending to his sister who was visiting, and taking care of her boys, who were almost thirteen years old.

During the same month, Humberto lost his job because he had failed to attend to an apartment so he could accompany me to the hospital. In truth, that was the drop that tipped the bucket, because the landlady had told him months before, "If you leave a job unfinished again, I am going to fire you." That was that; he had one month to leave the apartment.

The day that Radesh was released from the hospital, Humberto went along with me to pick him up. On the way home, without knowing exactly how Radesh would take the question, I asked, "Is it okay if Humberto stays a while with us?" I clenched my teeth nervously. "He doesn't have a place to live, and he also doesn't have a job." I clenched my teeth again.

I felt in debt to Humberto for having helped me and listened to me.

"Yes, that's fine," Radesh answered as if I had asked him if he wanted tea.

He was even enthused with the idea.

A few weeks later, Humberto sold a few pieces of furniture and gave away others. He brought his orthopedic bed to our house and put it in the boys' room. He slept on the floor, I slept in my room, and Radesh slept on the armchair, as always. He liked to sleep there, maybe to take care of us, or maybe not to feel so alone in his bedroom. After each stay in the hospital, he got better. He recovered so easily that we were all surprised. One night, the least expected happened. Radesh went into the boys' room, woke up Humberto, and said, "You want to sleep with Lili, right?"

Humberto looked at him, unable to say anything.

"Go! Go! Hot little bed," Radesh said, pointing to my bedroom door.

Humberto continued staring at him without saying anything but thought, *Who gets free bread and doesn't eat it?* and went to my bed.

Humberto became our support in raising Mathew and Kent. In fact, he brought moments of joy to our house. Radesh also included him in our vacations. In each trip, he made sure to leave us a room, and got another for him and the boys. I didn't feel good about those decisions, but he insisted on leaving us alone. He said that he did so because he loved me, and that if I was happy and satisfied, then he was happy too. Yet I was somewhat perplexed by Radesh's contentment with the situation. It was an illusion for him to think that all I needed from a relationship was intimacy.

Sometimes I felt affection toward Humberto and was thankful for everything that he did for us. Yet sometimes I hated him for having interfered in our household, especially when problems with the boys became more and more evident. It became more and more difficult to control them, especially when they had to obey not only me, but Radesh and Humberto as well. Their father wanted to continue treating them like children; he kept an eye on them at school and was alert to what they did in the neighborhood, and they reacted very badly to his discipline. Humberto spoiled them and sometimes even went along with their mischief. The very different ways in which they were raised were contradictory. Radesh didn't want them to grow up too quickly, whereas Humberto encouraged them to learn to drive a car at only thirteen years old.

Things got worse and worse among us. I saw Humberto as an outsider, and I felt distant as well. In front of others, we were a family, yet even at home I could barely stand to get close. I felt full of shame that Radesh would permit something like that, and that I had accepted it.

With the passage of time, Humberto felt more authority over Mathew and Kent, and conflicts began. When Radesh ran out of patience to deal with them, he said, "Take care of this; I cannot."

So Humberto decided and applied his rules in the house. When Radesh saw that he was losing all of his authority, he would back down. "Don't get involved. Better yet, leave them to me," Humberto would say. The boys grew up confused, and even with a little bit of anger, I think, against me and Radesh for having let this person intervene in our home. Everyone had an opinion about this experiment, but we had our reasons.

Despite Humberto's presents and the flashes of joy that I felt with him, my depression continued to progress. Knowing that I lived with my husband and my boyfriend was something crazy people did, and I continued to feel guilt. The addiction to beer made Radesh send Humberto and me to meeting of Alcoholics Anonymous. After that experience followed psychological therapy for me, which would last more than five years. I also had to go to the psychiatrist to control my brain convulsions and bodily symptoms of stress with medication. I trembled, I wanted to run away, but I was walking in the clouds with the calming drugs and antidepressants, which I sometimes mixed with beer.

I couldn't go back to work anymore because I could have a nervous breakdown at any time. Radesh got money from his siblings living in the United States to support us. One of his brothers was a pediatric surgeon, and the other was a physicist who worked with atomic bombs. We were lucky enough to help us during that difficult time.

Charito had already given birth to my grandson, but the baby spent more time with us. Humberto and I would take care of him while Charito went out with her friends and fixed her issues with drugs. Besides, she had problems with Sam; she had even slept in her car for a couple of days because the young man had kicked her out of the house. She came and went, and I didn't know how to help her. I couldn't help her, or else I would lose my head.

Sam, who also had a past with drugs, lived with his seven-year-old son and his brother. On the outside, it seemed like he wanted to change his life. I never found out details about that relationship, but I knew something was wrong and that my grandson was caught in the middle; the baby came to know tragedy in his first year of existence.

❧

One Thursday I called Charito to ask her about the baby, because he had seemed restless days before.

"He is very strange, Mom," she said. "He is behaving differently; he is screaming and gets distressed," she said as I hear my grandson scream through the telephone.

Charito promised to take him to the doctor the next morning. I called her all day to see how the visit had gone, but her cell phone was turned off. I felt that something was going wrong. Around ten in the evening, she answered, and her tone of voice was an answer to my worry.

"Did something happen to the baby?" I said in a hurry. "Tell me, please. Say something."

"There is a problem," Charito said without changing the rhythm of her speech.

"What happened to my grandson?" I said as the hand holding the phone to my ear trembled.

"My son is okay, Mom," she said, waking from her lethargy. "But Sam committed suicide."

We had barely finished talking when I ran to take the calming drugs. Upon hearing the news, I reacted in the worst way possible; I began to shake and cry, and was restless without knowing what to do. That night and on subsequent days I couldn't sleep. I woke up because of nightmares and asked myself what had happened in that house.

Charito didn't want to talk. We called Sam's cell phone; his cousin answered and told us the details. On the day he committed suicide, Sam's younger brother was in his room and Sam was in the kitchen preparing breakfast for my grandson and his other son. It was almost seven in the morning, and Charito was just arriving home with alcohol on her breath. She began to argue with Sam, who tried to control her. He didn't want to end the argument as some weeks before with a glass broken over his head (in the hospital they preferred to say that it had been an accident). When they ended the argument, Sam told her that he had tried, that he couldn't live that way, and that he would commit suicide.

"I don't think you have the balls," said Charito.

A few minutes later the house was calm and no one heard a sound. The boys remained in the kitchen. Charito went to the bathroom on the second floor and came back down. She saw the door leading to the parking open and walked toward it slowly until she saw Sam hanging from a rope. She went to the kitchen for a knife, cut down the rope, and tried to revive Sam, but it was too late. We never spoke with Charito about that day; instead, we dedicated ourselves to taking care of the little one and making a home for him. Charito also returned to our home.

Life with Humberto had its days numbered. Between us, one plus one didn't add up to two. He had his own tormented past and I was not good company; neither of us was good for the other. The boys were getting bigger and bigger and were aware of the disorder that we had in the house. The medication took away my desire to do anything, and I stopped seeing Humberto as my companion. The saddest phase of our time together began; we made each other suffer with reproaches and blame. Humberto had tried to kill himself even though I wasn't doing anything bad.

He was disappointed because although he proposed that I divorce Radesh to marry him, I had not jumped at the idea. So one day when I left the house to go grocery shopping, he took pain pills that had been prescribed for a spinal disc injury from one of his past jobs, ground them up, and took them all. When I returned from the grocery store, I saw him passed out with a letter nearby and took him to the hospital to have his stomach pumped. His letter said that he had no more love for life and that his decision to kill himself could not be attributed to or blamed on anyone, and was solely his decision.

I continued to drink beer, and one day I threatened to take my life with a knife. Humberto tried to control me while the ambulance and the police arrived. I felt trapped in something for which there were no words to describe. I remembered my father, my aunt Barbara, the doctor who tricked me, Leandro, and the men who beat me in Tijuana, and I felt more fear than I had in any one of those episodes. I lost control and began to say things that didn't make sense, until a policeman came into the room.

"Do you know anything about psychology?" I asked the policeman, after finishing my eighth cigarette in less than a half hour.

"Yes," responded the policeman. "I studied a bit of psychology."

He grabbed a chair and sat down. Humberto stood there listening. I told the policeman about all the things that had happened in Ario de Rosales, Morelia, and Tijuana. I told him of my childhood traumas and the fear I had about life. Humberto sometimes commented. The policeman listened to me with so much attention that we sat talking calmly for almost an hour. But suddenly Radesh got up from his chair, came into the room, and began to demand that Humberto leave because that conversation was none of his business.

"Who is he?" asked the policeman.

"I am Liliana's husband," responded Radesh.

"What?" the policeman said. "It isn't this man sitting here?" He gestured toward Humberto.

"No, that is her boyfriend," answered Radesh, furrowing his eyebrow.

"Go sit down," said the policeman. "This is a delicate subject."

"It's true," said Humberto to the policeman. "This man is her husband."

The policeman sat in silence.

He thought that we were tricking him; he couldn't comprehend why a husband would allow his wife to have a boyfriend within his own house. The policeman asked me to stay calm and, without another word, left. My mother was another person who thought that Radesh was crazy. But these decisions must be understood within their context and considering my husband's reasoning.

"Radesh loves me in his own way," I answered my mother. As with many things in my life, Humberto's presence was a consequence of decisions that others made for me. What was interesting at first turned into a veritable nightmare. We argued several times and I wanted to throw him out, but I also didn't have the courage to leave him in the street.

My second attempt at suicide was with pills. That night, I was in my bedroom, thinking about what had happened with my grandson's father and Leandro's death. I remembered my father's words when he said, "This is my destiny." I convinced myself that I was condemned to suffer and that I would never find peace or become a safe and happy woman. I thought that dying was the only way to give my children peace, to let them grow up alone without a mother who was so depressed, disoriented, and almost dead as I was. I looked at myself in the mirror, and even my eyes seemed to have abandoned me. I smoked almost two packs of cigarettes and drank two beers with a jar of pills. I lay down in my bed, imagining each of the people who had once loved me saying their good-byes. I felt myself rise slowly until someone shook me. It was Humberto trying to wake me while he yelled for Radesh to call an ambulance.

In the hospital I woke up to the sounds of machines and an intense stomachache.

"Don't tell them that you took tranquilizers," Humberto whispered to me in secret. "Tell them that you drank beer and that you mixed it with some pills for your stomach."

"Why?" I uttered slowly.

"Because they are going to put you into a mental hospital; that's what your husband wants."

"You are saying nonsense," I told him.

Radesh didn't want to lock me up in a mental hospital; rather, he was thinking about checking me into a rehabilitation clinic to cure me of my alcoholism and to clear my head. Yet nothing materialized. I returned home after three days. I wasn't sent to any rehabilitation clinic because I promised to make an effort to give up alcohol and continue with my psychological therapy and appointments with the psychiatrist.

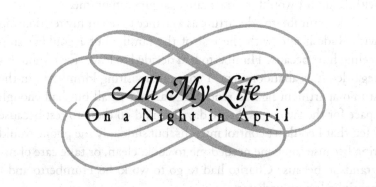

All My Life
On a Night in April

In 2009 Humberto left our house. The situation had turned from serious to critical. None of us could change our character, and we all ended up altered, including the boys and Charito. The yelling was like a knife in my head; each fight brought back the convulsions that didn't help to bring me out of my depression, even though the psychologist had made her diagnosis. "You have chronic depression," she said.

I had been seeing her for four years, but nothing had changed my attitude. I would switch from peace to sobbing for no reason. Sometimes I spent days without any symptoms of anguish; I remained serene and for some moments, I even felt joy. The presence of my grandson was a motivation for me to feel better, but other days I didn't want to get up in the morning, and upon any disagreement with Radesh I would see the giants ganging up on me.

I saw Humberto's departure as a chance to repair my relationship with Radesh and with the rest of the family, but I couldn't stop feeling hurt because Humberto had decided to leave. Even though I regarded it as abandonment, I continued visiting Humberto in the studio apartment he had rented. It was very small but had enough space for the two of us. Some days I would go there to rest because I felt that I couldn't control my sons, but suddenly the phone would ring because someone needed me to cook, clean, or take care of my grandson because Charito had to go to work. So Humberto and I continued to grow distant.

On a night in August, I locked myself in my room to think. Charito was visiting and was in the living room with Radesh and the boys, watching a television show; I could hear them all laughing and talking at the same time. I felt stressed and exhausted by the headaches. I felt like something was squeezing my brain and left it throbbing for several minutes. I was nervous, walked around and around my bed, went to the bathroom, and looked at the tranquilizers with the impulse to take them all at one time. I asked myself when I would be able to find meaning in my life, and when the ghosts that had followed me since my childhood would finally go away. I didn't live in Tijuana, Leandro no longer existed, I was in my own house, and was safe from everything except myself and my vices. My sons were about sixteen years old, and Charito was twenty-three. I couldn't understand why I wasn't content.

Suddenly, I had the impulse to go somewhere that would make me happy and give me joy, like the people in the streets and the restaurants; I wanted to be one of them. That night I changed out of my dark clothing and put on an evening dress. I put on makeup and came out of the room. I couldn't stop trembling, but I was anxious to exchange my enclosure for a place of enjoyment. When I came into the living room, everyone looked at me from head to foot.

"Where are you going all dressed up, Mom?" asked Charito.

"I'm going out for a moment," I told everyone, hastening my step so that they couldn't stop me. "I need to go out."

"But where are you going?" Radesh asked.

"I'll be back soon. Don't worry."

When I left the apartment, I drove the car to a place called El Caribe, a Mexican bar with a dance floor. It was nine at night and the locale was in full party mode. I sat at the bar and asked for a glass of white wine that helped me silence all the voices rolling around in my head. Many men came around asking me to dance, but I said no to all of them. I ordered another drink and called Charito so that we could share the moment. She, without any desire other than to rescue me from that place, arrived half an hour later.

Even though she didn't want to drink, I ordered a beer for her and sat watching how the couples moved to the rhythm of the *rancheras*, Mexican folk songs. I celebrated others' happiness while my head continued to spin. Charito seemed bored waiting for the moment in which I would get tired of the ridiculous idea of watching everyone else enjoy their evening. Two hours later, we left. I had drunk four glasses of wine, but I was calm and free of ghosts and voices.

On the way to the parking lot, a blond thirty-year-old man approached us. He said that he had seen us inside the bar and wanted to invite us to a party. Charito turned down the invitation and took my hand. We continued walking, but the young man followed behind us and insisted on his proposal.

"We don't want to go," said Charito in English.

"Yes! Of course we do!" I responded to the young man while I tried not to get dizzy. "Go, then, Charito," and I made a gesture to my daughter. "This young man seems nice, and I don't want to miss out on the party."

After many attempts to convince me, Charito got into her car and left. Later on, she told me that the young man and I walked to a white pickup truck that looked luxurious. What *I* remember, however, is that we got into my car and went to a place called Bonita. The man jumped the front gate of a house and then opened it. Inside, a man who spoke German greeted us. I asked what his name was, and he responded, "Call me Pablo."

The memories I have from that night are very vague. Two women were sitting in the living room with glasses in their hands … Pablo served me a glass, but I don't remember what it was, nor do I remember other scenes from that house. Later, I woke up in a motel, almost naked and with a video camera in front of me. I couldn't move; I woke up several times, saw that my head was still spinning, and would go back to sleep. I was so delirious that I could barely sit up, let alone escape. I was kept there for six days without eating. No one at my house worried because a man called, saying that he was a friend of mine and was taking care of me because I didn't feel well.

On the fifth day of my captivity, Humberto was working nearby because he had found a job near the hotel where I was locked up. When he crossed the street, he saw my car parked in the street, approached it, looked through the window, and saw my lighter in the unmistakable cigarette stash. He called my cell phone seven timesm but I never heard his call. With his suspicions aroused, he entered the hotel and asked to speak with me, saying that he was my son. He found the room I—without knowing—had paid for with my credit card. He returned with the police, but didn't succeed in rescuing me because Pablo created a story for the police, claiming that Humberto was persecuting him because he was jealous. The two even starting throwing punches until the police were able to separate them.

Humberto called the house to tell Radesh that I had been kidnapped by a man.

Mathew answered the phone. "Don't be possessive," he responded. "My mother is with a friend, and she is just fine."

"It's a lie, Mathew," said Humberto. "They have her hidden away, and I can't do a thing. I am not a family member, so you have to go to the police."

While Humberto tried to convince my family, the men injected me with alcohol and kept me unconscious. But one morning I woke up without restraints; I was alone and almost conscious. I called the reception desk, desperate to get a bottle of anything. A little while later, the cleaning lady came in.

"Are you doing all right, ma'am? You look very pale," she said, touching my cheeks. "Can I help you with anything?"

"I need wine, or tequila or whatever you can get …"

"Calm down, ma'am," she said while she covered my pale legs with a sheet. "You can't drink any more alcohol … Look at yourself."

The woman had returned to the front desk when Humberto came in again with a pair of policemen. They asked which room I was in, and the lady said, "I just saw that woman. She is so sick that she can barely move."

The police officers informed Radesh and took me to the hospital. They immediately initiated an investigation into the kidnapping; they showed me photos of several delinquents, one of whom I was able to recognize. Humberto recognized another one, the same one with whom he was involved in a fistfight when he first tried to save me. Both men had an arrest warrant for remaining in a gang that kidnapped women to rape them and steal their credit cards. The doctors didn't find drugs in my system, but did find an extremely high level of alcohol. My car was found a few days later, with various cables and a video camera inside.

After that unfortunate episode, Humberto returned to the house and we even all went together on a vacation to the Bahamas. Those days were spent in an incredible, heavenly place full of hotels, casinos, and clubs. The boys enjoyed the beach with Humberto while Radesh visited the casinos with the same luck as always. I preferred to stay in the room, controlling the chills and spasms I felt in my brain, which became more and more frequent. I couldn't have a normal life because I would react with sadness or rage to minuscule problems.

On one occasion Humberto accompanied me to exchange a garment that had been too large for my grandson. The cashier didn't want to exchange the garment because she said that a code was missing. She kept us waiting for ten minutes until anxiety hit and I started yelling that I couldn't wait any longer because I was ill in the head, and if they kept me waiting, I wouldn't be able to respond. I lost control and started screaming, and the poor girl started to cry. Those types of situations distanced me from people, changing me into a sick and lonely woman. I was headed straight for death, or worse, to a place where enclosure would be my worst enemy.

I arrived there on a night in April in 2010.

That was the worst day of my life. It was the moment in which I lurched down the ravine. It wasn't because I had jumped but because I had advanced slowly, step by step until I reached the precipice and couldn't stop. I had walked alone with a blindfold until I felt the blow that I first wished had ended my life. On that night in April, I touched the bottom of the sea, became tangled in the seaweed, and smelled rotten spoiled. In the end, what happened that night changed my life forever. At the end of that year, I would decide to write down the story of my life, a project that Radesh had encouraged since the day we met. I hadn't had the courage to do so, because of what it would mean to remember almost my whole life, and because of the fear I had of exposing my story to the world. Yet I was tired of carrying this weight and wanted to unload it on the pages of this book.

I swear that I didn't want to hit my own son that night, but it happened in a fit of desperation and fear. That day in April I had fallen into bitterness and was on the verge of crying with anguish. I had awakened depressed, as I had many of the previous days. It had become a routine. I spent almost the whole morning in my room folding clothes and organizing papers and my grandson's toys while he watched television.

The same old thing, I thought: making food, cleaning the kitchen, taking care of Radesh, and listening to complaints. Humberto had left for the third time. I wanted to leave and find a place to relax, but I couldn't with the stress of the city; I was unable to take a step out into the street. I was panicked. I spent the whole day restless, smoking one cigarette after the other, all while attending to the house.

In the afternoon, my anguish became more profound. My mind went blank as I sat facing the bed because my mind brain wouldn't obey my instructions. I wasn't taking antidepressants because an executive at the health insurance agency had made a mistake while signing my policy, and I hadn't been able to buy more. I went back to feeling suffocated and didn't know where to go or how to get out of that life. How could I get out of this world, split in two, and change to another planet? How could I get on the highway waiting for nothing, not even for someone to rescue me? I felt the weight of my past, of taking care of the house, of leading my children on the right path, of Radesh's illness, of dragging along the mistakes I had made in various point in my life.

In the room, as I cried in silence, I heard voices coming from people that were not real. I thought that I heard my sons' voices whispering, and then I heard the voices of many strangers in my living room. I got up, expecting to see my sons with a large party of visitors making noise. When I arrived in the living room, I was shocked to see it empty.

Charito, arriving home from work, and Radesh were in the bedroom attending to my grandson. I could hear their murmuring. Hours before, I had argued with Radesh about my life and my isolation from the world. I confessed that I was tired and bored. "I feel trapped," I told him. "I cannot continue like this." I started crying. "If you had given me more liberty, our story would be different. We wouldn't have had so many financial troubles, and you wouldn't be so sick."

Radesh looked at me with astonishment from the armchair. Maybe it wasn't the best way to say that, but if I had remained quiet,

I would have ended up in a coffin in the ground because something was choking me and I needed to be released.

Upon returning to the room, I continued crying. That was when I began to see the shadows that were circling around me. I covered my eyes. When I was able to get up, I went out of the room to see if Radesh needed anything; I offered him fruit and milk.

"Don't worry," he said calmly. "I'm fine."

"I am going to go out to smoke for a minute," I told him." He kept his eye on me at all times to make sure I wasn't buying beer.

I entered and left several times for an hour, and Radesh watched me the whole time. I was in a state of anxiety, which the cigarettes could contain only until nighttime, when Radesh began to get nervous because Mathew and Kent were not at home.

"When are they going to return home?" he asked.

"I don't know, Radesh. You let Mathew borrow the car; you should know when he is supposed to return."

"But he never arrives here at the time he says he will," complained Radesh. "I am annoyed that he takes my car and goes around with his friends."

"You need to talk with him," I said in a motherly tone.

"This is all because of that man whom you brought to live in our house," said Radesh, raising his voice. "He was the one who started raising them like this. All he did was create disorder in our family."

"But you were the one who asked Humberto to take charge when you couldn't. Don't you remember?" I responded.

"Yes, but that man damaged them. He really damaged them by giving them so much liberty," he continued to talk with his elevated tone of voice.

"We were the ones who did damage, Radesh, when we let another person into our lives," I said, and had the urge to light another cigarette.

That was the beginning of an argument loaded with accusations, resentment, and even insults. Radesh complained for the first time for my having brought a lover into the house.

I retorted, "It's your fault! You allowed him to settle in here. You approved of him from the first day!"

I went back to the room to try to rest, and periodically arose to run to the bathroom. One week before, intense pains of a stomach flu had come accompanied by diarrhea and vomiting. I covered myself with a blanket and put my hands around my neck, squeezing to alleviate the pain in my head and to stop seeing shadows. I thought that my head would explode and the crushing pains in my stomach had only intensified my anguish and anxiety and diluted my judgment.

After a couple of hours I heard Kent arguing with Radesh about why he had stayed out so late without asking for permission or answering his phone. I saw that it was after midnight. Then they started to argue about the past and the mistake that it had been to allow Humberto to interfere in our lives. In the middle of the fight, Radesh started to cough and couldn't stop. I went out to see him. Kent said hello to me and went to his room.

"Radesh, are you all right?" I asked him.

"It's midnight and Mathew hasn't arrived," he complained without addressing my question. "I already told you, Lili; that man came to ruin our family, and then he left."

"But you are in charge of the boys now. You have to talk with them and tell them to come back on time," I said, holding my head. "Besides, Mathew is riding around in your car because *you* lent it to him!"

"I called him ten times, but he isn't answering his lousy phone," answered Radesh, losing the little patience he had left but speaking better and better Spanish.

We returned to our previous argument. I went out to smoke another cigarette, continuing to pace in and out of the house like a caged cat. For a moment I thought about escaping, going far away with the clothes on my back and forgetting about everything. I even wondered what could be so bad about the life of a wanderer, without obligations, without worrying about anything besides finding a bridge under which to sleep at night.

From outside the house, I could hear the voice mails that Radesh was leaving on Mathew's cell phone. *What will happen if I disappear right now—if I abandon everything that I have accomplished after so many difficulties?* I thought. I rubbed my trembling hands together, lighted another cigarette, smoked it, and went back inside. As soon as Radesh saw me, he started up another confrontation.

"Why don't we have a peaceful life?" I cried desperately. "I cannot believe that, after so much suffering, we continue to make our lives impossible. My God! How long will this go on?!"

Radesh responded with yelling, and we began a noisy commotion that undoubtedly carried through several apartments in our building. Radesh started to talk about Humberto again. I was blinded by my fury and responded that I had tolerated all of his cheating with Pilar, which *was* actually infidelity, unlike my relationship with a man whom he himself had accepted.

"You were the one who allowed Humberto to come into our house, and you were the one who lied, saying that you were staying in a hotel in La Paz when you were really sleeping with another woman!" I yelled. Radesh tried to answer me while he dialed Mathew's number, but I continued yelling about Pilar. "You always defended her!" It was a true scandal that calmed down when Mathew answered Radesh's call.

"Bring me the car right now," Radesh ordered through the telephone. "I can't stand this shit anymore!"

I went to the bathroom, feeling sadder and sicker than ever. Then I lay down again on the bed to cry and to listen to the flurry of strange voices that I didn't understand but that kept repeating themselves over and over again. That's how I stayed for almost half an hour, until Mathew arrived and I went out to speak with him.

"Give me the keys! I am leaving!" Radesh yelled at Mathew.

"You can't go alone," I interrupted, shaking from fear and the feeling that everything was going to turn out badly.

"Give me the keys, Mathew!" Radesh yelled again.

Mathew extended his hand with the keys to give them to Radesh.

"Don't give him the keys! He cannot leave here!" I pleaded as I tried to take the keys.

"Give me the keys, stupid boy!" Radesh yelled one last time.

I grabbed Mathew's clothes to prevent him from giving Radesh the keys, but I didn't succeed. Mathew struggled with me until he pushed me and said, "The car belongs to him; he can do what he wants!"

When I fell into the armchair, I grabbed a bottle of perfume—the first thing I could find—and, without thinking, threw it with all my might. I ran back to my room without seeing what had happened. I covered myself with the blanket and began to cry. In the living room, Radesh tried to clean the blood from Mathew's face. The perfume bottle had struck near his right eye.

I continued to hear voices and see shadows as my head seemed about to burst. When I threw the perfume, my mind filled with memories of when I was a girl and would climb up to the roof of Grandfather's house and throw water balloons. I sat for hours listening to the conversations of men who passed by in the street. What caught my attention was the way in which they talked about women, to whom they referred with words whose meaning I didn't quite know, but understood that they were insults. When I didn't have water balloons, I used rotten eggs from the store, which Grandfather piled up in a wooden box on the patio. I got the idea from seeing carnival in the town. People had the habit of gathering eggs, emptying them, and painting them to later be filled with confetti. When the day of carnival arrived, the young people walked around dancing and singing until everyone chose a girl or guy whom they liked and broke and egg on his or her head. But there were men who broke real eggs, even forcefully, on women's heads, and one landed on me on one occasion. One year, my cousin Jennifer and I planned to take rotten eggs and do the same to those men, but from the second floor of the shoe store. I was not a troublemaker, but I got into mischief because I was bored and wanted to have fun and unload my fury on the world. That was the same feeling I had when I threw the perfume, without realizing that I had hit Mathew. In fact, I had no idea until the police arrived in my room and woke me up.

Kent, scared about the scandal and by how out of control we all were, had called. When I heard the sirens, I knew that something had happened, but I didn't know that they were even at our house until one of the policemen came into my room. Before he could say anything, I confessed. "I don't know what I did, but I need to pay for it," I said.

I didn't get up from the bed until they had finished asking me questions. Charito came in to see me, but they took her out immediately. She was only able to say to me that there were two police cars, a fire truck, and an ambulance outside the house, plus all of the people who had arrived to watch the spectacle.

According to the police, ten calls had come in complaining of the yelling that could be heard throughout the whole condominium. I felt like the worst human being on earth; I had hit my own son after everything that I had done to protect them so that they could grow up with a father and a good family.

The policemen came back into the room to ask more questions. When I left the room, I couldn't see Mathew because the ambulance had taken him to the hospital. Kent was outside the house, and the police were holding Radesh in his armchair in the living room.

"If you think I am guilty, take me away, please. Get me out of here," I told a woman who was in the living room.

I returned to the room to go to the bathroom again, but the woman—followed by Charito—grabbed me and said, "You are under arrest, ma'am. Don't move."

The other policeman tried to put handcuffs on me.

"Let me go to the bathroom," I requested, trying to get free.

The guy put on the handcuffs.

"I need to go to the bathroom!" I cried.

The man was gripping me so forcefully that he left bruises and bloody scratches on my arms and wrists. We continued to struggle until a woman joined in. Between the two of them, they tried to take me down, and she brought out a kind of iron to give me an electric shock. I stayed still.

"I am going to take you two to court," said Charito, afflicted by the policemen's violence. "She just wants to go to the restroom."

Kent and Radesh heard my screams, but the police wouldn't let them react to defend me.

"Your mother just scratched me," responded the female officer. "She is resisting arrest." They treated me horribly, like any mother or father who beats his child in the United States.

In the patrol car, my stomach continued to hurt, and on the way to the police department, I couldn't contain myself. I soiled the floor and the seats. When we got to the station, the policeman got out hurriedly and said to a female officer, "Take her inside ... She soiled the whole patrol car."

The woman sat me in a cold room, and a little while later, brought me men's underwear and a blue suit with buttons, which was the kind used by either a surgeon in the hospital building or by astronauts.

"Go in there and change your clothes," she said. I stayed handcuffed all night until seven in the morning, when they took me to the Santee jail.

Before locking me in a cell with twenty other women, they took my fingerprints, took photos of me, and asked me a couple of questions that I don't remember. I thought that I would have to stay there forever. In the cell, they gave me a piece of bread and a bowl of mysterious soup that I didn't want to eat. The women observed me and made comments. I didn't want to look at anybody, so I sat near the telephone and the bathroom, which was in a corner of the cell. I stayed there studying the floor until a group of women approached me. One of them spoke up.

"Why are you dressed like that?" she said so loudly that all of the women looked at me.

"Because I work for NASA," I said without thinking and without laughing.

"And why are you here?" she asked, even more interested.

"Because they sent my ship to one planet and I went to another planet. On the way, the CIA and the FBI stopped me."

"Oh my God!" several of them gasped.

Several women came up to me, formed a circle around me, and began to interrogate me. *Jesus Christ!* I thought. *Why did I open my mouth?* I repeated the same story again and again until I went to the bathroom, from which I didn't come out for an hour. How was it possible that they believed such a story? They started to talk among themselves, complaining of the injustice of locking up a scientist. They all shared their theories about my arrest, which served to keep them entertained. I thought, *These women are crazier than I am.* Nearly all of them were drunk or high. I realized that I was not as bad off as they were, and that I was capable of recovering my health and sanity.

"You can't be here," the woman who was most enthused by my story said to me when I came out of the bathroom. "You should call a lawyer."

"Yes, that's true," I replied. "It's a mistake, but you know how it is: they want to do experiments with us. In a little bit my colleagues will come to take me to my ship."

At four in the afternoon, a pair of policemen approached the cell. One of them yelled, "Liliana Kavianian. Out!"

They took me by the handcuffs and led me to an office in which I had to sign some papers. They opened a door so that Charito could enter. She hugged me, startled, and before she could say anything, I said, crying, "It was an accident, daughter; I didn't mean to hurt your brother. Forgive me ..."

Wearing that very astronaut suit, I was let free and walked with Charito to the parking lot, where Radesh was talking on the telephone. He had found a loan with which he paid 10 percent of the $100,000 bail. He would pay the rest through a bail officer. After I was released from jail, we went to the bail officer's office to find out what our next steps would be. I had recovered my liberty, but the punishment was not over.

What I wanted most was to see Mathew and beg for his forgiveness, to explain to him that it had been an impulse and I would never think of hurting him. I also wanted to promise him that I would make an effort to recover from depression and return our family's calm.

In the street where the bail officer's office was, I had to get out even though Radesh didn't want me to be seen in my ridiculous blue suit. The officer took new photos of me and made me sign more papers. Two hours later they called us to an office that seemed more like a pantry. The man who attended us said many things that I didn't understand. He spoke of a judge, of community service and training.

When we arrived home, Radesh and Charito explained the problem in which I had gotten myself. By order of the judge, Mathew and Kent—minors—were living in another place until I left the apartment. "You have to move somewhere else so that the boys can return," said Radesh.

Besides prohibiting me from living with my family for a year, I had to complete twenty hours of attendance in an anger management program and fifty hours of community service.

Two weeks after the incident and after looking for an affordable, nearby place to live, I moved to an apartment. There, I was faced with my very own sentence: loneliness. Every day I thought about the night of the perfume bottle. I couldn't sleep, thinking about the fact that I could have killed my son, which is why I continued visiting the family and attending to Radesh every day. That helped me make up for my absence in some way. I would go to the house, cook, clean, and return to my bubble, and sometimes stay to take care of my grandson.

The first weeks were filled with crying and desperation, but later I awoke from that bitterness and decided to face my punishment. First, I went to the psychological therapy for anger management, where I learned techniques and exercises to control my impulses and speak without wounding others.

I felt strange listening to words that I had never heard in my life, and responding to questions that I had never asked myself. I had been accustomed to lamenting and blaming the past for my present problems, but I learned that I had to focus on the present to make it worthwhile. I would have to think about the future and the consequences of my behavior. I learned that moments of stress and despair could be dealt with constructively by going on a walk or for a run, doing anything to distance myself from the volatile situation.

Besides learning that I had to deal with my bitterness and hate, *I had to want to change*. That was what helped me more than anything.

During that same time, the idea of writing a book gained momentum, so I started writing a few things in a notebook. As soon as I finished the therapy, I began the community service in a church. I cleaned the pews and the saints and prepared the church for Mass. It didn't cost me much to feel useful, because since I was a girl I had learned that cleanliness and order came first. If Pillita worried about anything, it was my wardrobe and tidiness. My aunt Barbara taught me with blows and curse words that every corner in the house had to be clean, and if it was already clean, it had to shine, even if the servants had already cleaned there. Living alone hurt me more than any of the blows I had taken in my life. As a girl, I grew up in luxury, but that was not sufficient to have everything that I needed in my childhood, and even less in my adolescence. Many times I thought that it would be better to be poor, without clothes or a house in which to live, but in exchange … to be calm, at peace. I didn't come to know happiness because there were always people and situations that worked to hide it from me, and I didn't have the courage to face those things. I saw things that no father or mother would be willing to show their children, and death was always circling about, lurking like a criminal outside the house. I was killed so many times, and just as many times I came back to life. Why …? I asked myself once and again, and now I can answer that it was so that I could write my story.

I did a thorough cleaning in my new house, but not one of those cleanings that requires hours to store everything away in a box. Rather, this cleaning involved rooting out bad feelings and experiences, breaking them and driving them away. This cleaning was deep and painful, but it had a purpose. Some people release their load by talking with a friend, but I had no one. Other people do it by dancing or exercising, but I could barely gather the courage to leave my house. Others lose themselves on the streets, but I wanted to find myself and did so in the best way I could think of. That is why I resumed the appointments with my psychologist and the psychiatrist and decided to share in a book everything that made me suffer so much, so that others can decide if what they are doing is what they want for their lives. The images of an ideal marriage and ideal family that I always had since my childhood were false; while trying to achieve that ideal, I ended up very far away from where I could have found it.

Now that I have remembered the past—and it hasn't been an easy process—I want to rest for a moment, but I won't stop building this new life. I will continue learning. In the meantime, I will continue living alone until my heart and my head are in absolute calm. Escaping, moving to another city or another country, did not help me leave behind my ghosts. I will not continue to look for the perfect place to be happy because I have realized that it is here, with me, and I had to discover that on a night in April.

Acknowledgments

This story, despite its sad experiences, is a gift for me. I always wanted to do something positive, which is why I wrote this, keeping in mind all the people who can identify themselves in my words. Each of us has a mission to accomplish, and to achieve it, we must trust in our creator, who gives us all chances and talents, which, because of destiny, we are not always able to discover. Any positive project can change a human being's life, and blessings for a better life come little by little. Anything is possible; I learned this. All that's necessary is to not have fear and to continue walking with a firm stride. We must block negative thoughts and give ourselves the opportunity to accept positive thoughts. Whatever happens, we must continue ahead and achieve our goals, because the one who perseveres will achieve success.

I don't have words to thank my husband deeply enough. During this whole project, he gave me all of his love and support, through the good times and the bad. He is my guardian angel.

With all my heart, I am deeply thankful to my children for having supported me all this time, and for respectfully understanding these unhappy moments that have passed like a storm over my life.

I give my most sincere appreciation to Doctor Dolores Rodriguez, my therapist, who for six years had the commitment and patience to listen to me and encourage me with good advice that transformed my life. With her support, I understood many things and transformed hate and suffering into love.

I thank God with all my heart for having put in my path the person who made my book into an excellent project. She had the courage to write my story. Thank you, Antonieta.

Many thanks to Deborah for all of her support in the publication process.

My voice comes from my heart to give my most sincere thanks to Olivia Holloway Salzano. She helped me give my story a touch of magic and listened patiently to me even during the most difficult moments of the project, because she takes her work very seriously. I thank God for putting her in my path. She is a woman with a big heart and excellent professionalism.

Author, Liliana Kavianian.